THE INSIDE STORY OF AUSTRALIA'S BEST LOVED BAND

POWDERFINGER

FOOTPRINTS

THE INSIDE STORY OF AUSTRALIA'S BEST LOVED BAND

POWDERFINGER

FOOTPRINTS

Powderfinger

with Dino Scatena

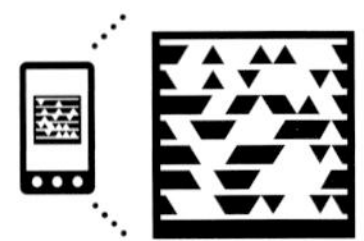

Get the free mobile app at
http://gettag.mobi

Publisher's note

Throughout *Footprints* owners of smartphones can scan the tags within the pages to connect with video footage relating to that particular moment in the book.

Just download the free Microsoft Tag app at http://gettag.mobi

Then hold your phone's camera about ten centimetres away from the tag images placed throughout the book, and it will play videos of the press conference, video clips and behind the scenes snippets.

If you don't have a smartphone you can still access the videos by visiting www.powderfinger.com/footprints

hachette AUSTRALIA

Published in Australia and New Zealand in 2011
by Hachette Australia
(an imprint of Hachette Australia Pty Limited)
Level 17, 207 Kent Street, Sydney NSW 2000
www.hachette.com.au

10 9 8 7 6 5 4 3 2 1

National Library of Australia
Cataloguing-in-Publication data:

Powderfinger (Musical group)

Footprints / Powderfinger with Dino Scatena.

978 0 7336 2897 9 (hbk.)
978 0 7336 2882 5 (pbk.)

Powderfinger (Musical group)
Rock groups—Australia—Biography
Rock musicians—Australia—Biography.

Scatena, Dino, 1968-

782.42166092

Front cover design by Debaser
Cover, text, packaging and limited edition collector's pack design by Christa Moffitt, Christabella Designs
Cover photograph by Ian Jennings,© 2003 Universal Music Australia Pty Limited, Licensed courtesy of Universal Music Australia Pty Limited.
Back cover photograph courtesy of Secret Service/S. Maughan
Typeset in Bembo 10.5/15
Printed in China by Imago Printers

Hachette Australia's policy is to use papers that are natural, renewable and recyclable products and made from wood grown in sustainable forests. The logging and manufacturing processes are expected to conform to the environmental regulations of the country of origin.

Powderfinger would like to dedicate this book
to fans past, present and future, and to all of the
people we have worked with over the last 20 years.

Contents

Contents

‘footprints on the other side remind me where I’ve been.’

INTRODUCTION

Sunsets

The show is over. Powderfinger is no more.

This is how it officially ends, in the heart of the band's hometown: A little after 10 pm on a perfect Saturday evening, 13 November 2010, under the stars, deep inside Brisbane's Botanic Gardens on the banks of the Brisbane River. A passionately patriotic sold-out crowd of 10,000 diehard 'Finger fans are packed all the way up the hill overlooking the Riverstage.

Backstage, the five very-soon-to-be ex-members of Powderfinger – Ian 'Hoggy' Haug, John 'JC' Collins, Bernard 'Bernie' Fanning, Darren 'DZ' (aka 'Darius') Middleton, and Jonathan 'Cogs' (aka 'Cogsy') Coghill – are crammed into a teensy brick enclave next to a concrete stairwell, preparing to return to the stage for their very last ever encore.

Usually at a Powderfinger show these moments before the encore are a pretty relaxed affair, reserved for a quick drink, a few general comments about the show, a chance for Hoggy to sneak in a ciggie, but mainly it's a volley of light-hearted smartarse quips the guys have stored up during the performance. That's the way it's been for virtually every Powderfinger gig over the past 20-odd years.

However, tonight, the mood backstage is intense, delirious, frenetic. All five guys are drenched in sweat and frantically talking over each other at a million miles an hour, their eyes wide open, peaking with adrenalin.

Even in these final moments of the band, with all that adrenalin pumping, with the crowd chanting, the end only moments away, the band's chaotic discussion is all about getting this very last bit of the show exactly right, a last check that everything is set to go down as agreed. They manically go over the basic plan one more time, everyone talking at once. '*How we going for time? How much time we got?*' They're all bursting to get back out. And then, off they go.

The short walk between the stairwell and the stage is lined by the band's nearest and dearest: Management, crew, wives.

Time for one last mass singalong, 10,000 voices as one.

'*These days turned out nothing like I had planned.*'

As the final crescendo evaporates, the blissful sound shatters into deafening shrills of exhilaration.

And that's it. The band members put down their instruments and uncharacteristically jump off stage, reach across the barricades, touching hands with as many fans as they can reach, embracing and being embraced. It's like they've just won the Ashes, or at least a State of Origin.

It's an extraordinary scene, so emotional, and yet, in a way, so unPowderfinger. They've never been a band for such grandiose rock & roll gestures … with the possible exception of Darius, who's always been a bit prone to pressing the flesh during a guitar solo, or climbing a speaker stack and striking the most audacious pose. In his younger days, DZ regularly did this without a shirt on.

This is it – the end of Powderfinger.

Cogsy was never much one for wearing shirts on stage either, back in the day, but that's just what drummers do.

Look, let's face it. We're all fans here, right? Let's be real about it. It's hard to stay humble when your band name is emblazoned on the side of a jetliner. And we all know that for all the 'shucks-we're-just-ordinary-blokes' stuff you've ever read about Powderfinger over the years, each member has quietly gone about the business of perfecting themselves a set of rock-solid patent rock moves. It's part of the reason we love them.

Bernie has his pout and his strut and that swinging mic-stand technique that he's obviously ripped straight off 1970s Rod Stewart. Hoggy plants his left foot forward as he does his making-love-to-my-guitar thing as often as he can. JC gets so low to the ground with his bass that he threatens to burrow through the stage, while Cogsy has his whole Cogs-the-class-clown/band-hunk act going on up the back. ('Imagine if we didn't have Cogsy's looks to prop us up through the hard times?' Bernie likes to point out.)

Still, jumping into the crowd at the end of the show? The 'Finger is no Jovi. For the hundreds and hundreds of gigs these guys have played together during the past two decades, this is unprecedented. But then tonight's show is unlike any other Powderfinger show before it. It's the final night of the staggering Sunsets farewell national tour – 34 sold-out performances over two and a half months in 21 towns and cities across Australia, playing to more than 300,000 fans.

Almost exactly 22 years since the embryonic form of the band played its first notes together, this is it – the end of Powderfinger.

There's no wall between the band and their fans. There never was. The hometown crowd reaches out as one. Everyone wraps their arms around the band and each other in an emotional last farewell. There are people in the crowd and in the crew and in the band with tears streaming down their cheeks. It's overwhelming, but the mood is not mournful. It actually feels joyous. Everyone has the hugest smiles on their faces. How can you be mournful when they're pumping Depeche Mode's 'Just Can't Get Enough' through the PA system?

Everything in the past few months – the past few years, actually – has been building to this moment.

'It's like a NASA countdown,' comments Paul 'Teaks' Piticco backstage just moments before the show, pacing up and down in the bandroom, nervously swinging around a toy inflatable caveman club. Teaks is the band's manager, the 'unofficial sixth member of Powderfinger', as he's introduced to the audience during the performance. Teaks has been with the band almost since day one, longer than even Cogsy, as a matter of fact.

What a perfect way to call it a day. Powderfinger was born, lived its life and now ends right here in the heart of Brisbane. Every early milestone in the band's history took place within a few square kilometres of this Riverstage. Four of the band members went to high school within walking distance of the venue.

Powderfinger, one of Australia's most enduring, loved and successful musical outfits ever. Australia's everyman band – and most women, too.

Now, it's over, for real, just like that. Finished. Which begs the question – why, why, why? Why break up? Why would they leave us?

Less than a week out from this final performance, Powderfinger won the national ARIA music awards for most popular Australian act and most popular Australian album of the year for what's turned out to be their last studio album, *Golden Rule*. Think what you might about such popularity contests, but after 22 years together the Australian public was still voting Powderfinger the most popular musical act in the land. You can't argue with democracy, right?

Not since Crowded House said farewell to the world in 1996 or Cold Chisel made its last stand back in 1983 has such a prominent group of local musicians made such a public declaration never to perform together again. While both of those other acts eventually reneged on their pledge and returned for highly successful reunion albums and tours, there are those within the Powderfinger camp who emphatically promise that they will never, ever perform together again, ever. You can make all the Farnsey jokes you want – they mean it.

But why? Why such a public, permanent split? Successful bands just don't break up any more, do they? Especially when they're still producing chart-topping albums and everyone is in agreement that they're probably playing better than ever.

As any true 'Finger fan will already have accepted, the short answer to 'why?' is, quite simply, the time had come. A group of mates, approaching or already in their 40s, after decades spent in each other's intimate company, and now most with young families, wanted time to do something different.

The long answer, well, we've got a whole book to deal with that. Let's just say, as the Facebook generation would put it: It's complicated.

Darius, the band's show pony, yet also its ex-hippy-navel-gazing consciousness, has penned himself a short note to try to encapsulate his feelings on this momentous last day.

'I understand today why bands who have been together for a long time keep going and going,' writes DZ. 'It's hard to let go, emotionally hard to let go, yet it's important, because change is important in life. It's essentially what living is ... loving and letting go. I'm feeling it today, but I know it's the right thing for us as a group and me as a person.'

Watching on from the side of the stage is Nic Cester, frontman of fellow Aussie rockers Jet, Powderfinger's opening act on the Sunsets tour. The four members of Jet, relative young'uns as they are (all in their early 30s), have treated these last ten weeks on the road as one non-stop party. They're a bad influence on older folk. Following tonight's show, Jet will take off into their own hiatus.

'Being in a band is essentially like being in a homosexual relationship with four guys,' ponders Nic. 'Like guy sluts, just without the sex stuff, obviously. One of the hardest things about being in a band is staying in a band because, inevitably, there are going to be issues with the relationships that exist within any band dynamic.'

If that's true, if the whole history of rock & roll has really just been about some sort of gay love thing, then ladies and gents, grab hold of something tight and ready yourself for one of the greatest Aussie musical bromances of them all.

Here is the previously untold story of the life and loves, highs and lows, hits and misses, and everything in between, of the almighty 'Finger.

DINO SCATENA

AIRBUS

CHAPTER 1

The End

To save you flicking to the back of the book to find out how this all turns out, let's start our story at the beginning of the end.

Surely it was obvious to everyone that something pretty big was about to go down when Powderfinger called a national press conference for the morning of 9 April 2010.

The venue was Sydney's Annandale Hotel, one of the town's traditional bastions of indie live music where the 'Finger played some of its first shows outside Queensland almost 20 years before.

The invitation to the media call-out suggested the purpose of the event was simply for the band to 'announce the full details of their upcoming, major Australian tour'. But since when did any Australian rock band call a press conference to announce a concert tour? Well, actually, we can tell you exactly since when – 12 June 2007, when Powderfinger and Silverchair did it to announce their joint Across the Great Divide national tour. But besides that one, rock bands call press conferences even less often than they break up.

So, at the most un-rock-godly hour of 10 am on a Friday, the five Fingers jumped up on stage together as they'd done so many times before. Only this time it's to take their seats at a long table in front of a room packed with cameras and reporters. There they were, the five Fingers all in a row. Left to right: Cogs, DZ, Bern, JC, Hoggy. Their manager, Teaks, watched on intently from near the side of the stage, as he'd done hundreds of times before.

It's left to Bernard to do the talking.

'Good morning everybody and thank you for coming out to see us this morning,' Bernie begins. 'I'm going to read a statement on behalf of the band which will include a few announcements with regard to what we have coming up.'

There are, specifically, three announcements. The first is that Powderfinger is preparing to embark on the most extensive Australian tour of its career, the Sunsets tour, taking in shows in every state and territory. Jet will be the support act for the whole tour, except for the first three dates, which will feature comeback performances by the Vines.

Secondly, Powderfinger will use this tour to help promote and raise money for a Queensland-based organisation called Yalari that sponsors Aboriginal and Torres Strait Islander children from regional, rural and remote communities to attend boarding schools around Australia.

Okay – part three. Bernie's voice appears to quiver momentarily. ('I don't remember being really nervous,' the singer swears afterwards.)

'Our third, final and biggest announcement today,' Bernie reveals, 'is that the Sunsets tour will be Powderfinger's last ever run of shows.' He looks up, briefly breaking from the script. 'Big surprise, eh?' he quips.

'We have decided,' he continues, back on script, 'after much deliberation and agonising, that after this final tour we will call it a day as a recording and touring band.

It was exactly 40 years before that the Beatles announced their split.

'After a career that has lasted for over 20 years, seven studio albums, a live album, two DVDs, 30-odd video clips, around 1000 shows, 16 ARIA awards and hundreds of thousands of kilometres travelled around the globe on local, national and world tours, we believe that the time has come to call an end to what we think has been an extremely privileged and rewarding run.

'We have always maintained that the important factor for us as a group is that our music remains relevant and that we continue to have fresh ideas that inform our new songs. With the completion of our last album, *Golden Rule*, we feel that we have said all that we want to say as a musical group. We firmly believe that it is our most complete and satisfying album and can't think of a better way to farewell our fans than with music that we all believe in and also with, hopefully, our best tour to date.

'Following the release of our last few albums there has been speculation in the press that we were breaking up. We have only come to this decision to "disband"' – Bernie looks up from the script again: 'That's a word we were asked to use by our management, by the way ... following our run of festival shows this last summer and even toyed with the idea of delaying this announcement until our tour was over. Finally we decided that it was much better mannered, and made a lot more sense, to give people the opportunity to come and celebrate with us as we make our way around the country one last time.

'There will be further releases made by Powderfinger in the future as there are obligations to fulfil with the great folks over at Universal, who have essentially been our label from the beginning of our recording career.'

Watch Powderfinger's press conference
www.powderfinger.com/footprints

AND THERE IT WAS – AT LAST, THE SECRET WAS OUT. No going back now. Within minutes, everyone knew. The news was flashed across websites and radio. It was all over that afternoon's television news bulletins and newspapers the following day.

A cultural happening: 'POWDERFINGER TO SPLIT!'

If any of the Fingers themselves thought saying it aloud would help alleviate the heaviness they'd felt from carrying this secret around for so long, it didn't pan out that way. Not immediately, at least.

Following the press conference, all the band members, as always, shared the media duties equally. Everyone in the whole country wanted a few words. How does it feel? Why, why, why? For the next eight hours, it was interview after interview after interview.

'I felt pretty emotionally drained,' says Darren. 'It was physically a long day and then callers ringing into radio stations going; "I can't believe it!" People were quite upset or disappointed.

'When you've got so many people around you going, "We can't believe you're doing it, we're really sad, we're going to miss you ...", it kind of rubs off on you. It annoys you and then it rubs off on you as well. Because we've never really paid much attention to how people attached us to their lives, in some degree. We were really finding that out at that time.'

'We only told our record company [Universal Music Australia] the night before,' says JC. 'We had dinner and drinks with George Ash [Universal's Australasian president] and he was like, "What the fuck?" Poor bastard. Hoggy and I had a few drinks with George, so we were a little bit dusty in the morning.'

It wasn't until afterwards that someone pointed out, coincidentally, or perhaps something a little more cosmically than that, it was exactly 40 years before to the day that the Beatles announced they were splitting up.

THE FINAL DECISION TO BRING AN END TO POWDERFINGER – and to go public with the decision – was only made two months prior to the press conference, in the week following the band's final appearance on the 2010 Big Day Out tour. This confirmation was more of a formality than anything else. Both Bernie and Cogsy had clearly indicated their long-term intentions in the lead-up to starting work on *Golden Rule*.

Diehard fans of the band will probably be in equal measures dismayed and bemused to learn that the seeds of the split go way back – perhaps as far back as the sessions for *Vulture Street* in 2003. As we all know, however, the Fingers have always kept private 'Finger business very much to themselves, avoiding non-music-related publicity and gossip at all costs.

Also, it must be noted, in this group that has always prided itself on functioning as a genuine democracy, the decision to split was by no means a unanimous choice.

Hoggy was not happy. Powderfinger was his band, he formed it, and now it was being broken up around him against his explicit wishes. Hog's argument all the way along was simple: Why break up? Why make it so finite? Why not just go on an 'indefinite hiatus'? Like, say, the Rolling Stones did in the 1980s. Or the Stooges in the '70s. Or Silverchair in 2011. Why make such a public spectacle of the fact that you will never, ever perform together again? Why make such a promise?

As late as the morning of the press conference, Hog was on the phone to his old mate Bernie, just checking one last time if he might reconsider. It *still* wasn't too late ...

'I was in denial, so I was trying to keep it together all the time,' Ian admits. 'I was like, "No, not gonna let you bastards break up a good thing!" I thought it was a really ridiculous idea. Still do, frankly.

'I was so fucking persistently in everyone's ear, like "Do you realise what you're doing? Do you realise this is never going to happen again if we do this? We are not going to be able to do this anymore."'

But one by one, Hoggy watched his allies drop away. Bernie and Cogs were already as good as gone. DZ, in turn, accepted that the fate of the band was sealed and he was okay with that. Even JC, the band's other founding member from day one of the Powderfinger trip, was wavering.

The first serious, open conversations about the long-term future of Powderfinger – or non-future, as it turned out to be – took place in October 2009 on the eve of the release of *Golden Rule*. The band had already committed to headlining the Homebake festival in Sydney in December, to organising acts and headlining the Queensland 150th anniversary concert at the Riverstage in Brisbane a week later, and then touring with the Big Day Out (BDO) festival around Australia in January. Beyond that, they agreed to reconvene after the BDO to talk about exactly what they were going to do.

Imagine everyone's utter shock (well, almost everyone's) when details of this very private band meeting somehow got into the hands of a gossip columnist at Brisbane's *Sunday Mail* newspaper. It was dumbfounding. The 'Finger had never sprung a leak. The words 'Finger and gossip very rarely mixed, full stop, so this didn't make any sense.

'That's news to me,' Teaks told the gossip columnist from the paper when quizzed about the rumours, although, of course, Teaks had been in the band meeting too. 'I can't imagine why they would split. I've had 20 journalists ask the same thing every time we are about to launch a tour or an album over the last few years.' Hahaha. Teaks added that the band was currently planning and booking shows in both Australia and abroad through to October and November 2010. Either Teaks is psychic or he was already formulating a plan.

So, how on earth did the details of such an intimate, private band meeting get to the media? Well, at the next rehearsal, the guys walked into their bandroom to find Cogsy waiting for them, wearing a boxing helmet and gloves. Turned out he'd been to a friend's wedding on the weekend after the meeting, had a couple and started telling some of his mates about his plans for the future beyond Powderfinger ... Yeah, the boxing gloves and helmet was a good gag, but no one was laughing too much.

'I didn't know it was meant to be such a big secret,' says Cogsy. 'Or maybe I did, but I wasn't going to bullshit my friends. People were asking me why I was at uni and I told them because I thought the band wasn't going to last much longer.'

Anyway, *Golden Rule* came out, topping the national ARIA charts for a week, Powderfinger's fifth chart-topping studio album in a row. The guys did some launch events, headlined

Maton

Homebake, organised the line-up for the Queensland 150 Concert and played the Big Day Out. (Both Hoggy and Bernie's wives had a child between these two events; Hoggy's second and Bernard's first. JC already had three children, including a set of twins, and DZ had two.)

Then the week after the last BDO show in Perth on 31 January 2010, the band members regrouped in their management's offices in Brisbane to put the matter to rest.

The band's recording contract with Universal was up for renewal following *Golden Rule*, so a final decision had to be made one way or another. How were they going to do this? Should they simply put out a press release saying it was over and be done with it?

Hoggy was still arguing that they didn't have to do anything, just quietly go off on an indefinite hiatus. What's the difference, he asked, you're just leaving the door open. But Bernie in particular, having just become a father for the first time, was the most quietly defiant about wanting to make it a completely clean break.

'When you say, "I'm in Powderfinger", then you are beholden to that schedule, whenever it is convenient for everyone to do what they are doing,' was Bernie's simple explanation. 'I don't want to be part of that schedule anymore and I think everyone, apart from Hoggy, everyone is going to say it out loud and be relieved to be free of that, to not have to answer to the idea of when you can go visit your family.'

Ian may not have accepted it yet, but Teaks had, and he came to the meeting armed with a road map, a manager's vision.

If this was really the end, if this was really what they wanted, then why not go out in the biggest way possible? How about staging a humungous national farewell tour – give every Powderfinger fan everywhere in the country, young and old, the chance to come out for one last hurrah? Also, obviously, if it was done right, it would set the guys up financially for some time to come.

'We sat there and talked about the differences in not coming back, about actually saying we are not coming back, or leaving the book open,' recalls JC. 'And Paul had a lot to say. He said, "For you to come back and do one show in five years' time – for example, playing the V8s [motor racing event], because they're the only people around with money at the moment – I think you will be able to get that income off this tour if you say you are finishing up. It will balance itself out and you won't have to do those one-off shows."'

The concept of a fully fledged farewell tour was not immediately embraced by the band. Coming straight off the back of playing every capital city on their umpteenth Big Day Out tour, some doubted they could still pull the sorts of crowds to justify another big national tour. Some also thought the idea of a farewell tour itself might be a bit morose, like 'carrying a coffin around the country'.

But Teaks explained his rationale. 'I used this as an example when I spoke to the band. I said there was a very famous Australian band I saw in Toowoomba in an RSL, playing to a

This was a decision for the five band members.

couple of hundred people. They were still really good live, but the feeling in the room, I thought to myself, was "You wanna be on that stage more than I want you to be on that stage."

'That's a point you never really want to get to, where the artist needs to be out there performing more than people want them to be. I thought it would be sad to get to a point where it was like that with Powderfinger. I think that some of the other guys felt the same way, not all of them.'

It went without saying that this was not Paul's call to make. As integral a figure as he's been to the band since the virtual outset, as much as he's guided and facilitated Powderfinger's success for so long, this was a decision for the five band members alone to make.

'My assessment of this wasn't based on how it feels to be a band member,' offers Teaks. 'For them, it's much more personal, a dismantling of their relationship, and I'm just the guy managing their relationship. I'm the counsellor – they're in the marriage. It's kind of a different feeling, a different sense of it being appropriate for me. I look at their career more like a whole project that started in the early '90s and here we are, 20 years later, and it seems to be a fitting end.'

The manager's pitch – along with the singer's insistence that he didn't want the spectre of Powderfinger indefinitely hanging over his and his new family's future, or worse, have the band return somewhere down the track as a nostalgia act – was enough to convince JC not to fight the will of the majority.

That meant the vote now stood at four to one. Regardless of what Hoggy thought and felt, Powderfinger was all set to split.

Piticco and the wider Powderfinger infrastructure immediately set about looking at the logistics of putting the band on the road for its biggest tour since its joint Across The Great Divide jaunt with Silverchair three years earlier. Indeed, that previous tour would act as the template for these farewell events, revisiting many of the same venues. Massive tents would again be used to take the show into regional areas without venues big enough to stage such a big rock concert. The rock & roll circus would travel to as many cities and towns as feasibly and fiscally possible, from Hobart to Darwin, Albury to Perth, Tamworth to Bendigo, and many places in between. This would be the biggest and most complex show Powderfinger had ever taken out on the road.

As always, everything would be kept in-house. Piticco's management company, Secret Service, would co-stage and co-finance the entire tour itself in conjunction with Village Sounds, the company run by Powderfinger's long-time friend and booking agent, Jessica Ducrou. Jessica's relationship with the band goes back to a fateful meeting of the minds and livers in Byron Bay way back in 1992.

With everything in place, the press conference was announced to reveal the break-up and details of the Sunsets tour. Initially, only 21 dates were revealed, one in each town and city, beginning at the Newcastle Entertainment Centre on 1 September 2010 and ending, as unusual as it might seem, in the North Gardens of Ballarat on 16 October that year.

With the blanket media coverage generated by the press conference, Teaks fulfilled step one of his vision to have all of Australia know that tickets for Powderfinger's farewell Sunsets tour would go on sale at 9 am on Friday 30 April.

'There was even debate about that, about whether we should do it that way,' says Bernie. 'That was Teaks' idea from the start – splash the fuck out of that story. Which he did. It just went berserko. And then when it went on sale, it just went nuts.'

Within hours, a mind-boggling 140,000 tickets were bought by fans across the country. Shows in Brisbane, Sydney, Melbourne, Perth, Adelaide, Townsville, Wollongong and the Gold Coast, as well as the first show in Newcastle and the last show in Ballarat, literally sold out in minutes. Second shows were immediately announced for Brisbane, Sydney, Melbourne and Perth. These also immediately sold out.

Paul Piticco, the band and everyone else were completely taken aback by the ferocity of demand for tickets. There was no contingency plan in place for such an overwhelming response.

'We got caught unawares,' Teaks says. 'The band wouldn't let me pin them down to the what-ifs of adding extra dates because they didn't want to talk about it: "We don't want to plan *that*, it might not happen – let's not jinx it." So when we were confronted with the sales as they were, we were flat-footed. We thought maybe we'd sell-out those shows in a week or two, and we'd have time to think about extra shows. But it all happened very, very quickly.'

'I thought we were going to sell a lot of tickets,' says Bernard, 'but I didn't think it was going to sell-out like crazy. I think the message hit home to people that, okay, they may have missed Chisel's last tour and they missed the Oils' last tour. It was like, "I'm going and I'm taking my 12-year-old kid." All the way through, families have liked the 'Finger. People have always told us how their kids are crazy about Powderfinger when they're about four. Which I think is awesome, because it's like that thing with the Beatles, where if you can appeal to four to 74-year-olds, you're obviously making good music. If that many people like it, it can't be all bad.'

It took a week to announce an additional final round of shows, by which time the ticket count was up to 175,000. More concerts were put on in Sydney, Melbourne, Adelaide, Perth and Cairns. Again, they were instantly snapped up.

It was also confirmed that the tour would not end in Ballarat as first stated, but in the band's hometown of Brisbane, with an additional three shows at the Riverstage and the official final-ever Powderfinger performance taking place on 13 November. The tickets to all three of these shows were gone within minutes, making a total of five sold-out shows at the Riverstage alone.

In the end, the total ticket count topped 300,000 for 34 shows across the country. It was a breathtaking response. Even more shows could have been added, if they wanted. Teaks guesses there was demand for a minimum 500,000 tickets, easy.

However, he explains, 'The band said, "We agreed we'd do one final lap – that's it." And they're of their word. I'm very proud that greed didn't kick in: "No, no, no – this time it's *really* the end!" That would have been maybe a bit *too* Johnny Farnham of us.

'Personally, from a manager's perspective, I feel the response to the announcement, the tour and towards the band since making that statement has validated the idea of winding things up, to exit gracefully.'

WITH THE SECRET OUT AND ALL THOSE TICKETS SOLD, grossing over $30 million at the box office, Powderfinger got on with the business of readying itself to say goodbye.

There was less than five months between the press conference and the scheduled opening night of the Sunsets tour in Newcastle on 1 September, with several key events on the band's agenda in between. First of all, there was an international tour, a short run of dates through Ireland and the UK, scheduled long before going public with the split. The basic idea was for the band to be on a plane out of Australia the week following the press conference, but those best-laid plans fell over when an Icelandic volcano grounded all flights in and out of Europe. The tour was hastily rescheduled for the start of June.

The seven overseas shows included two sold-out nights at London's O2 Brixton Academy, playing to a combined total of 10,000 rowdy expats and Poms. International touring stopped being a priority for the band years ago, but all those endless months they once dedicated to travelling the world in crappy tour buses with leaking toilets meant they could always draw out pockets of loyal fans in markets as far apart as Germany and Canada.

Following those UK dates, the 'Finger headed to South Africa in time for the start of the football World Cup. This was a particular thrill for Bernard, Cogsy, Darren and Teaks, all of whom, as kids, had dedicated many a Saturday morning to local soccer competitions.

The band performed a couple of unforgettable private shows for the Fanatics, the thousands of Aussie soccer fans who had travelled to South Africa for the event, as well as playing their first-ever club show in Cape Town. The band members then witnessed the Socceroos get annihilated by Germany in the opening round of the competition. Fortunately, none of them were sober enough to remember anything that happened in the game. 'I was so maggoted that I didn't even know until the next day that [Australian star striker] Tim Cahill had been sent off,' says Bernie.

On their return to Australia in mid-June, the Fingers set aside a week to catch up with their long-time American record producer, Nick DiDia, to put down a handful of recordings for possible inclusion in a future greatest hits set. Four new songs came out of these sessions at Sydney's 301 Studios, the same room in which they'd teamed up with Nick and recorded a little gem called *Vulture Street* seven years earlier. One of the new tracks, 'I'm On Your Side', ended up being released shortly after the band's split as a charity single to aid victims of the Queensland floods.

'It was our little *Abbey Road*, if you will,' says Nick of the final sessions. 'Everyone knew it was over, so it was a celebration of making records together. There was lots of talk about how it was going to be, but once we got in there, we could have been working on our first record.'

When that was done, throughout July and August, the group hunkered down in its rehearsal room, a converted paint warehouse in a semi-industrial area north of central Brisbane, to prepare for the tour.

One last time, just the five of them, alone in a room.

So much of Powderfinger's entire existence was spent like this, but it's impossible to encapsulate this painfully protracted element of their story in a book. If you truly want to see a rock democracy at work, or the intimate machinations of a five-way marriage at play, you'll need to go teach yourself an instrument and then spend 20-odd years in a semi-padded room with four of your best mates. It's rock & roll heaven or hell, depending on the given day and everyone's mood.

These were happy days, these final days of Powderfinger. It wasn't always this way, of course, especially in recent years. In the end, however, any negatives were far outweighed by all the wonderful and occasionally absurd experiences these five Fingers shared with each other and with their fans.

And now, over 300,000 of those fans were waiting to personally say goodbye, to experience and share the magic of Powderfinger for one last time. Who could have imagined it would play out like this? Certainly no one who was lucky enough to be present at Powderfinger's first-ever performance over 20 years earlier …

TELEPHONE

CHAPTER 2

The Beginning

To the best of everyone's fuzzy collective memory, the first-ever Powderfinger public performance took place under a house in Crestgarden Street, Macgregor, about a 20-minute drive out of central Brisbane, on 18 March 1989.

There weren't 10,000 people there – more like 10 or 15.

The band was only a three-piece at this stage: Hoggy on lead vocals and guitar; JC on bass; and Steven Bishop, JC's best mate from high school, on drums. They were still all in their teens and had only jammed together for the first time a few months earlier, at the end of 1988. After that, the trio started rehearsing fairly regularly in a practice room at Queensland University before this debut venture out into the real world.

The occasion? It wasn't really an occasion, as such. Peter 'Garts' Gartner, one of their mates from high school, was living with his mum and she'd gone out of town, so he invited a bunch of friends around for a piss-up.

'It was just mates hanging out – there weren't a lot of us there,' recalls Garts. 'The house had quite a big rumpus room downstairs, which I used as my bedroom. It had a bar at one end and they played down the other. Usual shenanigans.'

The band brought along its own homemade PA system and played a rough and ready set of a bunch of fairly eclectic covers, including a couple from Neil Young ('Like a Hurricane' and, of course, the song 'Powderfinger'), as well as songs by R.E.M., Bad Company and Aussie bands the Sunnyboys, Screaming Tribesmen and Lime Spiders. They also premiered a couple of songs they'd penned themselves.

Powderfinger was Hoggy's idea. It was Hoggy who pulled all the pieces together.

After the less-than-sober show, the party erupted into an all-out tennis ball fight. The rumpus room got trashed. None of Garts' collection of commemorative beer glasses from Brisbane's Expo '88 survived. Nor did the table tennis table. Mum wasn't rapt.

But Powderfinger was on its way.

Powderfinger was Hoggy's idea. It was Hoggy who pulled all the pieces together. There was never a question of whether the young Ian Haug would form his own rock & roll band, it was just a matter of when.

LAGER

CHAPTER 3

Hoggy

Ian Haug

John Collins, future bassist of Powderfinger, clearly remembers the first time he really took note of the lanky, long-haired lout who would soon enough become his lifelong rock & roll blood brother – the young and strapping Ian David Haug. It was back at their old high school, Brisbane Grammar School, in year nine, right in the middle of the 1980s. They were both about 15 – JC was relatively new at the school, a full-time boarder, while Ian was what they called a 'daygo', a day student. The two groups rarely mixed and the only thing the pair shared at this point was an English class.

So, JC looks over one day during English to see Ian with his head on his desk, his long fringe covering his eyes, weakly trying to cover up the fact that he was asleep. He distinctly remembers thinking to himself: 'Who is this fucking idiot?'

Coincidentally, in the same year, Bernard Fanning, future lead vocalist of Powderfinger, also laid eyes upon the formidable young form of the teenage Ian Haug for the first time. It was at an inter-school swimming carnival. Bernard, a year older than both Hog and JC, went to the neighbouring St Joseph's College Gordon Terrace private boys' school, Grammar's traditional rival at everything.

Sitting in the stands with the rest of the Terrace cheer squad, you couldn't miss Ian – already at 15 he physically towered over the competition and almost everyone else. He looked like a natural-born swimmer, a strapping young Viking Queenslander. But it wasn't Haug's physique that made the opposing team's cheer squad focus in on him. It was his hair.

'He had a haircut like Feargal Sharkey,' Bernie says. 'He came out in his dick trunks to swim and the whole of Terrace started sledging him: "We've got such-and-such, you've got Feargal Sharkey!"'

The taunts from testosterone-fuelled school boys dripped straight off the young Haug. Feargal Sharkey? Idiots. After all, Ian's haircut at the time was so obviously in the general long-fringed fashion of hip alt Oz rock bands of the day – namely the Stems, Hoodoo Gurus, the Sunnyboys or Brisbane's very own Screaming Tribesmen. But there was no way those uncool kids from Terrace were to know that. And let's face it, the swimming cap Hog was forced to wear didn't help his overall look.

It didn't matter – the school and swimming stuff was just something Ian did to fill those daylight hours when he didn't have a guitar in his hands. Out of school uniform, you'd find Ian always immaculately decked out in winklepicker boots and a paisley shirt with the top button done up, his fringe almost covering his eyes, a sort of modern-day mod.

Already by his mid-teens, Ian's nights were increasingly spent playing gigs in pubs, living the nightlife, well on his way to fulfilling his destiny as a rock star and guitar god.

ALTHOUGH THE TEENAGE Hoggy looked for all money like a State of Origin Queenslander, he was actually born way down in the deep, deep south. No, not Byron Bay, rather the Royal Hobart Hospital, Tasmania, on 21 February 1970.

There are three Haug boys and Ian is the youngest of the brothers by almost a decade – Chris is nine years older than Ian and Greg is 11 years his senior. Being the youngest by so much came with its perks. As soon as he was old enough, Mr and Mrs Haug, John and Lynn, had no qualms leaving Ian in the care of his studious and responsible teenage brothers, both of whom would grow up to be doctors. However, naturally, once the parents were out the front door, Ian was free to do pretty much whatever he wanted.

One of Ian's earliest memories is of his teenage brothers having all their mates around for an evening of beer and poker while their parents were out, and him being given the task of sorting out everyone's one- and two-cent coins. In the background was a weird and wonderful sound, which at the time Ian called 'the sneezy song', but he later discovered it was in fact – 'ah-ha, ah-ha' – Led Zeppelin's 'Whole Lotta Love'.

There was always lots of music in the Haug household and, indeed, musicianship runs in the family. Lynn is a piano teacher. Ian's grandfather on his dad's side was a violinist in the Oslo Philharmonic Orchestra before the family emigrated to Perth. John's side of the family is all Norwegian going back generations, while Lynn is of French and Lithuanian descent. Her maiden name was Redgrave – actresses Vanessa and Lynn Redgrave are Hoggy's distant aunties.

Aside from his mum's piano, Haug's parents had a considerable collection of old '33s and '78s. Mum listened to the likes of Carly Simon, Roberta Flack and Nina Simone. Dad preferred old-time big band music. He was a fantastic whistler and, as a younger man, ran local dance hall nights in Perth. Both his parents loved to dance and actually met when John taught Lynn how to dance the jive.

But for Ian, growing up through the 1970s, it was his older brothers' vinyl record collection that contained the magic that enchanted him – classic albums by Neil Young, Led Zep, the Stones, Creedence and T.Rex. There was still lots of Beatles music around too, of course.

The age difference between him and his brothers played a huge role in forging the independent spirit and early music leanings of the littlest Haug. Freedom and rock & roll – what else could a young man want out of life? Growing up, the answers to everything could be found in his brothers' vinyl.

The Haugs had uprooted from Perth to Hobart just before Ian's arrival. Then, when Ian was six, due to his father's work in the groundbreaking new field of computing, the family again moved house and states, this time from Hobart to Mount Eliza on the outskirts of Melbourne.

It was at Mount Eliza North Primary School that Ian got his first experience with the world of entertainment. There was a teacher, Mr Fildes, who played guitar and sang songs to the class and it mesmerised little Hoggy. It was also here that Ian made his celluloid debut, playing the role of Dan Kelly in a Super 8 'tween remake of the Ned Kelly story.

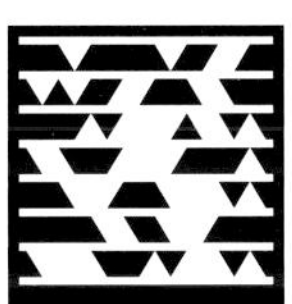

Watch Ian's debut performance
www.powderfinger.com/footprints

IAN'S ELDEST BROTHER, GREG, HAD STAYED BEHIND IN TASSIE to continue his studies, but he regularly trekked across Bass Strait during school holidays to visit the new family home on the mainland and he'd always bring along his guitar.

It was during one of these visits that Greg, himself a formidable musician, first put a guitar into Ian's hands. He taught the six-year-old some basics, how to play a riff. The pair were soon jamming out a blues number together. It wasn't long before Ian's tiny fingers could etch out a decent version of 'Jumpin' Jack Flash'.

When Ian was 10, the Haug family moved again, for one last time, to the suburb of Indooroopilly, some seven kilometres west of central Brisbane. It was the perfect setting for an idyllic, carefree suburban childhood. Much of Ian's time was spent out with his mates skateboarding, BMXing, playing backyard cricket, or exploring the mangrove swamps on Indooroopilly Island, making sure to avoid the wild boar that lived there. Weekends were taken up by surfing trips with the family.

On weeknights, Ian regularly met up with his mum at the local neighbourhood theatre, where she was involved in staging amateur productions of musicals such as *Cabaret*. It wasn't

quite rock & roll, but it wasn't that bad either. He'd do his homework in the dressing room as actresses in various states of undress hurried around him. Lynn also took him to see a professional performance of *The Rocky Horror Show*, which made quite an impression on the emerging alt-rocker and future diehard fan of the Cramps.

On his 11th birthday, Ian got his first guitar, a gift from his folks, and he rarely put the thing down. That instrument, a nylon-string acoustic, still holds pride of place in the grown-up Hoggy's expansive guitar collection.

Outside the family, if there was a defining moment in shaping the future tastes and general global outlook of young Ian, it happened at the local pool one morning in the early-'80s, when he was about 12. He was already well into his swimming by then, loved it almost as much as he loved his guitar, and he swam up to six hours a day.

Among the other dedicated tads at the pool, there was an older kid, Scott Lambert, who must have been about 15 or so. One morning, the pair got talking about music, and Ian told Scott how he was still listening to lots of '70s rockers like Slade and Status Quo, but he'd just discovered this amazing new band out of America called R.E.M. – with their jingly jangly guitars, they sounded nothing like anything on his brothers' records.

'Have you heard the Sunnyboys?' Scott asked. The next day, Ian's new mate lent him the self-titled debut album by the Sydney rockers (actually, trainspotters, it was both versions – the blue and yellow covers). Ian went home and taped it onto a cassette and it was like this bristling new edgy sound and attitude swung open a big door in Ian's musical consciousness and he marched straight through it and never turned back.

Ian immediately became obsessed by the new wave of Oz rock. One of the first records he remembers buying with his own pocket money was 'Big On Love' by the Models and from then on he spent whatever he had on music.

He got himself added to the mailing list of the seminal Melbourne-based independent music store Au Go Go Records, and he regularly sent off cash in the post for the latest vinyl discs by underground Aussie acts of the day such as the Moodists (Dave Graney's original band), Tuffmonks (a one-off collaboration between Brisbane's Go-Betweens and Nick Cave's Birthday Party) and Wet Taxis. This soon led to the discovery of '60s psychedelic garage rock revivalists the Stems of Perth and the Lime Spiders of Sydney, defining acts for the burgeoning artist and rockers upon which the young Ian would fashion his personal look and early guitar stylings.

This growing obsession with music coincided with Ian's earliest days at Brisbane Grammar, where he met and bonded with another guitarist and his first true rock & roll blood brother. No, not JC – not yet. Before JC came into his life, Hoggy had another musical compadre. His name was Macca – Cameron McKenzie.

The Valley was still pretty seedy back in the mid-'80s.

HOG AND MACCA met in year eight in a guitar class and, from there on, were pretty much inseparable. They lived close to each other in Brisbane's western suburbs. Every morning and afternoon for years, they'd share the long bus and train rides across town to and from school. Not that either of them was ever that much into the concept of 'school'.

With each passing semester, the pair attended fewer and fewer classes. The powers-that-be at Brisbane Grammar mostly overlooked this truancy. Ian and Macca might not turn up to class much, but at least they were at school. Everyone always knew where they could find them – in the Organ Room, practising guitar. (Or out the back having a smoke.)

These high school glimmer twins had a co-conspirator in their pure rock pursuit, someone looking out for them inside the staff room. Rick Purdie, the pair's music teacher, was an accomplished guitarist and professional session player in his own right. He immediately recognised the passion and ability in both young musicians. It was in Purdie's guitar tutorials that Ian and Macca truly bonded – initially pushing each other on to higher skill levels on their fret boards, and soon after diving headlong into the underground Brisbane music scene together.

Purdie taught the pair how to play by ear and feel. Initially, they'd bring along whatever new song they wanted to learn, Purdie would help them work out all the parts and the boys would then go away and master it. Stray Cats, Hoodoo Gurus, early U2, circa *Under A Blood Red Sky* – whatever the early-to-mid-'80s had to offer. Older stuff too, of course.

In one shape or another, day-in, day-out, this went on for years. In effect, Ian and Macca's high schooling was all about one thing – readying themselves to be rock & roll guitarists in a rock & roll band.

Before they'd even turned 15, Hog and Macca were both playing in bands in pubs on school nights. 'Brisbane was awesome back then,' Ian says with a laugh. 'No one asked for I.D.'

There were a couple of venues around town – especially in the Valley (Brisbane's Fortitude Valley) – that would happily take on blindingly obvious underage bands to fill in their late-evening weeknight slots. This was back in the days when all you needed to show a pub bouncer as proof-of-age was a photocopy of your birth certificate. So anyone with access to an older brother's birth certificate, some Liquid Paper and a photocopier was technically old enough to get into a licensed, over-18s venue.

The Valley was still pretty seedy back in the mid-'80s – 'sketchy', as Ian likes to describe it. It was the city's red-light district and certainly no place for 14-year-old school boys to be

hanging out late at night. Initially on gig nights, Ian and Macca would cover for each other by telling their parents they were having an innocent sleepover at the other's house. It didn't take long for their folks to work out what was going on and they begrudgingly gave their conditional support, as long as it didn't affect the boys' school work. Which, technically, it didn't.

At first, Ian and Macca played in different bands. Ian's earliest outfits included the Vibrants (who auditioned to headline the school dance at the neighbouring Terrace College by playing Sex Pistols covers but surprisingly didn't get the gig).

There was another band called the Jury in which Ian and Macca separately played at different times. Then Ian had his heart broken when he auditioned for his dream band, the Huntsmen.

The Huntsmen was made up of a bunch of Ian's mates – Dalton Gentner, Tim Mawson, Kerry Flood and Adam Wood. Dalton and Tim went to Indooroopilly High and although the guys were a couple of years older than Ian, they treated the 14-year-old as an equal, except for the fact that he was a private school brat. The band needed a bass player and Ian was willing to turn for them and swap instruments. It was all set to happen when Ian's parents forced him to go on a summer holiday back to Tasmania, and the band didn't wait, they took on another bass player, Chris Anderson. Ian still went along to rehearsals, remained a bit of a groupie.

'They were my idols, those guys,' says Ian. 'All these fantastic musicians. A couple of them, Dalton and Chris, are no longer with us, God rest their souls – I was in contact with Dalton until the day he died and it still upsets me. But I was so cut when I got thrown out of the Huntsmen. I knew I had to eventually start my own band.'

In the meantime, Ian joined Macca in the pair's first serious outfit together, the Fossils (along with bassist Jason Williams and drummer Nick Naughton), and they were soon regularly playing gigs at parties and venues such as the Outpost, Club Sensoria and the Love Inn.

'I reckon we were really good,' Ian says. 'I have a suitcase of tapes. One day they will see the light of day, maybe.'

They were essentially living their rock & roll dreams.

The Fossils' set-list included a selection of originals, but was mainly cover versions that reflected Ian and Macca's ever-expanding and increasingly sophisticated musical tastes – songs by their favourite Australian acts, including the Sunnyboys, Hoodoo Gurus, the Scientists, Lime Spiders, Celibate Rifles, Screaming Tribesmen, plus some music from the rest of the world. There was some Beatles, and as he moved into the second half of his teens, Ian – the Fossils' lead singer – particularly loved the likes of the Gun Club and Iggy Pop & the Stooges; the set-list always included Ian's take on Iggy's 'I'm Loose' and 'TV Eye'.

While they often performed to virtually empty rooms or just a small group of friends, they didn't think it could get much better than this. Get drunk and play some rock & roll. What more could a couple of Queensland teenage boys want out of life?

By years 10 and 11, Ian and Macca's façade of being interested in anything academic entirely disappeared. They were still physically turning up to school, at least most of the time, but it proved difficult to stay awake all day when they'd been up all night.

By this stage, not only were the mates living their rock & roll dreams by playing in a rock band, they were essentially living out a rock & roll lifestyle, too. Along with their mates from Indooroopilly High who were also in bands, Ian and Macca's weekends were spent either gigging or hanging out in the city's hip pubs and clubs – drinking, smoking ciggies, getting stoned and generally living the high life. A favourite hangout was the legendary White Chairs inner-city club in Elizabeth Street, which had been Brisbane's alt-music central hub for over a decade, the guys sneaking in their own booze and hiding it under their chairs.

Occasionally, Hoggy, Macca and their mates didn't turn up to school at all, instead taking off for a day trip and finding somewhere they could play guitar all day. Ian found yet another distraction when he became one of the first guys in his crew to have a serious girlfriend, Ingrid (Neilson), who would be his partner from age 14 through to 24. They're still good mates.

Macca remembers when he and Ian got into seriously deep shit one day in year 11 when the school swimming coach caught them and a few mates red-handed, drinking and smoking at the pub on a school day. Not just *any* school day – it was during the annual swimming carnival, which was going on at the pool across the road from the pub. 'We were not liked from that time on and were told there was something seriously wrong with our year and our generation,' says Macca. 'Ian was in trouble a lot.'

Yes, it was all fun and games, until someone had to repeat a year.

THE FIRST INDICATION IAN'S PARENTS GOT OF THE GULF BETWEEN what they thought Ian was doing with his life and what he was *really* doing with it, came crashing in when they saw his results. Up until this point, Ian had been able to stumble his way through the school curriculum, relying pretty much on his street smarts rather than study. But that was never going to cut it in year 12. His folks were genuinely shocked, they'd never had to deal with anything like this with their other two boys. There was only one remedy – Ian would have to repeat the year.

It was a devastating reality check for Ian too, a real body blow. He was by no means a dumbski – quite the contrary. It's just this teenager couldn't see the point of wasting his mental energy on formal schooling when all he wanted to do was rock. What was wrong with that?

So, as all of his mates took off into the real world, free from school forever, either starting jobs, taking gap years or going to uni, Ian had to suffer the indignity of being stuck at Grammar for a whole extra year, although he made lots of new lifelong friends.

This unexpected turn of events made Ian sick, quite literally. He was struck down by a chronic case of glandular fever for much of 1988. The only upside was that his illness meant he got to miss a lot of the extra school year and skip several exams.

If there was one true positive to come out of this truly horrible year for Ian, it's not that Brisbane was hosting the World Expo or that Australia was celebrating its bicentenary. No, the only good thing to come out of 1988 was that, later in the year, Ian would form another rock & roll band, the group that would eventually take on the name of an esoteric country rock classic by the American performer Neil Young – 'Powderfinger'.

IF WE ARE TO TRY TO PINPOINT THE first spark in the story of how Powderfinger came to be, that moment takes place one bright afternoon around 1985 on the sporting fields of Brisbane Grammar.

Ian was trudging around the bottom oval when he spotted one of the boarders running towards him, out of uniform. It was JC. He was wearing a grey shirt instead of the school's training jersey. JC's shirt had a logo on it, a hand-drawn logo. As he got closer, Ian realised what it was – a Sunnyboys logo!!!!

'He had a home-printed Sunnyboys shirt,' says Ian, clapping his hands at the memory. 'And it was like, "Hey man, how are you doing? What's your name?"

'And that was it.'

CHAPTER 4

JC

John Collins

It wasn't until they were in years 11 and 12 at Brisbane Grammar – 1986/87 – that JC and Hoggy finally started to bond, forging the foundations for their future life together in rock.

Before they became inseparable, it was almost as if JC and Hoggy were living parallel lives on different planets, their orbits rarely crossing, despite being in such close proximity to each other, in the same year at the same school.

As Hoggy rock & rolled and rampaged his way through his time at Brisbane Grammar as a 'daygo', over in the full-time boarders' dorm, John Collins, forever simply 'JC' to his mates and everyone else, was drawing himself a considerably more disciplined, clean-cut, electro-tinged stairway to rock & roll heaven.

The similarities between JC and Ian at this early stage of their lives were as stark as the differences.

Like Hoggy, JC was the youngest in a family of three brothers. JC's siblings, Jeff and Peter, were six and four years older respectively. This, of course, had a massive influence on JC's early tastes and general lifestyle.

Like Hoggy, JC started playing guitar as a youngster and by high school was playing in bands, even illegally performing in exactly the same dodgy licensed clubs around Brisbane as Hoggy did.

And also like Hog, the young JC had another partner-in-crime before bonding with monsieur Haug. JC's best bud Bish – Steven Bishop – would go on to become Powderfinger's original drummer.

And yet, even though they shared a guitar teacher later in high school, JC and Hoggy's paths very rarely crossed prior to that fortuitous meeting on the football oval. Same universe, different planets. JC was a live-in boarder, Hoggy was a daygo. JC was brought up in the country, Hoggy in cities. JC was clean cut, Hoggy wasn't.

But these young men were two sides of the same coin and destiny was paving the way so that their separate paths would soon become one.

PRIOR TO BEING PACKED UP OFF TO BOARDING school in Brisbane in his early teens, JC's childhood played out like a boy's own adventure.

John Andrew Collins was born on 27 April 1970 in the tiny and remote Queensland country town of Murgon, about 250 kilometres northwest of Brisbane. The Collins family lived in the neighbouring town of Wondai (population: about 1000). Before JC turned two the family relocated to another country town, the slightly larger Beaudesert, only about

Playing guitar? He wasn't sure how cool that would be.

90 kilometres south of Brisbane (population: about 5000), where JC's dad, Ross, a pharmacist, had bought his own business. The family finally settled on a farm in a place called Kerry, in the Beaudesert hinterland, and it's here JC did his growing up.

JC and everyone he knew attended the Beaudesert State School, followed by Beaudesert High. Music wasn't an overwhelming feature in these early years. Like his brothers, JC was forced to take piano lessons as a child (their mum, Cheryl, could play quite well and their grandmother had been a piano teacher), but they all dropped out as soon as they could.

Sport was JC's religion as a kid. His great loves were, in rough order, playing cricket with his mates, playing rugby league with his mates and riding his BMX or motorbike around the paddocks with his mates. Even before hitting his teens, JC was riding his motorbike to school in the mornings. 'The best thing ever,' he says, 'with my leather jacket on thinking I was Fonzie.'

Beaudesert was the sort of place where kids had to make their own fun. The town's old picture theatre had long ago blown over in a storm, so if you wanted to see a movie you had to get yourself all the way across to the Gold Coast, which was 60 kilometres away.

Saturday was always JC's favourite day – sports day. During summer it was cricket, of course. For years, like his brothers before him, JC played for the Kerry Cricket Club in the local regional competition. One of the highlights of his early life came when, as a six-year-old, he was called up as a last-minute substitute to play in an under-14s match. He was bowled third ball that day, but still, what a thrill.

In winter, the whites stayed in the cupboard and his rugby league jersey came out. His under-13s team won the grand final the year before he left for boarding school. It was another highlight of his childhood. His team included good mate and future professional rugby league player Andrew Gee.

If they weren't occupied playing cricket or rugby, JC and his mates would be out riding their bikes, building their own dirt track ramps with an earthmover. They also had access to an old beat-up car in which they could bash around the paddocks.

His was a postcard country Aussie upbringing. School holidays were spent with mates camping in the forest on the edge of the family property, sneaking along bottles of their parents' wine.

It was during these camping trips that JC's musical journey began in earnest. Like Hoggy, JC had the benefit of older brothers with contemporary record collections, as well as the bonus extra parental freedoms that come with being the youngest of three boys. But it was while camping with his mates, staying up all night, drinking stolen wine, listening to his friends' compilation tapes and making his own, that JC began to experience the alternative universes

that music could reveal. Human League, Devo, Madness, David Bowie – to kids in Beaudesert in the early 1980s, these were enchanting, alien sounds.

For JC and his mates music started becoming an obsession. 'We found our own little world,' he says.

By year six, he was playing DJ, putting on lunchtime discos to raise money for class excursions. Once puberty hit, JC and his gang started hanging out at the local Beaudesert Blue Light Discos – under age dance nights put on in town and in school halls by the local constabulary. Trips across to the Gold Coast became a much more regular activity; surfing, loitering on the beach, trying to act cool. According to his mates, the teenage JC, with his blond pretty boy-band good looks and impeccable manners, was quite smooth with the young ladies.

At 14, just before he left for boarding school, JC's mum surprised him by booking him in for guitar lessons. JC was caught completely off guard. He was into his music, but playing guitar? He wasn't sure how cool that would be.

'I was really embarrassed because back in Beaudesert it was daggy to play an instrument,' says JC. 'These two guys I had lessons with were like Redgum hippies – they liked to smoke a few cones. And they were awesome guys, big Ned Kelly beards, that kind of look. They were fantastic, and from that first day, I thought, "This is cool, I'm going to play guitar", because they made it really fun.'

ANYONE WHO'S EVER MET JC WILL TELL YOU he's seriously just about the nicest bloke you're ever likely to meet.

Tim Prescott, the man who down the track would sign Powderfinger to their first major recording deal, tells the story of being out with the band one night early in their career, back when all the members were still on the dole (as they were for years). They were at a bar somewhere, JC came up to him, saw Tim didn't have a drink, and offered to give him the rest of his own beer. JC said to Tim, 'I can't afford to buy you a drink, but I want you to have mine.'

That might sound a little over the top, right? But that's genuinely what JC is like. So sweet and it's no put-on.

JC was always one of the most popular kids at school during his years at Beaudesert. Aside from his on-field sporting obsessions, he helped organise school events and starred in school plays. But once he took off to the big smoke to start life as a full-time boarder at the prestigious and very 'old school' Brisbane Grammar, life suddenly wasn't as sunny and fun-loving as it used to be.

JC was one of three new boarders to start year nine at Grammar at the beginning of 1984. He was instantly popular among his new classmates, following in the footsteps of his similarly popular two older brothers. But a big part of 'old school' culture – which JC says was pretty much as depicted in the movie *Dead Poets Society* – is about breaking the spirit and confidence of newcomers. It was generally a rough initiation at Grammar for everyone. Kids in the lower grades were routinely terrorised by some of the older kids, who acted like army sergeants. These hazing sessions might include JC and his classmates being made to stand in the middle of the hallway in the boarding house as the bullies took turns running up and whacking their elbows into the little kids' backs. On one occasion, JC remembers a senior tried to bash him senseless with a football boot because JC dared answer back.

Yet it wasn't all misery at Grammar. In fact, far from it. With time, JC's personality shone through. 'He was a pretty confident sort of bloke, mixed very well with a wide group,' says Tim 'Doiza' Kelly, a fellow boarder and lifelong mate. 'He was socially aware and didn't let school get in the way of a good time. He's very, very bright, Johnny, but he probably didn't enjoy the academic side to school that much.' JC became the students' social coordinator and made a name for himself playing cricket and rugby (union now at private school, not league). Later, when it came JC's turn to play senior prefect and help run his boarding house, he and his mates set about changing the culture of abusing younger students, making it an altogether friendlier and more welcoming experience for the juniors. He was also elected as a member of the school's Student Representative Council.

Even through the darker days at Grammar, JC was never entirely alone. For just like Hoggy and his best mate Macca, JC also had a proto-rock & roll blood brother. His name was Bish – Steven Bishop.

Bish started boarding at Grammar on the same day as JC and the two were paired off immediately, assigned bunks right next to each other in the dorm.

Bish came from the far northern Queensland coastal town of Mackay, 1000 kilometres north of Brisbane. Bish describes himself as the antithesis of cool on his arrival at Grammar, with a flat-top hair-do and a wardrobe made up primarily of AC/DC and Iron Maiden t-shirts. 'I was a complete bogan, a Bevan from Mackay,' he says. He was 'treated like a leper' by most of the other students, but not by JC, who Bish says, with the benefit of hindsight, was himself a bit of a country bumpkin.

It was never going to hurt their chances at friendship that Bish was a budding drummer and JC a budding guitarist. Still, it took more than a year for everything to fall into place so that fate could put JC and Bish in their first rock & roll band together. And that first rock & roll band was called the Undertakers.

Formed late in 1985, the Undertakers only ever played one show – the end-of-year boarding house social, held in Grammar's opulent Grand Hall. The Undertakers were the night's headlining act, playing to an audience of a few hundred kids, including all the young ladies from the neighbouring girls' colleges. It was a big deal.

The Undertakers featured Bish on drums and his older brother Mark (now a university professor in the United States) on lead vocals. JC played guitar. The band members rehearsed their arses off in the school music room for weeks leading up to the show. JC and Bish, in particular, became obsessed by their upcoming debut. 'We had a pretty good band, we thought,' says Bish.

JC, whose other ballooning passion at high school was graphic art, would hide up the back of classes, filling exercise books with potential logos for the Undertakers. One of his hand-drawn 'UT' insignias featured on Bish's kick-drum at the big gig.

The Undertakers' one-and-only show went down a treat. It was JC's first chance to show off his big beautiful new guitar – a 16th birthday present from his parents, a Westone copy of the classic Gibson 335. The set was all-killer, no-filler. What a way to see out 1985. Talking Heads' 'Psycho Killer', Hoodoo Gurus' 'My Girl', as well as some classics – 'Wild Thing', 'Lola' – plus a couple of tracks from everyone's favourite, Sunnyboys. 'Very '80s,' JC says with a laugh.

There was no going back. Music instantly moved to the centre of JC and Bish's universe. That same year, they attended their first-ever rock concerts. They saw Melbourne band Models at the peak of their popularity playing Brisbane's Festival Hall, as well as Bob Dylan and Tom Petty together at Lang Park. Bish's lasting memory of the Dylan gig was of a considerably older woman, probably in her 20s, trying to pash JC.

The Undertakers didn't survive beyond that end-of-year social mainly because Mark Bishop graduated from Grammar and was gone. So come the start of 1986, year 11, JC and Bish had to find themselves a new band, which proved easy enough.

They hooked up with two other mates in their year – Bass (Andrew Bassingthwaighte), a fellow boarder, played keyboards and Taras Misko, a daygo, took lead vocals. Taras's little brother Yarema, who was in the year below, played bass.

Bass and Taras had known each other since they were young kids and shared a hardcore love of all things Joy Division/New Order. This would heavily influence the new band's sound, as well as the choice of band name – the Eternal was borrowed from the title of an old Joy Division track.

Taras describes the Eternal's sound as 'goth meets jangle meets electro'. They started out playing covers by all their favourites: 'Alone With You' and 'Happy Man' by the Sunnyboys; Joy Division's 'She's Lost Control' and 'Love Will Tear Us Apart'; 'Mongoloid' by Devo, to name a few.

'We had quite decent taste and quite wide ranging,' says Taras. 'We had a really good time together, it was a fun band. It had a little bit of a gang feel to it, because we were *the* band at school. We'd meet during a geography lesson or English or whatever and we'd be sketching ideas out for posters. John in those days was into his art and was always designing the next Eternal poster and the imagery we should use.'

Taras was also a close mate of Hoggy's dating back to primary school days. Ian credits Taras with being a big influence on expanding his musical tastes, introducing him to the likes of XTC, Stiff Little Fingers, Sex Pistols and, of course, Joy Division and New Order.

The members of the Eternal spent all their time together: school during the week, sports on Saturdays, band rehearsals on Sundays. The boarders required special dispensation from their dorm masters to leave the school property to go rehearse downstairs at Taras and Yarema's parents' house in the inner-city suburb of St Lucia on a Sunday afternoon.

Music instantly moved to the centre of JC and Bish's universe.

Soon enough, the Eternal was playing its first gigs. Friends' parties to start off with. They had a most memorable debut performance, playing in the backyard at their mate Michael Hintz's 16th. Things got pretty messy pretty quickly. Bass and Taras got so pissed that, at one point, they were playing different songs at the same time – Bass was bashing out 'House of the Rising Sun' until he knocked over his keyboards, while Taras was trying to sing 'Alone With You' and shouting out 'fuck' a lot. It only got worse from there. After the performance, JC walked out the front of the house to find his girlfriend pashing one of his best mates. JC went home early – something he'd never get to say about his Powderfinger years. By midnight, the police arrived and shut the whole thing down. So rock!

The Eternal started writing their own songs and, with time – which they all had plenty of – developed a full set of original stuff to play. The band wore its influences proudly, Taras's vocal style was very reminiscent of one Ian Curtis.

Midway through year 11, the Eternal scored a proper debut gig, playing as opening act on a Tuesday night at the Outpost in the Valley, the very same seedy joint that just over a year earlier hosted the debut gig by Hoggy and Macca's band, the Fossils.

There was no sneaking about for JC and Bish to get to their debut show like Hoggy and Macca had done. The boarders again had to get permission from their dorm masters to be allowed to leave the school grounds. They dutifully waited for the afternoon school bell to ring before getting changed out of their uniforms and into their gig gear.

Taras and Bass organised for their older brothers and parents to pick them and their instruments up and drop them off at the venue. The boys managed to get in a couple of sneaky beers at the neighbouring Shamrock Hotel before the show. A small group of mates and relatives came along to the gig. 'I can't remember it being amazing, but it was a lot of fun,' says JC. 'We got home about 11.30 pm and we were a bit tipsy. But we were responsible, just had a few beers.'

The young band made a good first impression on the shadowy figure of Tony, the bloke who ran the Outpost. As it happened, Tony was a huge Joy Division fan and invited them back to play at a tribute night he was in the process of organising.

From then, until the end of high school the following year, the Eternal had something of a meteoric rise, in relative terms compared to, say, the Fossils. There were lots of rowdy friends' parties, school functions, loads of rehearsing, Friday-night support slots at the Outpost and gigs at other venues like the Rec Club at Queensland University.

In 1987, things got quite serious. In March of that year, the Eternal spent a Friday evening in a small Brisbane studio called Music Systems, putting down a demo of four of their original songs: 'These Silent Days', 'Misty Life', 'Court in the Act' and 'Discard'. The recording helped them score a prized Friday night live-to-air session on Triple Zed, Brisbane's legendary independent community radio station – the epicentre of the city's indie music scene.

All this activity didn't go unnoticed by Hoggy. In fact, by this point, Planet JC and Planet Hoggy were whizzing about in such close proximity it was inevitable that they would soon crash into each other.

By year 12, JC and Bish were sneaking out of boarding school whenever they could and getting themselves a feel for the real world and Brisbane nightlife. They'd see Hoggy and Macca out and about at parties and in the coolest local watering holes, like White Chairs and the RE – the Royal Exchange.

Soon, all their worlds converged and new friendships bloomed. So much so that back at school, JC, Bish, Hoggy and Macca were now all regularly taking naps together on their desks during classes whenever possible. On one occasion, they were all asleep in a classroom next to the quadrangle as Friday lunchtime assembly was about to take place. One of the teachers sent in a year nine student to wake them up and they arose from their slumber to the sight of hundreds of students staring and laughing at them through the windows. 'It was pretty funny,' says JC.

AT THE END OF THE YEAR, THE END OF HIGH SCHOOL, naturally everything changed for everyone. Except for Hoggy, of course, who had to repeat his final year.

The Eternal didn't survive the transition out of school, especially once keyboardist Bass took off to continue his studies in Lismore. The rest of the guys kept the band going for a short while as a four-piece, but slowly everyone's interest waned.

'We weren't really popular,' says JC. 'It was hard music for people to get into. We were pretty dark.'

'I don't think we actually ever called it quits, it just sort of faded away,' says Taras. 'We were a school boy band and we had a great time ... we were okay, but we were never going to set the world alight. And we all had different tastes and wanted to do different things.' (Taras and Bass still make music together today in an outfit called Schimmelbusch.)

The simultaneous conclusion of high

school and the Eternal left both JC and Bish at a bit of a loose end, especially JC. While Bish went on to study agriculture at Gatton Agricultural College, JC unsuccessfully applied to get into art college. Knocked back, he was suddenly without a band or a clear career path.

He ended up getting some work as an assistant in a graphic artist's studio, while his brother Pete had a word to a mate who ran the Regatta Hotel on the banks of the Brisbane River, a popular hangout for students from the nearby University of Queensland (UQ).

Fortuitously, the Regatta (which has since been renovated into one of Brisbane's mega pubs) needed to put on some live entertainment as part of its liquor licence requirements to stay open until midnight, so the manager agreed to let JC and Bish perform as a duo in the downstairs bar for 20 bucks each, plus beer. Deal.

JC played guitar and Bish sang – all acoustic. The pair didn't even have amplifiers to start off with.

'I remember the first night we played, it was all AJs [army jocks] there and they wanted us to sing "I Was Only 19",' says Bish. 'Because we sang it, they chucked money at us, which really hurt because they were chucking 50-cent pieces at us. So we put a hat out in the corner of the Regatta and it progressed from there.'

JC and Bish made a pledge to each other that, no matter what the future might bring, they would always perform together.

As a duo, they proved popular enough with the AJs and uni students that the pub manager moved them into a bigger space upstairs, increased their pay to 80 bucks each and this became JC and Bish's main gig, every Thursday night, for much of 1988.

The duo wasn't to everyone's liking, though. 'I actually saw JC and Bish playing at the Regatta and hated them,' says ex-UQ journalism student, Bernard Fanning. 'They were doing a Sunnyboys thing, on acoustic guitar, and the Cure, things like that. I remember thinking they sucked.'

JC and Bish's regular set also included some Bob Dylan and Violent Femmes covers, plus the odd original. There was one self-penned ditty about how Expo '88 was shutting down all the pubs.

A regular face among the drinkers at the Regatta gigs was Hoggy's. He invited the pair to come along and play support at an upcoming Fossils show. Then Hoggy asked if the guys would mind if he came down to the Regatta one Thursday night and played a few songs on his own before the duo went on. Of course they didn't mind.

'And that,' says Bish, 'was really the catalyst for getting the early Powderfinger together.'

'They chucked money at us, which really hurt because they were chucking 50-cent pieces.'

CHAPTER 5

The Birth of Powderfinger

POWDERFINGER (MK I)
NOVEMBER/DECEMBER 1988

IAN HAUG - VOCALS/GUITAR
JOHN COLLINS - BASS
STEVEN BISHOP - DRUMS/VOCALS

Shelter me from the powder and the finger
Cover me with the thought that pulled the trigger
Think of me as one you'd never figured
Would fade away so young
With so much left undone

'Powderfinger' by Neil Young

If 'Powderfinger' wasn't the very first song they played together, then it was one of the first.

No one is exactly sure precisely when the initial jam took place – it was around the end of November or the start of December 1988. It was definitely after schoolies' week that year, because Hoggy had finally graduated from high school and wanted to party, even though he still couldn't drink because of his lingering glandular fever.

There's also no doubt about the location for this historic session. It happened downstairs at Jacinta Loos's parents' place in Kenmore, the suburb neighbouring Indooroopilly where Hoggy lived.

Jacinta was Steven Bishop's girlfriend at the time and by late 1988, almost a year out of boarding school, Bish and JC were both living at Jacinta's.

It was Hoggy who initiated the jam, asking Bish if he was up for a play. This was quite a turnaround from Bish's earlier relationship with Hoggy – rather, non-relationship – throughout most of high school.

'I was a bit scared of Ian,' confesses Bish. 'He was with the radical kids. Very arty, very rebellious, wouldn't cut his hair, was a fashion leader with his colourful paisley shirts, top buttons done up, all at 15.' Hoggy hung out with the tough kids at the school, like Martin Lee, future drummer of Regurgitator, who got expelled at one point for being a bit too rebellious, although Bish remembers Martin was treated rather unfairly in the incident.

Bish never imagined he'd end up in a band with Hoggy, let alone form an enduring mateship. Bish's instant reaction to Ian's proposal for a jam was that JC had to be involved. After all, Bish and JC had made a pledge.

'It's important. Almost as important as music. *Almost.*'

This posed a bit of a problem for Hoggy. JC was a guitarist and he didn't need another. Hoggy's plan all the way along was to get his best mate, Cameron McKenzie, to play second guitarist in any future band. 'Macca is an awesome guitarist, like Hoggy,' says JC.

Hoggy came up with a possible solution. How would JC feel about trying his hand at bass guitar? JC didn't need to be asked twice. 'Shit yeah, love to,' was his instantaneous response. JC immediately went out and got himself a bass and bass amp and was onboard.

But there was another glitch in Hoggy's original concept: Macca wasn't interested in joining a rock band. He was already over rock – hardcore blues was now his passion – but on top of that, all he wanted to do was to get out of Brisbane and see a bit of Australia and the rest of the world, rather than be holed up in rehearsal rooms for the next few years.

So, instead of joining Powderfinger, despite occasionally jamming with the guys early on and repeatedly being asked by Hoggy to change his mind during the first year and a half of the band's existence, Macca chose to take off travelling around Australia. His plan was to cash in big time on the booming covers band scene – tour non-stop with a variety of top-notch tribute bands and slowly work his way around the entire country. And that's exactly what Macca did – he was gone for the best part of the next two years.

'I ran the other way,' says Macca, laughing. 'Possibly the greatest mistake of my life, missing out.'

This, however, was by no means the end of Macca's close relationship with Powderfinger. Whilst he went on to become an in-demand international session musician and successful screen composer in his own right, Macca would remain very much a core member of the extended 'Finger family right to the end, even stepping up as the band's official substitute twelfth man (or technically sixth man) on several occasions when injury and illness struck the team.

AT THE BEGINNING OF 1989, Ian started a degree in architecture at the University of Queensland. Unlike his later years at high school, this wasn't just a time-killer for the youngest Haug. 'I think architecture is one of the most important things there is, except for being a teacher,' he says. 'The space you live and work in affects the way you feel. It affects how your brain works. It's important, almost as important as music. *Almost.*'

Coincidentally, January 1989 saw the first-ever Livid music festival staged on the grounds of UQ, headlined by three legendary Brisbane acts – the Go-Betweens, Ups & Downs and Chris Bailey, former lead singer of the Saints. In the ensuing years, Ian would forge a close

friendship with Grant McLennan of the Go-Betweens. The pair would go on to form a side-project, Far Out Corporation, which released an album, entitled *FOC*, in 1998.

Hoggy's enrolment at UQ in 1989 also coincided with one of the most turbulent years in student politics in the campus's history. Indeed, the whole of Queensland was in a state of political upheaval.

The Fitzgerald Inquiry, a long-running Royal Commission into political and police corruption in Queensland, handed down its findings in the middle of 1989. It recommended corruption charges be brought against several of the highest ranking figures in state politics, including the state's recently deposed leader, Sir Joh Bjelke-Petersen, who'd run Queensland with an iron fist for 18 years. After Bjelke-Petersen was forced to resign in 1987, Mike Ahern took over the ultra-conservative National Party. In the state elections at the end of 1989, the ruling National Party was finally swept from power for the first time since 1957.

Bjelke-Petersen's repressive reign throughout the 1970s and '80s meant Queensland more closely resembled a state in America's Deep South or apartheid-era South Africa rather than a state of Australia. It wasn't much fun being young, open-minded and living in Queensland during this time. It was the sort of place where hanging out with a group of mates or even having the wrong haircut would get you frisked by the cops.

However, in the years leading up to Queensland's cataclysmic political and sociological change, life had started to lighten up in the Sunshine State. While all the future members of Powderfinger say they never personally felt victimised by the oppressive regime, it provided the fuel for the emerging counter-culture movement which, come the turn of the decade, helped breed an adventurous new crop of Brisbane bands, a genuinely alternative music scene within which Powderfinger grew and ultimately prospered.

'Politics got in the way of a lot of stuff in Queensland but we never found it heavy as a band,' says Ian. 'It was a pretty weird time in Queensland, but we were probably five years too young for it really to affect us. People Grant's age [McLennan was 12 years older than Hoggy] were really affected.

'I got in trouble from the stationmaster for having a cigarette in the dunny with a punk, but it wasn't because I was walking three abreast up the mall, which is what used to happen. The whole politics of Queensland when we were starting as a band was all based around student union politics.'

Indeed, while the rest of Queensland was basking in the glow of its post-Expo '88 social enlightenment, this was directly contradicted in campus life at UQ where, in 1989, the student arm of the right-wing National Party wrested control of the student union from its traditional office bearers: hard-left-leaning activists.

Hog, JC and Bish had no interest whatsoever in the campus politics of UQ, yet one day, in the not-too-distant future, this heady political atmosphere would unexpectedly pop up and bite the young Powderfinger right on the butt, inadvertently altering the band's trajectory and, in turn, changing the course of Australian music history.

SOON AFTER HOGGY STARTED uni, Powderfinger – the original trio – moved its rehearsals out of Jacinta's parents' place and into a small practice room under the student union building in the middle of the university's main campus in the inner-city suburb of St Lucia.

The cancer of the 'tribute' band was spreading.

The rehearsal room cost only $13 to hire per session, but the guys had to haul all their gear in and out each time they played. The room was down the corridor from the Triple Zed radio studios, the same studios in which JC and Bish performed their live-to-air show with the Eternal a few years earlier. Triple Zed had broadcast out of the university since the mid-'70s.

It's here that Powderfinger's early sound and attitude started taking shape. Three became one. The guys already looked and dressed quite differently to the way they had back in high school. Hoggy's beloved paisley shirts and winklepicker boots were long gone, replaced with a much more relaxed jeans and t-shirt/casual shirt approach; Bish grew his hair out; JC still looked a bit like a perfect pretty prefect but was doing his best to rock it up by ripping the sleeves off his shirts.

Alongside all the political upheaval going on in Queensland, another, more disturbing, cultural phenomenon was taking place in the late '80s, not just in Queensland but right across Australia. The cancer of the 'tribute' band movement was spreading.

Of course, cover bands had always existed, and most rock bands have traditionally included a few covers in their sets, but in the mid-to-late-'80s, the number of bands specialising in mimicking the hits of other acts took on epidemic proportions.

With these outfits no longer confined to the dingy dark corners of clubs and RSLs, it seemed that almost overnight the majority of pubs and clubs in Australia were no longer interested in hiring bands that played their own songs. Everyone just wanted to hear the classics.

Fortunately, like most budding young musicians, all three members of Powderfinger had grown up refining their crafts by mastering the songs of their favourite musicians and songwriters. Their tastes had broadened somewhat since the days of the Fossils and the Eternal, but the infant 'Finger was still playing a lot of covers.

With Hoggy on lead vocals, early set-lists included songs by the likes of, naturally, Neil Young, as well as Bad Company ('Shooting Star'), Ian Hunter ('Once Bitten, Twice Shy'), the Only Ones ('Another Girl, Another Planet') and the Kinks ('You Really Got Me'). They also

held onto a few favourite covers that had helped define their recent pre-Powderfinger pasts: 'Wave Goodbye' by the Stems; 'Beyond The Fringe' by the Lime Spiders; 'Ice' by the Screaming Tribesmen; and their eternal ode to the band that brought them all together, 'Alone With You' by the Sunnyboys.

Such a set-list was designed to assist the baby Powderfinger compete with other cover bands in securing gigs in the Brisbane scene. More significantly, however, ever since that very first jam at Jacinta Loos's house at the end of 1988, the 'Finger also started working on original songs, initially based on self-penned pieces that Hoggy brought to the rehearsals.

Some of these earliest Powderfinger originals, all but lost to the annals of history (Hoggy reckons he's probably still got them all on cassette tapes somewhere), included titles such as 'Do Anything', 'Made Up My Mind?', 'Same Old Trick' ('That was our big number,' says JC), and 'Take Me Away'.

Take me away
From this place
Where I'm livin' …

WHAT'S IN A NAME? WITH A GIG'S WORTH OF SONGS worked up, and a start made on building a repertoire of original material, they were ready to unleash their new band into the real world. All the guys needed was a name.

According to Hoggy, the name came very early in the piece. In fact, he thinks it might have been the very same night as the first jam. As JC remembers it, the question of a name didn't arise until they were forced to come up with one to put on a demo tape to enter into a local band competition.

They might be a bit sketchy about the date it happened, but they all remember where and how the christening went down. It was following a band rehearsal and the trio headed to the Story Bridge Hotel at the foot of the iconic central Brisbane landmark. They were drinking in the legendary Bomb Shelter at the back of the hotel, enjoying the smooth acoustic stylings of one of their favourite local artists at the time, the bluesy singer/guitarist John Malcolm.

'He was a hot guitarist and we were there watching him one Friday night, and we talked about a name,' says JC. 'Bish had already thought that Powderfinger was a good name, and so did Hoggy, independently of each other. Bish went, "Yeah – love it!"'

'We were drinking $5 jugs of beer and we thought, "What are we going to call this little outfit?"' adds Hog. 'All I remember thinking was we need a name for the band that isn't "The" something. We came up with the idea of Powderfinger, and Bish graffitied it on the toilet door in the Story Bridge Hotel and that was it.'

Alongside John Malcolm, another of the guys' favourite local live acts around this time was a hard rocking outfit from Byron Bay called Bourbon Street. In particular, Hoggy and his best mate Macca were big fans and would go watch Bourbon Street perform whenever the band came to town, even occasionally travelling down the coast on a weekend to watch them play taverns on the Gold Coast.

Hoggy makes no secret of the fact that Bourbon Street was a huge influence on this earliest stage of Powderfinger. 'Bourbon Street covered, pretty well, all the bands that we loved: Creedence [Clearwater Revival], [Led] Zeppelin, [Rolling] Stones,' he says.

Most tellingly, perhaps, Bourbon Street also opened all their shows around this period with a stunning version of a classic Neil Young track … 'Powderfinger'.

THE INITIAL THREE-PIECE VERSION OF POWDERFINGER only ever performed a handful of shows – maybe a dozen, tops. Mostly the band played at friends' parties – boozy, raucous affairs in backyards and lounge rooms in and around Brisbane, most often ending in the police rocking up and shutting the parties down after receiving predictable complaints from the neighbours.

Following the band's debut performance at their mate Garts' place in March 1989, their next gig was at Jamie Webb's 22nd birthday party on 29 July 1989, held in a house in Bent Street, Toowong (a five-minute walk up the road from the family home of future 'Finger vocalist, Bernard Fanning). Webby shared the Bent Street house with JC's older brother, Pete Collins (aka PC), and it also ended up being JC's de facto home.

The guys invited a few dozen people around for the big bash and it was a typical student party – lots of booze, lots of dope. There was another band on the bill that day too, a group of crusty older professional players calling themselves Free Spirits. Webby remembers the drummer from Free Spirits coming up to him at one point and saying, 'I reckon these kids have got something good here – they might get somewhere.'

After their set, the young rockers switched into party mode and set about writing themselves off. Almost on cue, the cops arrived while Free Spirits were playing and shut the party down.

There was another party around the same time at Tim and Kylee Douglas's place on the river in St Lucia. The trio set up their amps down by the pool, their music wafting across the water. The PA blew up after a few songs, before the cops showed up as per usual.

'As a three-piece we were limited in what we could do,' says JC. 'It was really good fun – fuck, it was good fun. This wasn't a big career decision. It was just hanging out playing in a band, for the love of it. Seriously, if we could get a good gig in front of a few people, that would make our day. That's how we were at the time.'

The band's first break, in relative terms, came in the middle of the year when the trio entered the annual Queensland Rock Awards. The awards were a pretty big deal at the time, drawing around 100 entrants from across the state.

Powderfinger's heat at the Spring Hill Hotel on 25 August was the first time the band had ever performed together on a proper stage and they put on an impressive enough show, winning the runners-up prize in the encouragement awards section.

This effective showing at the rock awards led to the band getting booked for a bunch of other gigs. In fact, according to JC, after that night, Powderfinger never again had to go out in search of work – the gigs always found them. One of the judges from the awards, a guy called Rod McLean, took an immediate shine to the guys.

'From the word go, they had something,' says Rod. 'You get a feel about a band. I just liked the way they went about it, the whole attitude of the guys won me over. It came across to me that they could be really professional. So every bit of work I could find, I'd give to Powderfinger. Any job I had going anywhere, I would give to them. They would always do the right thing.'

'Through Rod, we got offered work all the time,' says JC. 'He'd go, "I got a gig, will you do it?" And we were like, "Okay."

'So Rod McLean was basically our first agent, in a way, in terms of booking our shows. I'm not sure if we paid him commission. He was good to us, and so were a handful of others, like Andrea Donohue [née Smith], who used to run the Orient Hotel. She would ring if they had a cancellation, or wanted to put a night on. Work was not hard to come by, for some reason. Hoggy was managing the band then. It wasn't that hard, just taking calls and turning up.'

'Rod was this big dude who loved rock & roll,' says Hog. 'He looked like [Led Zeppelin manager] Peter Grant – he was a pretty scary looking guy. I remember JC and I, and later Bernard and I, going around to his house to pick up our pay and he'd be sitting on the couch in his undies. It was pretty weird. But he was a cool guy who was always really good to us.'

The three Fingers ended up playing the inner-city Orient Hotel a few times as a trio – it would become a regular haunt for the band over the next few years – and there were a couple of other gigs, too, including a particularly disastrous show, a pyjama party at Gatton Agricultural College, where Bish was studying.

'We were terrible and they'd paid all this money for us,' says Bish. 'They'd paid $400 or something. We ended up playing Guns N' Roses covers. I think we did "Patience".'

Back at the band's rehearsal room at UQ, everything was about to get turned upside down. Early one evening, as the band was jamming away, they noticed a disturbance brewing outside the student union building. Actually, it was the makings of a fully fledged riot. The right-wing-run student council had passed a motion to get the leftie radio station Triple Zed thrown off campus. In retaliation, station supporters stormed the building – which also housed the band's rehearsal room – to forcefully occupy the studios. All hell broke loose.

'We saw from the windows in the bandroom that it was going to happen,' says Hoggy. 'So we loaded our amps and the drums into our cars and we were out of there, because the skinheads and the student union were about to have a major clash. The whole student union building at the uni got absolutely trashed. If we'd stayed, we would have been caught right in the middle of it. It would have been awful.'

'The skinheads and the student union were about to have a major clash.'

Soon after, once Triple Zed moved from the uni, Powderfinger was forced to find a new place to rehearse.

Before the band left the student union building for good, two significant events took place in that practice room – well, actually, one significant, the other quite frivolous.

One night while the trio was rehearsing, rocking out on 'Ice' by the Screaming Tribesmen, a shit-faced science student stumbled into the place uninvited and started slam-dancing around the small room like a mad man. This crazy bastard, everyone would work out years later, was future Powderfinger drummer, Jonathan Coghill.

'I was a student at UQ, and I used to go to the Rec Club and get drunk,' confesses Cogsy. 'I was walking home one night and I heard this band rehearsing and it was Hoggy, JC and Bish. I went in, I was so drunk, and I pogoed around the room while they were playing.'

The other historic thing that happened in that room, very shortly before the riot, was one afternoon when Hoggy brought along a new mate to rehearsal, a journalism student he got to know during a particularly boring economics class.

Hoggy had recently started thinking that Powderfinger might need a new lead singer, to free him up to concentrate wholly on his guitar playing. Hoggy didn't know if this new guy could sing or not, but the pair had quickly worked out they shared similar tastes in lots of music. Like, for instance, believe it or not, a love of Byron's finest, Bourbon Street.

As fate would have it, turns out this guy could sing a bit. And this guy was … well, you know who he was.

CHAPTER 6

Bernie

Bernard Fanning

Back at Bernard Fanning's old primary school, St Ignatius in the Brisbane suburb of Toowong, there is a building named in honour of the singer's first proper piano teacher – Sister Mary Leonard. No, not because she gave our Bernard his first music lessons in life, but rather because Sister Mary Leonard was an institution at St Ignatius, around long enough to have taught the parents of several of Bernie's classmates. All the little kids assumed she was immortal.

Aside from teaching piano to a couple of generations of local children, Sister Mary Leonard was famous in the parish for her annual school musicals. To the students involved in her shows, she was the sternest of theatrical directors. At rehearsals, she had her upright polished to such a gleam that, while she played, she could keep an eye on all the children behind her through the piano's reflection. Act up and she'd come around and give you a whack in the back. This was the '70s, when corporal punishment was still cool.

Bernard was by no means a natural star at this early stage of life and managed to wangle his way out of most of the big productions throughout primary school. Indeed, Bernie's only appearance of note in a school musical was back in year two, when he was given the supporting role of King Bombo in *Gulliver's Travels*.

Following that, at the tender age of seven, Bernie got out of the entertainment business and essentially retired from any kind of public performance. Instead, he decided, he would dedicate his life to the highest calling to which any young Aussie boy could aspire – cricket.

It would be more than a decade before Bernard drew himself out of his self-imposed retirement and managed to grow enough balls to step on a stage again. This happened only a matter of months before he officially joined Powderfinger, his first-ever band, in August 1989.

ASK IAN HAUG TO DEFINE THE COMPLEX PERSONALITY of the guy who took over his role as lead singer of Powderfinger, this man whose voice and words would help provide the band its soul, reflecting an innate sense of spirituality and human empathy and Hoggy thinks he can just about sum up his old mate in a few words. 'Irish Catholic, lots of guilt,' says Hoggy with a cheeky laugh.

Bernard Joseph Fanning was born at the Royal Brisbane Hospital on 15 August 1969. Like Hoggy and JC, Bernard is the youngest member of his immediate family. Also like Hoggy and JC, Bernie grew up with at least one much older brother, John, 10 years his senior. He also has two other siblings much closer in age: His sister Carmel is three years older and a mere 16 months separates Bernie from his only slightly older brother, Paul Fanning.

The Fannings come from tough traditional Irish Catholic stock. Both mum and dad,

Margaret and John senior, were born in rugged North Queensland townships and moved to Brisbane as children, ahead of raising their own family in Toowong (a short bus ride up the road from the Haug childhood home in Indooroopilly).

The local church and its community played a huge role in the Fanning family's life in Toowong. Both Bernard and Paul were altar boys and the parish church of St Ignatius, which included the primary school, was right next to their house, so it doubled as their own private playground and skateboard park outside school and church hours.

Growing up, Bernie and Paulie were inseparable, only one year apart at school. They both describe their childhoods as idyllic. 'A classic neighbourhood experience, an awesome way to grow up,' says Bernard. All their mates from around town went to school and church together. All their older brothers and sisters had done the same, all their parents were friends – everyone knew everyone.

'We're probably the last generation to have that privilege,' says Bernard. 'To grow up that way, where there was still a little bit of the old world. Kids could just piss off for the whole day and come back at night, and mum would send them out again if they did come home before dark.'

From infancy into their early teens, Bernie and Paulie shared a bedroom at the back of the family house. They were the very best of mates who spent virtually every minute of every day together. And what did these two youngest Fanning brothers do with all of that time? Mostly, every spare second, every day, went into playing cricket in the backyard. The matches often drew a brew of regulars from around the suburb.

This was the era of World Series Cricket and the Fannings were utterly obsessed by the sport almost all year round (soccer briefly took over in the winter months). Normally, the only things allowed to interrupt a game of backyard cricket were school, church, Bernard's piano lessons or, during the summer months, a Test match or a one-dayer on the telly.

Bernard and Paul didn't need a TV to follow their sporting hero, though. He lived down the hallway. While both boys were still in primary school, their big brother John was already out playing first-grade cricket with the West Brisbane Cricket Club.

'Johnny was a big influence,' says Paul Fanning. 'He was a good bloke. We idolised him growing up. He was one of those people who infectiously motivate you. He was always doing something.'

The eldest Fanning also had a massive influence over his younger siblings' other major obsession. Music.

While neither Bernard nor Paul were too keen on learning to play an instrument, they were besotted by Johnny's vinyl record and cassette collection. It was pretty standard classic mid-1970s fare: Alice Cooper's *Welcome To My Nightmare*; Steve Miller Band's *The Joker*; Elton John's *Goodbye Yellow Brick Road*.

There were a couple of discs in particular that the youngest Fannings listened to endlessly, namely best-of albums by the folky James Taylor and the freaky David Bowie. There were also several old Beatles 45s lying around – 'Come Together'/'Something'; 'Hey Jude'/'Revolution'; 'She Loves You'; 'Please Please Me'; 'Ticket To Ride'. It was these Beatles singles that did the most to mould the early tastes of the youngest Fanning.

For a while they were utterly obsessed by KISS.

Whereas Paul somehow managed to get out of music lessons from fairly early on, their mum insisted Bernard stick with it. She'd initially taught him some basics when he was five. There was always a piano, which belonged to their grandmother, in the house and throughout his primary school years, Bernard would get called in every evening from the backyard cricket games and be made to practise his scales.

Piano lessons weren't much fun for Bernie – Sister Mary Leonard didn't believe fun and music theory should mix. She was more one for knowledge through discipline. In his final year at St Ignatius (in which he was joint school captain), Bernard gave his mum an ultimatum. He would continue his piano lessons on one condition – all he wanted to learn to play was Beatles songs. That's it. His mum and his new piano teacher, Marcia Corcoran, agreed to his conditions, but the arrangement only lasted a year. By 1981, when Bernie took off to start high school at St Joseph's College Gregory Terrace in the city, he'd given up piano lessons for good.

'The awesome thing is that it was such a good grounding for me,' says the grown-up Bernard. 'Just having the basics of the language of music there when I wanted to write songs.'

Before moving on to high school, Bernie and Paulie's music tastes began expanding beyond the confines of Johnny's record collection. There was always *Countdown* on the telly, of course, but in the late-'70s, the two Fanning boys, along with a lot of their mates, discovered the first music act they could truly call their own – KISS.

For a while, they were utterly obsessed by KISS. 'When [drummer] Peter Criss left the band, I remember my mate Stevie Pratt coming out after mass and telling me that KISS had got a new drummer and he apparently had double-jointed wrists,' recalls Bernie. 'I was in year six when Eric Carr joined the band [in 1980]. Double-jointed wrists: I was super-pumped about it because that meant he was going to be really super hot.'

Throughout their childhoods, alongside all the cricket and church and school and music, the youngest Fannings were always encouraged to go out and work for their pocket money. Margaret and John had grown up through the Great Depression and World War II and put great value on the idea of earning and looking after your money. Bernard's dad had left school at 15 and got a job at the Commonwealth Bank, which he kept until his retirement 45 years later.

The family owned acreage down south in Jimboomba, where Bernard's sister Carmel kept a horse. John Senior came up with the idea of the boys shovelling up all the horse shit and selling it as garden fertiliser to their neighbours back in Toowong for a dollar a bag.

The Fannings also had a beach house at Nobby Beach on the Gold Coast, where many a summer holiday was spent playing cricket. Sean 'Foggers' Fogarty, Bernie's best mate since grade one, was often invited along. He remembers one trip in particular during which he, Bernie and Paulie stayed up late listening to Bad Company's 'Shooting Star' over and over, a song about a rock & roll star who takes it too far. The boys theorised about its hidden meaning.

This was long before it had crossed Bernie's mind to be a rock & roller himself, but Foggers says, even this early in life, there was never any chance that Bernard would be allowed to take anything too far. The Fanning household was always a strictly bullshit-free zone. 'Not allowed to be a wanker, not allowed to be a poser,' says Foggers. 'That was just not on.'

Aside from selling manure, Bernie and Paulie shared two other main jobs throughout their high school years. The first was delivering junk-mail to neighbourhood letterboxes – supermarket brochures, free pizza coupons, that sort of thing. They made thousands of pamphlet drops over the years.

Their main job, however, was mowing lawns around the neighbourhood. Brother John had started his own lawn-mowing business back when he was in high school and he'd handed down the work to his siblings once they were old enough to handle it. Paulie complains that most often he'd end up doing all the work while Bernie schmoozed all the neighbours walking past. (Bernie would continue mowing lawns part-time right up until Powderfinger released its second album, *Double Allergic*, in 1996.)

The end result of all this childhood labour was that the brothers had enough money to buy any new album they wanted. Their music tastes expanded exponentially. Paulie in particular started building a sizeable record collection, with an emphasis on harder rock – Led Zeppelin and Black Sabbath were a couple of particular favourites – and he also splashed out on a decent sound system. During their teen years, there was always music blaring out of the brothers' bedroom. Bernard also went through a phase of being obsessed by the film version of *Jesus Christ Superstar*, watching the video over and over. But despite all the new sounds coming into the house, Beatles and Bowie remained the core staples.

In this whole period, Bernard still never showed any inclination to actually play music himself. That only began to change when he was about 15. It was Paulie who started taking some guitar lessons, using Johnny's old guitar that hadn't been touched by anyone in years. Paulie came home one afternoon and showed Bernie how to wrestle out a clunky version of Bowie's 'Space Oddity'. C-major, E-minor. Johnny's old acoustic wasn't the easiest instrument to play, but Bernie started to get a feel for it pretty quickly.

ALL THE WHILE GROWING UP, BERNIE WAS A short-arse with a big mouth. His dad's nickname for him was Stumpy and he was always the kid made to sit in the front row of class photos.

The adult Bernard Fanning stands at five foot ten, but the boy-teen Bernie was stuck down at closer to five foot all the way through school, before finally enjoying a dramatic growth spurt around year 12. Needless to say, the extra inches did wonders for his cricket bowling action.

'He was pretty lippy and feisty, due to the fact that he was a little short bloke,' says Paulie. 'He was a scrappy little fucker, too. He'd go you in a heartbeat. He wasn't afraid to throw a punch, not at anyone other than me and his mates, but he certainly wasn't timid in those stakes. He wasn't violent by any stretch, but he was no shrinking violet either.'

Small-man syndrome aside, what Stumpy lacked in stature, he made up for in natural charisma. He was a smartarse: sharp, funny, who could charm the pants off anyone and talk to everyone. Soon after starting high school he'd befriended the seniors and school jocks on the bus rides to and from school, quickly earning the prestigious junior position of ball boy for the Terrace First 15 rugby team.

Unfortunately, his height issues meant Bernie struggled a bit with the señoritas early on, not for lack of trying. 'He was very good with the women but they didn't take him seriously because he looked too young,' says Foggers.

Bob Dylan, Cat Stevens, Rodriguez and, of course, Neil Young.

Bernie also got left behind as all his mates started sneaking into pubs and clubs to get pissed and watch live music when they were still only in their mid-teens. Sure, it was easy to fake IDs back then, but no bouncer anywhere was going to buy that Bernard was 18 when the short-arse still looked like he was 12.

He wasn't too fussed about missing out, though. There were enough opportunities to get wasted at friends' house parties. Anyway, by now, his first love was that old guitar and he was happy to stay at home by himself, either listening to records or trying to work out how to play songs out of his Beatles and Bowie song books, teaching himself the chords, even making some clumsy attempts at writing his own songs.

He'd strum that guitar endlessly. Foggers remembers Mrs Fanning regularly complaining how her youngest would sit at the kitchen table playing the same few chord progressions over and over and over. 'Why doesn't he play a song?' Mrs Fanning would beg.

'I never really progressed with the guitar for a long time,' admits Bernie. 'I just wanted to be able to write songs, I think.'

While he missed out on hanging at pubs and clubs with his mates on the weekends, the ex-altar boy was no saint. Paulie remembers that by their mid-teens, the brothers' pamphlet-drop job became a total piss-take.

They had an older cousin who lived just around the corner from their house. 'We used to take all the pamphlets around to the incinerator at her place and burn them and then just hang out,' says Paulie. 'I think we started smoking there. All the stuff you shouldn't be doing at that age.' They also had hundreds of pamphlets for free promotional pizzas, so no one they knew ever went hungry. 'Made us quite popular,' says Paul.

With all that time spent in solitude in his bedroom, Bernard's musical tastes expanded further. He loved all the hard rock stuff that Paulie was right into – Led Zep, AC/DC, Black Sabbath, etc – but when it was just Bernie alone with his guitar, it was the folkies who swept him away. He fell hard for the masters: Bob Dylan, Cat Stevens, Rodriguez and, of course, Neil Young.

'We were never kids who went around singing the whole time or anything,' says Bernard. 'But once I started playing the guitar, I just started singing along with it. Then I got into Neil Young around that time. Because I was such a pre-pubescent disaster area, my voice was still really high, so I tried to teach myself to sing like that [Neil Young]. Probably explains the really nasal and high-pitched squeaky nature of all the early Powderfinger stuff.

'I remember Dad hearing Neil Young once and just going, "That guy, I am telling you now, that guy cannot sing."

'It's fun to think back on those times, especially thinking about music and how deep it cut into you when you were a kid, and a young adult. I used to take it really seriously. I really hated some music, and I loved the music that I loved. There were these guys at school who were into Joy Division and New Order – they were mates of mine. One would give me a lift to school occasionally, and he'd play a Joy Division song and I'd pull his tape out and put on a Led Zeppelin song and go, "Listen to this, mate – not that crap!" But we came together on the Doors.'

It was around this same time, 1985, that Bernie and his circle of mates discovered dope. Is there anything better than getting stoned and strumming your guitar? Or listening to music? Or strumming your guitar while listening to music? Bernie didn't think so.

Denis Sheahan, another of Bernie's close mates from Terrace and Powderfinger's future long-time tour director, remembers inviting Bernie over to his house on the night of the global Live Aid concerts in July 1985.

'I think he smoked his first joint at my house when we stayed up all night and watched Live Aid,' says Denis. 'He recorded the stuff he wanted and I recorded the stuff I wanted onto our combined VHS tape. Bernard was doing all his Zeppelin and Black Sabbath stuff and I was recording U2 – we had very different taste.'

More and more, Bernie's daydreams had him out in front of a crowd, either as a folk singer, just him and his guitar, or up the front of a rock & roll band. Aside from the odd ramshackle lunchtime jam in the school music room with a bunch of mates (including Paul McGarry, future guitarist of Brissie band Webster, which Paul Fanning would end up managing), Bern was doing absolutely nothing about turning his musical dreams into reality. 'I wanted to get in a band, absolutely,' he says, 'but I had no real idea how that would happen.'

Also, there were other things to occupy his energies during these final couple of years of high school. There was the increased academic work, obviously, plus Bernie had achieved one of his other ambitions, to play in the First 11 of his school cricket team. 'We still don't know why he was in the team,' offers Foggers. 'Probably for his companionship.'

It wasn't until Bern started at university that everything began to change.

BERNARD FINISHED UP AT HIGH SCHOOL, DID PRETTY WELL and got into journalism at the University of Queensland. He'd just missed out on scoring a journalistic cadetship at Brisbane's only daily newspaper, the *Courier-Mail*, which would have seen him go straight from high school to working for the Rupert Murdoch empire. Imagine that.

Bernie had lofty visions of life as a journalist. Perhaps he could work for *Rolling Stone*, get to hang out with his favourite bands. Or, even better, become a sports writer, spend the rest of his life covering international cricket matches. Even to this day, Bernard reads everything he can about cricket and retains an encyclopaedic knowledge of the sport. He is a true cricket tragic.

Soon after starting his university course, however, Bernard got a much clearer sense of what life as a journalist would really be like – predominantly soulless drudgery.

'Going to uni and studying journalism gave me a different picture of it,' he says. 'I thought being a journalist was writing features. You wrote long bits of prose, but I was wrong. I was pretty naïve about it, really.

'I wasn't a particularly worldly person, had a pretty easy life growing up, never any big dramas or big problems, a pretty happy existence. And I'd gone to a private boys' school. There was kind of a general expectation that you would go on and do some tertiary study or whatever and have a career. Also, Johnny, my older brother, had gone to uni. He was an architect, so he'd set the path and I wasn't diverging very much.' (Paulie, meanwhile, followed his father's footsteps and went from high school straight into banking.)

Having finally grown up – physically, at least – Bernie was now always out and about with his mates, hitting the clubs and pubs, seeing bands, generally enjoying the boozy, carefree social life that comes with being a uni student. His favourite pub was his local, the RE, the Royal Exchange Hotel, located just down the road, within stumbling distance, of the Fanning family home, which was handy.

Bernie, Paulie and another of their oldest mates, EZ – Eric Simons – became regulars at the RE. There was a guy who used to perform there every Tuesday and Saturday night, Matt Buglar (stage name Matt James), who was also an ex-Terrace boy.

Matt started giving Bernie guitar lessons and also taught him some ground rules about performing. 'When I was playing guitar and learning from him,' says Bernie, 'I used to keep time with my foot, but also with my teeth, I would click my teeth together. I remember him saying to me, "Well, how are you going to sing?" Yeah, okay, fair enough.'

After a while, Matt and the other regulars at the RE began hassling Bernie to get up and sing them a song. He staunchly refused. 'I had a desire to do it, but I didn't have the guts at this stage,' he says. But the guys wouldn't let it go.

'They would always be daring me to get up,' says Bernie. 'Eventually they made a bet with me. They had a basketball team or something, and they were hopeless, they used to get thrashed every week, but they said if they won a game, I had to get up and sing a song. I agreed to the bet. And they fucking won a game.'

The idea of physically singing in front of people sent Bernie into a panic. He had to get himself shit-faced to go through with it. Whatever the means, sometime early in 1989, Bernard Joseph Fanning emerged from his decade-plus self-imposed retirement to perform to a tiny group of drinkers. Accompanying himself on guitar, he sang Cat Stevens' 'How Can I Tell You'.

And how did it go? 'Put it this way,' says Bernard. 'I'm glad there were no mobile phones around then.'

Regardless of how it really went, this single three-minute performance was enough to finally break the hoodoo. It helped Bernie come to the astonishing realisation that if he really wanted to try his hand at being a performer, then he would need to actually start performing.

'It wasn't a conscious decision,' he says. 'It wasn't like, "I am *going* to do this!" I was at uni, studying to be a journalist, but my focus was not on that at all. I just loved playing music, couldn't get my hands off the guitar, and working out new songs.'

Certainly by this stage, Bernie had basically blown off all ambitions to become a journo. He was barely making the effort to show up to class or hand in any assignments. When he did bother to hand something in, it was half-arsed at best. On one occasion, he told a lecturer he'd been kicked out of home and was living out of his car. Which, of course, was a load of crap.

What he was doing with his days was pretty much nothing, other than playing his guitar. Paulie had moved out of home by this stage and was sharing a place with EZ.

'Instead of going to uni,' reveals Paulie, 'he'd leave Mum and Dad's – "See ya Mum, see ya Dad, going to uni now" – and he'd come straight over to our house. We'd be walking out the door to go to work and Bernard would be walking through the door to do his thing at our place. We'd get home at night and there'd be no beer left, no grass left and shit everywhere, 20 records out of their covers. Just classic Bernard being the pig that he was. He spent some quality hours down there.'

What Bernie did manage to achieve with all this spare time was build a repertoire of material with which he could finally launch himself onto Brisbane's live scene.

'I eventually started getting my shit together and learnt 30 or 40 songs,' he says. It was basically a set made up of all his favourites: Young, Dylan, Bowie, Stones, Beatles, Stevens, Rodriguez. 'I think that my first love is the singer/songwriter. In that sense, I was always planning to do that, which I suppose I eventually did.'

A mate who worked at a pub called the Gap Tavern, not too far from where Paulie and EZ lived in Ashgrove, organised for Bernie to come down and play on a Sunday afternoon.

Bernie can't remember exactly how many times he ended up performing at the Gap – it was only two or three, max. For it was very soon after these debut performances that Hoggy invited him to come and have a sing with his band, effectively putting Bernard's solo career on hold for another decade and a half.

CHAPTER 7

Four Fingers

POWDERFINGER (MK II)
SEPTEMBER 1989

IAN HAUG - VOCALS/GUITAR
JOHN COLLINS - BASS
STEVEN BISHOP - VOCALS/DRUMS
BERNARD FANNING - VOCALS/RHYTHM GUITAR

'Powderfinger is a very ambitious band,
with a determination for longevity in this industry.'

(From the first official Powderfinger press release)

Brisbane at the end of the 1980s was like an adolescent Bernard Fanning going through a huge belated growth spurt. It used to be a much smaller place than it is today. It wasn't as if everyone knew everyone, but everyone knew someone who knew someone who knew someone.

'It's hard to understand Brisbane back then,' says Bernard, 'how connected it was, if you didn't live there. People all knowing each other. It's not like that anymore.'

Certainly, say if two people of a similar age at that time in Brisbane were into the same music, liked the same bands – chances are they'd at least know of each other or occasionally find themselves together in the same room.

Point is, it was sort of inevitable that Hoggy and Bernie would eventually cross paths, get into a conversation about music, and suddenly feel like they'd found a soulmate, a sort of musical love at first sight. So obvious, in hindsight, that they were always meant to be together.

Soon after Bernie finally stepped out into Brisbane's nightlife, he kept seeing Hoggy's face everywhere about town. At Bourbon Street shows, down at the RE, at parties. He recognised Hoggy from that time at the swimming carnival. He'd spotted him on the train on and off throughout their high school years. Hoggy was hard to miss. And Bernie already knew Hog's girlfriend, Ingrid.

The two guys finally got into their first proper conversation during an economics class at UQ around the middle of 1989. Bernie and Hoggy in the same economics class – the Lord works in mysterious ways, if you believe that sort of stuff.

Hoggy and Bernie caught up again soon after at the RE and got to talking. Neil Young this and Bourbon Street that, this Beatles song, that Stones record. It was like Hoggy was meeting the personification of the left side of his brain.

Hog invited Bernie over to his place – Hoggy was still living at the family home, but his parents were often away. He and Bernie smoked some grass, listened to some music and played some guitar.

'I went to his place,' says Bernard, 'and he was playing me these awesome Pink Floyd licks on his Jackson Charvel with the pointy headstock through his Peavey amp. And Hoggy was hot in those days. We used to call him Lightning Haug, because he was such a shredder. Became instant mates with Hoggy, basically. He told me about the band, and said, "Mate, do you wanna come and jam?" So I did.'

'It was such an organic meeting,' says Ian. 'An economics class, really boring. I have no idea why I even ended up in this class. Initially I had never heard Bernard sing. I didn't even know if he *could* sing. I said to JC and Bish, "I just really want to play guitar and I just met this guy."'

Hoggy organised for Bernie to come in and have a play with the band in their rehearsal room at UQ. It was September 1989. No one called it an audition, as such, but that's obviously what it was.

'Hoggy came and picked me up, and was a few hours late,' says Bernie, 'which was the sign of things to come. Then I walked into the rehearsal with Powderfinger and there's JC and Bish. And I thought, "Oh, fuck, it's those guys from the Regatta – great!"'

JC recognised Bernie's face, too. Bernard was a year older than the rest of the band members, so was a year above all of them at school. 'I'd met Bernie briefly somewhere at a party when we were still at high school,' says JC. 'He looked about 12, but he was 16. I knew he went to Gregory Terrace.'

Bish, too, recognised Bernie from around the traps, but for his part, he felt a bit weirded out having a virtually complete stranger come in and sing with them. 'Bernard thought I was laughing at him,' says Bish, 'but I was just really nervous.'

All this made for a strange mood in the room.

Well, what to sing? How about a Neil Young song? No, it wasn't 'Powderfinger'. The first song they played together was 'Like a Hurricane'.

'We start playing "Hurricane",' says JC, 'and 30 seconds in, I look at Bish with that feeling: YES!!! Fantastic! Bern sounded like Neil Young. The guy could hold a tune, it wasn't a struggle.

All this made for a strange mood in the room.

'We were looking at each other and we just knew. And 10 seconds after that, my bass amp blew up, and that was the end of the rehearsal.'

'JC's amp blew up in the middle of it,' confirms Bernard, 'and that was also another kind of a sign of things to come, because his amp has been blowing up ever since. He went through about seven on the last tour. I am not fucking joking.'

'So Bern joined the band,' says Hoggy.

For Bernard, this was perfect. From his first-ever solo performance a couple of months earlier, now he was a part of a pretty good sounding rock & roll band playing music he loved. Suddenly, he was living the dream.

He instantly felt completely at ease with his new mates. 'They were really cool guys and really fun to hang out with,' says Bernie. 'I started hanging around with Hoggy quite a bit and jamming with him, going to rehearsal, and then just started doing gigs around the place.'

WITHIN A MATTER OF a few weeks, on 14 October 1989, Bernard made his live debut with Powderfinger. The band was booked to play a friend's party – Kylee Douglas's 18th. One of the trio's first-ever performances had been at another Douglas family party. It was a big event, held in a venue called the Speakeasy in the middle of the city and attended by more than 100 boozed-up teenagers.

As far as Kylee Douglas was concerned, having this early version of Powderfinger play at her party was the greatest 18th birthday present she could have wished for, although she didn't know it at the time. Her brother Tim was good mates with Hog, JC and Bish from Grammar, so Kylee knew the guys really well, especially Ian, who she says was like an older brother. Soon after her 18th, Kylee took off overseas and never lived in Australia again. So she didn't get to witness what became of this band of drunken teenagers who played at her birthday party.

'Living in Canada, I didn't realise how big Powderfinger got in Australia,' says Kylee. 'Every now and again, I'd meet someone who'd say they love Powderfinger and I'd say, "Oh yeah, they're my friends." And they'd be like, "Oh my God!" All these friends I went to high school with are really big fans and they all still remember that party.'

'That was my first proper gig,' says Bernard. 'I would have played eight or nine songs: "Like a Hurricane", "Wish You Were Here", "Sympathy for the Devil" and "Fortunate Son" – lots of Stones. Eventually, I was up there playing the whole set.'

One of Bernie's other major early performances was the band's return appearance at the Queensland Rock Awards, where they'd been so well received the previous time around. Again, the new line-up performed in a preliminary round at the inner-city Spring Hill Hotel.

'I got up and played three songs with the Fingers out of their set of nine or 10 songs,' recalls Bernard. 'And we failed to go through to the qualifying round.'

'They hated us,' Hoggy says, laughing. 'They thought we were shit.'

The judges' observations were harsh.

> *Image (Dress): Not much effort 4/10*
> *Stage presence: No real audience involvement 4/10*
> *Entertainment value: Good pub band 6/10*
> *Quality was reasonable, but you need to decide on a direction. There seem to be both Bon Scott and Neil Young influences – too diverse for a consistent direction.*

Another judge was even more severe:

> *Sounds like Neil Young revisited! Lead vocal lacks control. Pretty average. Didn't feel much happening there. Just OK. Your vocal arrangements tended to let you down on your performance. Just working on your music doesn't always do it. Good luck guys!*

Bish admits the band's performance that day was 'very amateur'. 'It took a long time for us to get a decent sound going,' he says. 'Things started to get serious when Bernie arrived, but it took a while. Bernie had to learn to be in a band.'

Obviously, Bernard's introduction into Powderfinger instantly changed the dynamic of the group, bringing about a massive shift within the ranks. Going from a three-piece to a four-piece is a big deal for a rock & roll band. Naturally, it caused a notable shift in sound and direction. For starters, Bernie brought along a whole new bag of influences – all that singer-songwriter stuff and his Beatles obsession.

And then there was that voice. A voice still very much in its infancy – a voice in search of a voice.

'They hated us. They thought we were shit.'

'He had a really ridiculously high-pitched voice all the time,' says Ian. 'Pretty much copying the Bourbon Street guy, Col [lead singer Colin Germano], trying to be like Robert Plant. And it just didn't work. That's how he nearly fucked his voice up forever. Yeah, the Rock Awards people thought it was terrible. But we liked it. It was totally different to what I had been singing, that's for sure.'

HOTSHOT
SHOT
HOTSHOT
MAD
BARRY'S

'Hoggy, when he sang, was more like the Screaming Tribesmen,' says JC. 'Bernard was more Neil Young, Led Zeppelin, Acca Dacca, that sort of stuff. We actually started playing some AC/DC when Bernard joined. We played "Whole Lotta Rosie".'

The four-piece version of Powderfinger took a long while to get its act together. Not that they were working ridiculously hard at it. They rehearsed once, maybe twice, a week, but at the same time, dived straight into the deep end of the Brisbane live scene.

There was an awkward crossover period as the band altered its song list to suit Bernie, who was taking on more and more of the lead vocalist role. A lot of the songs Hoggy sang, including the band's earliest originals such as 'Same Old Trick' and 'Take Me Away', simply didn't work with Bernie's voice, so slowly those songs were dumped.

Initially, with the batch of originals being dropped, it felt as if Powderfinger was becoming more of a covers band than ever before. To remedy this, the guys took a week off together and headed up to the house Bish rented near his college in Gatton. They set up their gear in the lounge room with the sole purpose of writing a bunch of songs custom-made for Bernie's squeaky tone.

'I think we just wanted to keep moving forward,' says Ian. 'And pretty much it was an excuse to drink beer.'

Nonetheless, it was a productive week; the guys came away with a bunch of new material that formed the backbone of their original set for the next little while. Songs such as 'Clear Water', 'Mercedes Eye', 'Love Jammer', 'Manson Gun', 'Free Stone' and 'Move On'. Again, all these songs served their purpose at the time but would not survive long enough to be captured in proper recordings.

Bernard recalls the first song of his own that he brought into the band was called 'Speak Your Mind'. The very thought of it still makes him cringe.

The men in the white coats came today
Came to carry my soul away
And all the turncoats came to pray
All looking for another way to speak their minds

HEADING INTO 1990, THE BASIC PLAN WAS FOR Powderfinger to start gigging as much as possible. Bernie, Hoggy and Bish were still all at uni and they also all had various part-time jobs, while JC had a full-time day job as a salesman working for a books wholesaler.

Every show felt like you were at a mate's party.

One of Powderfinger's first shows in the new year, the new decade, came in February at the Sherwood Aussie Rules Club, playing alongside a band called the Tomorrows, who would soon become another significant Brisbane band of the period under the name Puzzlehouse.

Powderfinger and Puzzlehouse had a strange sort of symbiotic-cum-competitive relationship in these early years. It dated back to Puzzlehouse's frontman, Brendan Cassidy, hogging all the limelight as the recognised singing talent at Bernie's primary school. Steve Bishop had also taken drum lessons alongside Puzzlehouse stickman Peter Reeves while the pair were at Grammar together. Peter Reeves also did lights for the Eternal. Brisbane in the '80s – everyone knew everyone.

Gradually, the regularity of Powderfinger's gig bookings started picking up. 'Early on as the four-piece, we were playing twice a week on average,' says JC. 'We were playing at the Ship Inn [in South Brisbane, off Vulture Street] and the Treasury [in the city]. Sometimes we would do two shows a night, Pineapple [Kangaroo Point] and Dooleys [Fortitude Valley] – we did that a couple of times.'

The new Powderfinger was moving away from its traditional alt-indie influences and taking on more of a '70s roots-rock flavour – essentially leaning on the Neil Young side of its personality, rather than the Stems and Screaming Tribesmen.

'We were just full-on blues rockers,' says Bernard. 'We were still doing lots of covers. We were always doing some originals too, which went down a complete bag of shit as opposed to "Sympathy for the Devil". We were playing a lot of Stones, bit of Led Zeppelin, early AC/DC. I don't think we did any Beatles. JC always had some problem with the Beatles, so we didn't do much of them. I remember him saying to me before *Odyssey Number 5*: "No Beatles this time." No Beatles? Fuck off, no Beatles!' ('I don't hate the Beatles,' clarifies JC. 'I just hate copying them.')

'Those early gigs were probably pretty ragged, I imagine,' adds Bernie. 'We used to get pretty pissed, it was part of it.'

JC doesn't argue that point: 'We were playing the Orient one time and I think we went on stage about 11 or 12. Bern had come around to my place at four o'clock that afternoon and we started drinking beer; we were maggoted by the time we got there. We played and we walked off stage and we were like, "Man, that was awesome!" Someone had recorded the show and we listened to it the next week and thought, "Fuck, how bad was that?" We were shithouse. But we had such a hot time. It was all so much fun, we didn't take it too seriously.'

'We weren't even touring,' says Hoggy, 'just playing around Brisbane, not considering saving money. But we ended up playing heaps of gigs, the four of us, absolutely heaps.'

Powderfinger began to establish itself as a popular live act on the local Brisbane inner-city music scene. They were building themselves a reputation as a good time band – every show felt like you were at a mate's party.

Before that, however, early on, there were countless nights when they basically played to no one – one or two punters plus bar staff. There were lots of gigs like that, but often they could regularly rely on a bunch of loyal friends to show up and help fill most rooms.

'There was already a group of maybe 16 or 20 people who were mates of the band,' says Bernard. 'Mates of Hoggy or JC, their mates from school, and girlfriends, stuff like that, and they would be at every gig. And then my friends started coming as well after I joined and we got going. So we kind of knew lots of the people and then you would also play with other bands, so you get to meet them and their friends, and the people who would come and see them play. It kind of just developed into a scene. And it was really fun.'

Powderfinger was now frequently sharing the bill with other popular young local Brisbane indie bands, including the Toxic Garden Gnomes, the Tellers, Purple Avengers, Aloha Pussycats and the Worms. The band also buddied up with Bernie's idols, Bourbon Street, and supported them on a run of shows through Lennox Head, Byron Bay and the Gold Coast.

Back in the heart of Brisbane, the four Fingers were now regulars at the central hub of the Orient Hotel. The band's first few shows at the venue were erroneously advertised as 'Powdafinger' until one of them built up the courage to point out the mistake to management.

The venue's live music bookers, Andrea Smith and Donnie Burke, absolutely loved Powderfinger.

'Donnie and I used to say all the time, "This band is going to make it, this band is going to be really big",' says Andrea. 'We used to give them quite a few gigs, partly because we liked them and because you could see that they were starting to build an audience.

'There was also a really interesting progression with their songs, from starting out singing a lot of covers to presenting their own songs and having them really well received, both by the audience and other bands.'

Donnie, better known as Blind Dog Donnie, a legendary figure in the Brisbane live scene in his own right, regularly invited the 'Finger to play support to his own band, the Howlin' Moondoggies.

'I loved them – I thought they were fucking great,' says Donnie. 'I liked them from the very first time I saw them and I put my money on them. I made a point of getting them a Saturday-night spot. They were really rootsy and chunky and their original stuff was good shit.

'I loved them – I thought they were fucking great.'

'It was a great gig, the Orient. It was sex, drugs and rock & roll. It was a full-on moshpit and lots of sex on the dance floor, sex backstage. They definitely had pussy power. You can't buy that shit, that likeability. That's a magic spot. They were loved, they had a great rapport with the audience. The crowd and the pub loved them, so I promoted them above everyone else that was around.'

Supporting Donnie was a personal thrill for Hoggy, who used to sneak out as a 14-year-old to go watch him play at Club Sensoria. 'He'd sing Lou Reed's "Vicious" and I remember I used to think, "That guy is sooo cool!"' says Ian. 'He's an amazing guitarist.

'So he used to ring up on my landline, I was still at my parents' house, and say, "Mate, a band has cancelled – can you come and do a gig?" And we'd go do the show, never any question. It was like, "Yep, we'll be there." We were the go-to band, if anyone ever called us, yep, we would be there. We rarely got paid, maybe free beers. We'd call a few friends, say come down to wherever.

'I was still studying at that stage, but I was also delivering pizzas, everyone was doing something. We weren't on the dole yet. JC was selling books, Bernard was mowing lawns; he had the lawn-mowing company. He was pretty good, too – he used to do the stripes.

'But Powderfinger played whenever we could. We just did as many gigs as possible.'

WITHIN A YEAR OF BERNIE JOINING THE BAND, POWDERFINGER had sorted out its sound and established itself as one of the brightest new lights on the Brisbane live music scene. As with most of its contemporaries, the 'Finger's live sets still featured lots of covers, along with a constantly expanding selection of originals. Not surprisingly, the band was being lumped in with old-school rockers like Bourbon Street rather than the new hip-cool indie bands such as Puzzlehouse.

In August 1990, ahead of another gig at the Orient, the band received its first-ever media coverage in a local music fanzine called *B.U.M.S.* (Brisbane Underground Music Scene).

> *'Raunchy rock & roll with a bluesy feel' is a very apt self-description of the band Powderfinger. Many of the originals have a distinct Neil Young sound. 'The Free Song' stands out as an interesting fusion of 'rap, rock, funk and reggae'. All the originals are co-written by Ian and Bernard (except for 'I've Heard' by Cameron McKenzie) and have a tendency to be about girls; how unusual.*
>
> *So what does the future hold for the band? Well, they're contemplating taking time off next year to concentrate solely on their music and playing around SE Queensland and Northern NSW. Ian says: 'We would like to be successful in Brisbane before we conquer the rest of the cosmos.' Ambitious, yes?*

Yes, ambitious. Incidentally, this article was penned by a budding young writer named Sara Herald, who aside from being Powderfinger's first champion in the media, went on to become better known as Sahara Herald Shepherd, one of the driving forces behind the Big Day Out music festival and wife to Hoodoo Gurus guitarist Brad Shepherd.

B.U.M.S. became a major Powderfinger supporter, long before any other media even noticed the band existed. In the magazine's end-of-year poll, its readers voted Powderfinger as one of 1990's most improved acts.

There were strange gigs and lessons to be learned all the way through this early stage for the young Fingers. Bish remembers a bloke who ran a music store in Spring Hill asked the guys to act as his back-up band at a festival up north. They agreed and played away as he strummed a mandolin and sang Steve Earle covers.

On another occasion, in September 1990, the band performed its biggest show to date, playing opening act on a triple bill also featuring the Toxic Garden Gnomes and the Tellers. It was a party cruise on a converted barge that ended up with a show on North Stradbroke Island in front of some 500 punters.

After they played their opening set, the Fingers headed backstage to say hi to the headliners, the Toxic Garden Gnomes, who were at the top of their game at this point and were about to relocate to Melbourne in an effort to break nationally. The Gnomes' overzealous manager told the Fingers to piss off – his stars were not to be disturbed.

'And we're like, "What?"' grizzles Hoggy. 'Because they were all friends of ours. So we got thrown out of the backstage area after we'd played. When the band found out, they were cut at their manager. But we thought, "Wow, this is wanky."

'Lots of stuff like that happened to us early on, crews treating us like shit, and we were like, "We have to make sure that we will never do this to people." And as far as I know, we didn't. And whenever our crew did shitty things to others, we pulled them up on it. I like to think that we, along with a few other bands, helped break the cycle of that bully mentality.'

THE NEXT YEAR WOULD PROVE TO BE both momentous and turbulent in Powderfinger's formative phase.

Life was complicated for almost everyone back in 1991, the future looking decidedly bleak: Australia was entering its worst recession since the Great Depression; youth unemployment was at record highs; Gulf War I was in full bloom. Generally, one year in, the 1990s was looking pretty crap all round.

With all this negativity about, in the spirit of the burgeoning international grunge movement, what should a group of young blokes do other than throw it all in, grow their hair out and dedicate themselves to a life of rock & roll?

Brisbane in 1991 wasn't quite Seattle, but there was definitely something in the beer. A bold reaction to the all-pervasive cover band movement was brewing and, not for the first time, this relatively small Australian city was about to spew forth a whole new scene of inventive original music.

Independently of this, the four members of Powderfinger, with encouragement from some wiser heads in the Brisbane music establishment – such as Blind Dog Donnie – and a visibly growing fanbase, took a leap of faith to make the band their full-time focus.

Hog and Bish deferred their studies at uni. Bernie was basically already out of his course and working full time, first as an office clerk, filing evidence for the Director of Public Prosecutions, and then driving a forklift in a paper bag factory.

'The work was just a means to play music,' says Bernard, 'but there was never the idea that I would just be a full-time musician. That wasn't a justifiable existence at this stage. But then I worked at this factory for six months and I just hated it and decided I was quitting and told my parents. I said to them, "I'm quitting this job, I'm not going to uni, I'm becoming a musician."

'At first it was not greeted with very much applause, but eventually – I don't know how long the process was – they said to me, "If you are doing it, you're doing it properly. Don't muck around. Work – work really hard at trying to be a musician. Try to get recognition." It was really encouraging advice, actually.'

JC threw in his full-time job, too, and together, all for one, one for all, Powderfinger went on the dole. 'The dynamic definitely changed when the guys left uni and I left my job,' says JC. 'We thought, "We have to go for this, this is our job now, we can't just pretend we're in a rock band, do two shows a week and not rehearse. We're not going to get away with that." We spent a lot of time getting together and rehearsing. We were just trying to save money so we could go travelling and put a CD out. We needed cash and you're not going to earn money sitting on your hands.

'We used to play these gigs with Toxic Garden Gnomes, the Tellers, and they were fucking awesome. They had an agent and they'd get their own bandroom and I thought, "Look at these guys – they're killing it!"'

Since leaving behind the rehearsal room at UQ following the riot, the band tried out a couple of different practice rooms around town, including the rehearsal space at the famed Red Zeds studios, where Powderfinger would later record its *Transfusion* EP. The band's old mate Cameron McKenzie was caretaker of the rooms at Red Zeds and Bernie also worked there briefly as a nightwatchman on Friday evenings.

The band finally rented a room above a music store in Barry Parade, Spring Hill, where it based itself for six months. It was the first time they had a place where they could permanently leave their gear set up, rather than lugging it in and out each time they wanted to play. This changed everything and marked the start of a disciplined routine the band would follow right through to its break-up: When not on tour, they'd rehearse virtually every day, from 10 am to 4 pm.

Talent aside, a lot of the band's future successes can be credited to this strict and unwavering work ethic. Artistically, however, it was the band's next rehearsal room, in an abandoned shopping centre in Fortitude Valley, which unexpectedly provided the energy, environment and inspiration that helped catapult Powderfinger into the national consciousness.

BY THE MIDDLE OF 1991, POWDERFINGER was working harder than ever, playing loads of shows, writing more songs, watching its fanbase grow from gig to gig. The band even started scoring the odd support slot for major label artists visiting from interstate such as Weddings Parties Anything.

To help spread the word further, the band sent out an official press release to venue bookers and local media, belatedly introducing Powderfinger and detailing its history thus far.

The band bio read in part:

> *Each member has made a full-time commitment ... to enable the band to work on the road wherever work is available throughout the country. A production crew of two (sound, lights) has already been arranged in anticipation of road work as soon as possible.*

It concluded:

> *Powderfinger is a very ambitious band, with a determination for longevity in this industry.*

Meanwhile, Bish spent the money he got for his 21st birthday on a Bedford van so they could start performing further afield than just inner-city Brisbane. His parents also lent him money so they could buy their own proper PA system.

Despite everything this line-up of Powderfinger had achieved in little more than a year, Hoggy still felt like something was missing. He had it in his head that the band needed to expand its sound further. At first, he was thinking they might need to bring in a keyboard player, a sort of lead keyboardist like the Doors or Steppenwolf.

What they actually needed became blindingly obvious when Hoggy and Bernie went out one night to catch a young Brisbane wannabe metal outfit called Sonic Tapestry playing in a local football team's clubhouse. The band was okay, but the long-haired show-off they had shredding on lead guitar, this kid looked like he might be something seriously special.

POWDERFINGER

TRANSFORMERS

THURSDAY 18th OCT.

CHAPTER 8

Darius aka DZ

Darren Middleton

Visualise, if you will, a mid-1980s heavy metal video clip.

A guitar case opens, an electric guitar shimmers and shines, a young boy's face lights up. He lifts that magical instrument out of its case like King Arthur pulling Excalibur from its stone. Cue the sickest guitar solo ever, a metaphor for a metaphysical transposition, a rebirth into the world of rock & roll.

This is only a slightly embellished version of what happened to our Darius.

Darren Middleton had never touched a guitar until he was in his mid-teens, had never contemplated the idea of playing an instrument. Then came the fateful afternoon in 1986, DZ was 15, when his mate Fitzy (Alex Fitzsimmons) showed up to soccer practice carrying a guitar case. As Darren remembers it, Fitzy took the guitar out of its box, placed it into DZ's unsuspecting hands and said, 'So, what do you think? Have a go …'

What happened next might best be described as a transcendental experience. Some could call it a miracle, or perhaps it was a darker force at play, with horns in a school uniform (ie: AC/DC's Angus Young). Here on the sidelines of the soccer field, a young boy stood at the crossroads.

One of DZ's oldest mates, Andrew Sands, was on hand to bear witness. 'I remember it vividly, actually,' says Sandsie. 'Darren was like, "Oh, what's in there?" And Fitzy said, "I've started learning guitar at school and I've got this old electric guitar." And Darren goes, "Oh, give us a look." He was holding it and staring at it, going, "Wow, this is cool – can I take it home tonight for a bit of a play?"'

Fitzy was fine with that. The guitar came with beginner's sheet music for the party classic 'He's Gonna Step On You Again'. Darren didn't get much sleep that night, couldn't put the guitar down. The next day, he brought the instrument into school to give back to Fitzy and showed his mates how he could already eke out a half-decent version of the lead riff to 'Step On You Again'. By the end of that week, according to Sandsie, Darren had that riff nailed.

From then, and this is no exaggeration, every living, breathing moment for our Darius was all about guitar.

Darren's introduction to the instrument coincided with his recent discovery of a new god – ie: again, AC/DC's Angus Young. 'I was idolising Angus Young at that stage,' says DZ. 'He was in a school uniform, I was in a school uniform. I basically picked it up from there.'

Out of school uniform, Darren spent his evenings and weekends working part-time at Toys 'R' Us, bolting together new bicycles while daydreaming of the moment he could afford his own guitar. 'With a little amp with delay effects, that would be the best thing ever,' recalls Darren. 'I started dreaming about it, playing, practising. School work kind of went out the window for me.'

It was indeed a miraculous transformation for Darren, because up until this point, his interest in music had been – at best – very, very dubious.

DARREN STUART MIDDLETON WAS BORN on 4 October 1971. Like future band mates Hoggy, JC and Bernie, Darren grew up in a household with two brothers (Chris and Matt, two years apart in age), but unlike the others, Darren is the eldest of his clan rather than the youngest.

The Middletons' family home was set on acreage in the fringe suburb of Moggill, about 20 kilometres southwest of Brisbane, where Darren attended the local state primary school. His dad, Doug, ran his own business as an electrical engineering consultant on major construction works, while his mum, Sandra, stayed at home looking after the kids. When Darren was at high school, the family relocated to the suburb of Chapel Hill, next to Indooroopilly where Ian Haug grew up.

During these early years, music barely made a bleep on DZ's radar. He pretty much hated all the Shirley Bassey, Glen Campbell and Beatles records his parents used to play. 'I'm the biggest Beatles fan out there now,' DZ hastens to add. 'I came full circle. Once you learn about music, you can appreciate music.' Although in DZ's case, that would take some time.

His only other musical memories as a child are of videotaping film clips off *Countdown* and taking them on family trips to visit his cousins in Sydney. While his own family wasn't musical, his cousins down south had a piano in their home and DZ's aunty played a guitar, which fascinated the little fella.

'I was about 12 and I'd play my cousins video clips of stuff I thought was cool,' says DZ, 'which was not really cool: Dynamic Hepnotics, stuff like that, Split Enz, although they were always pretty cool. I'd try to impress my cousins, but they were older and wiser than me and they'd tell me: "That's rubbish, that's rubbish."'

During these early years music barely made a bleep on DZ's radar.

Not that we're here to pass judgement, but that stuff was gold compared to what Darius got into in his early teen years. The first music that really made an impact on him, the first music that reached out through the TV screen and touched his soul, came courtesy of the great hair metal movement of the mid-'80s.

Before he discovered AC/DC, his favourite bands included – and there's no gentle way to put this, so we're just going to say it – Twisted Sister, Cinderella and Dokken (look them up). There was also early Bon Jovi and Guns N' Roses, which is like rock & roll Mozart compared to

that other stuff. It wasn't until later that Darren was introduced to the likes of the Exploding White Mice, the Cult, Peter and the Test Tube Babies, as well as other cool local indie bands. Although it should also be noted that DZ's favourite band before he discovered metal was Huey Lewis and the News.

'I was listening to some bad '80s bands by the time I was 15,' Darren says, cringing. 'Pretty ugly stuff. I was listening to a lot of hair product being sprayed into hair. I had a lot of hair product of my own. In years 11 and 12, I was in a private boys' school and I wanted to grow my hair, but you couldn't have it over your collar, so I used to gel it and curl it up under itself, so it sat above the collar. It looked hideous. But I was playing within the rules of the private school I was in.'

For high school, Darren attended BBC, the Presbyterian Brisbane Boys' College in Toowong. (That makes five out of five Fingers so far from private schools, for anyone keeping count of those sorts of things.) Call it coincidence or just another example of the compactness of old Brisbane, but BBC is on the same street – Kensington Terrace – as the Catholic parish of St Ignatius. Which means Darren went to high school within a few hundred metres of Bernard Fanning's family home and primary school. Weird, right? However, due to their different religions and, more so, their difference in age – Bernie is two years older than DZ – the pair's paths never crossed in these early years.

Before music took over, Darren's main teenage passions were the usual stuff of young Queenslanders – skateboarding, surfing, hanging out at the beach, camping trips with mates. His folks had a place up at Kings Beach, just north of Brisbane, and then later a beach house down on the Gold Coast, so DZ and his mates spent many a weekend hanging out on the sand.

But it wasn't long before DZ fulfilled his daydream of getting himself a guitar, a red and white Reflex (a cheap copy of a classic Fender Stratocaster), plus a little amp. And from there, he was off.

Darren spent hours upon hours practising and learning his instrument – before school, after school, every spare second. He started taking lessons from a high school music teacher, but his main tutorials took place on his own in his bedroom, watching his heavy metal videos over and over and learning each guitarist's intricate licks. Soon, he could perfectly mimic the most complex of lead breaks from the world's greatest heavy rock guitarists.

It wasn't only playing the notes that DZ was mastering. 'I watched AC/DC video clips, I had my little amp at home, and I would stand on it and jump off, 50 centimetres from the top of the amp to the ground, writhe around the floor like Angus used to. That's where my showmanship and jumping around on stage came from. Definitely from Angus Young.'

The voracity of DZ's passion for playing guitar was obvious to everyone who knew him. At home, he was driving his mum insane, eternally locked away in his room making noise that sounded nothing like Shirley Bassey. Not to mention what was going on with his hair.

At school, Travers Murr, another of DZ's best mates at BBC, recalls their music teacher being taken aback by the sudden emergence of Darren Middleton's advanced musicality.

'Darren didn't pop up as a good guitarist until years 11 and 12,' says Trav. 'He had six months' worth of lessons at school and then the teacher said, "Mate, I've shown you about as much as I can – you're already as good as me. You're on your own."'

Around the same time, Andrew Sands remembers a similar instance at a local music shop. He and DZ would regularly drop into Palings, one of Brisbane's premier instrument stores, to fawn over the top-of-the-range guitars that DZ never expected to be able to afford for himself. There was the obligatory *Wayne's World*-esque sign hanging on the wall: 'PLEASE, NO STAIRWAY TO HEAVEN'.

But DZ wasn't into Led Zep at this point. The latest long-form music video he'd absorbed was the live version of Joe Satriani's *Surfing with the Alien* – a favourite among all techy guitarists at the time.

DZ asked the dubious shop attendant to let him try out one of the $1000 Ibanez guitars. DZ plugged in and started showing off, doing his best Satriani, shredding the hell out of that instrument, tapping and hammering the fret board like a virtuoso.

'I remember this guy in the shop going, "Geez, mate, you're pretty good – how long you been playing for?"' says Sandsie. 'And Darren goes, "Maybe six months." This guy's jaw dropped and he goes, "Are you serious? Oh my God!" And he said, "Mate, you keep up with it because one day you're going to make it." We just had a bit of a laugh, put the guitar down and did what boys did – went out and checked out some chicks.'

IT WASN'T TOO LONG AFTER PICKING UP a guitar that DZ joined his first band. It never crossed his mind to go out and try his hand as a solo artist. Angus Young would never have contemplated that so neither would he. 'I didn't really think about it, but I guessed that's how it was done – you get other people and make a band,' says Darren. 'I always saw myself as part of a band, as opposed to trying to go at it on my own. I never thought about it that way, probably because at that stage I wasn't listening to solo artists like James Taylor or Neil Young. I was always into rock bands.'

The first band Darren joined was called Pirate. It was primarily a hard rock covers band and DZ was brought in as a second guitarist. All the other guys in the group were a couple of years older and had already been out playing in the real world for a while.

Darren says he can't remember too much about his time in Pirate – he was only in the group for a short while. He says the band's sound was in the vein of British rockers the Cult. Fortunately, we can cover off DZ's amnesia on his time in Pirate thanks to the eyewitness account of another young man who would grow up to become a heavyweight in the Brisbane music scene.

Lachlan Goold, better known under his working name Magoo, is now one of Australia's leading music producers. Back in his high school days, several of Magoo's mates were also in the band Pirate – who would later change their name to Scarlet Fever – so Magoo regularly sat in on rehearsal sessions as an observer. He describes Pirate as swampy rock, somewhere between the Rolling Stones and underground rock, with a singer who was a bit of an indie-styled Mick Jagger.

He remembers the shy, tiny, boyish figure of DZ suddenly showing up to rehearsals one day back in 1987. DZ had a 'Shattered Rock' Washburn metal guitar covered in lightning bolts and a tiny Ross brand practice amplifier, which immediately earned DZ the nickname of 'Rossi' among the other band members.

'Darren was quite good at playing guitar and he would happily just noodle away in the corner in the rehearsal but nobody could actually hear him, probably because he had that tiny amp,' says Magoo. 'We would look at each other a little bit puzzled. Nobody actually said anything. Also, he had this habit of just playing lead solos constantly. He was really good at lead but couldn't play rhythm guitar – he didn't have a great sense of rhythm.'

According to Magoo, Darren ended up playing about three shows with Pirate, his first-ever public performances as a guitarist. There were, however, personal issues to be overcome before DZ could take to the stage – namely his hair.

'Darren had short hair and at Pirate gigs he would wear this wig under a hat,' reveals Magoo. No wonder Darius has blocked a lot of this out.

DZ does, however, have faint memories of playing those shows with Pirate. It was at the long-gone Atcherley Hotel on the edge of Fortitude Valley, downstairs in a room known as the Stardust

Club. 'I always looked sort of youngish for my age,' says DZ, 'but I looked *really* young when I was 15. I don't know how I was actually allowed into these venues to play these shows, but we turned up on a Wednesday night to play our first gig, and didn't realise at the time that it was a heavy metal night.

'We were kind of a rocking band, but we weren't heavy metal. So between the sound check and the gig, we just turned up all the knobs, turned up the distortion, and learned a couple of Wasp songs really quickly.

'It was pretty scary, that first gig at the Stardust Club, but it was good fun. I think it went pretty well. I used to literally wear a kind of Confederate cap, the way Angus Young used to wear a cap. I was highly influenced by Angus in every way at that stage.'

'The band needed a second guitar to fatten up the sound and it didn't quite work with Darren,' says Magoo, who would go on to become good mates with DZ and also work closely with Powderfinger. 'It was an awkward period for Darren. It was an awkward period for all of us, but we all thought we were cool and Darren was trying to be cool. I would say we were all dags.'

FOLLOWING HIS SHORT-LIVED, BAD-HAIR DAYS WITH PIRATE, it took Darius a while to find himself in a band he could comfortably call his own and start to shine. There was a group of mates at his high school who would irregularly jam together, with different members coming in and out. Darren remembers they occasionally set up in his parents' garage in suburban Chapel Hill and blasted the earwax out of the neighbours.

'We rehearsed whenever we could,' says DZ. 'Probably once a week. We were literally a garage band at first. We'd set up in the garage, doors open, not to annoy the neighbours, but because you're 15, you've got this new guitar amp and just cranking it. It was great fun. The cops came around a few times to tell us to turn it off – that was pretty cool.'

It wasn't until towards the end of high school that this rotating line-up of mates coalesced into the band that would affectionately christen itself the mighty Tap – Sonic Tapestry.

The band featured Darren's good mate Travers Murr on lead vocals and rhythm guitar, plus two other BBC students, Aaron Daniel on bass and Bernard Catt on drums.

'We weren't very good, but people liked us,' says Trav. 'Darren led the way and we tried to follow and not fuck up too badly. Everyone could play but I wouldn't rate myself a very good singer. By about 18, Darren was an awesome guitarist – there wasn't much he couldn't do.'

According to Darren, Sonic Tapestry's musical style wasn't too dissimilar to what Powderfinger would eventually end up sounding like. He credits Travers with broadening his musical tastes beyond his beloved metal, introducing him to the sounds of artists such as Neil Young, Led Zeppelin and Rodriguez – exactly the same acts that had such an influence on early Powderfinger.

Pearl

WOR
PEACE

'We were playing rock, but it wasn't super heavy,' says DZ. 'We had songs that were a bit rocking and songs that were a bit more ballady. There was quite a bit of light and shade going on, which is what the Fingers have always done. Maybe that's why I fit into the Fingers.'

Even at this very early stage, the similarities between the Tap and the pre-DZ Fingers were obvious. For instance, both were covering the Rodriguez song 'Hate Street Dialogue' and both had a couple of AC/DC songs in their set – the 'Finger played 'Whole Lotta Rosie'; the Tap threw in a 'Highway to Hell', 'Hells Bells', or 'Jailbreak'.

The few covers aside, what made Sonic Tapestry different from virtually every other young band in the Brisbane music scene of the late-'80s/early-'90s, Powderfinger included, was that the Tap predominantly played original material.

'We started out writing our own songs,' says Darren. 'I always found it quite natural. I wanted to create rather than copy, as a starting place. We did a couple of covers, but primarily we wrote our own songs with the aim, "Let's do a recording, it would be amazing to do a recording."'

The Tap's set of originals included titles such as 'Never Trust a Hippy', 'Waimea Bay', 'All in One Night', 'Now You're Gone' and 'What Do You Want?'.

What do you want
I'm what you need
You can get it from me
If what you want
Is what you need
You can get it from me

Sonic Tapestry also took a slightly different approach to its live performances. In addition to playing at friends' parties and pubs and clubs around Brisbane and as far afield as Ipswich, the Tap also occasionally promoted its own events, hiring out a venue and pulling in a bunch of other bands to share the bill.

A regular venue for these shows was the Wests Leagues Club, a football clubhouse not too far from the boys' high school in Toowong. 'You would book the place and throw a party,' says Darren. 'Invite all your mates and everyone from other schools. Those early days in Sonic Tapestry were a great experience, good times.'

It was at one of these gigs, with everyone crammed in on bench seats knocking back a few beers, that a couple of members of Powderfinger, Ian Haug and Bernard Fanning, first copped an eyeful of the outlandish, firebrand shredding style of the one they would come to know as Darius.

'I was into the idea of showing off. Shredding it up.'

STRAIGHT OUT OF HIGH SCHOOL, for almost the whole time he was in Sonic Tapestry, Darren was also studying at TAFE, doing a two-year course in cooking and hospitality management. He also worked part-time in a bar in the city, pouring drinks and washing dishes. 'Work was purely a means of getting money to buy music stuff, that was its sole purpose,' says Darren. 'Not money to buy clothes or a car, just musical gear.'

Once he'd sorted himself out with a decent amp and some effects pedals, top of DZ's wishlist was to get himself one of those fancy new wireless pick-up systems to free him from the constraints of guitar leads. That was the dream. Imagine what he could do once he was unleashed!

'I was into the idea of showing off,' says Darren. 'Shredding it up. Not many people in Brisbane were doing that at the time. There was another guitarist who was an inspiration – his name was Raymond [Dobson] and he played in a band called Love Child. [Love Child won the cover band category of the 1989 Queensland Rock Awards, the same event where the trio version of Powderfinger made its official debut.] He was a showy guitarist and I was pretty impressed with his showmanship. It's meant to be entertaining and fun. This was before all that '90s shoe-gazing stuff came along.'

A couple of years out of high school, Sonic Tapestry was still only averaging about a show a week. The closest the band ever got to making a proper recording of its original material came when it spent an evening in the studio at the School of Audio Engineering in Milton. A friend of the band was a student at the school (Darren later did a course there, too) and got them a free night to make a live-to-tape recording of their songs. Unfortunately, the only copy of that recording has since been lost.

Heading into 1991, it didn't appear as if Sonic Tapestry was going to be setting the music world alight any time soon. Not that the guys were giving up hope. Trav, who was studying graphic design, decided he should put some more work into his musicianship and set about finding an instructor who could give him guitar lessons and also teach him how to play harmonica.

Trav's girlfriend at the time, Kerry, was working in a bookshop. One of her colleagues also played in a band, so Kerry asked him if he knew anyone who could help Trav out. The guy told Kerry that the singer in his group was a pretty good guitarist and a great harp player. The guy who worked with Trav's girlfriend was none other than JC. And JC's recommendation was, of course, Bernie.

Trav and Bernie hooked up and hit it off immediately. Why wouldn't they – they shared almost exactly the same taste in music. Trav and his mates, including Darren, started showing up at Powderfinger shows and were impressed. 'We thought they were a pretty good band as far as Brisbane goes,' says Darren. 'There were a few good bands at the time, like Garden of the Prophet, but Powderfinger just had something special about them. Bernard had a charisma that made you want to watch him and listen to him.'

In return, Trav invited the Fingers to the Tap's upcoming show at Wests Leagues. Bernie and Hoggy showed up and the Tap members were quite excited by that. As usual, there were a couple of other bands on the bill, including Pirate.

'It was a free gig,' says Trav. 'Everybody bought beers and sat on long tables in the football club – not the most rock & roll of venues. But we got up and rocked as hard as we could, knowing that Powderfinger had turned up.'

When it came time for DZ's trademark show-stopping solo, he let rip even more than usual. He'd finally bought a wireless guitar system and there was no holding him back. 'I was all over the place. Playing out in the crowd. So much fun, I loved that,' says Darren.

'He jumped onto Powderfinger's table,' recalls Trav, 'and walked up to the middle of it, kicked off all the beer glasses in front of them and just shredded. And then hopped back on stage again. We were all looking at each other, going, "That was fucking hot!" We were cheesy little metal heads.'

If the purpose of this spectacle was to blow those Powderfinger guys away, well, it had the desired effect. 'We saw him play with Sonic Tapestry and we asked him to join, because he was too good for them,' says Bernie.

'At the time,' adds Hoggy, 'I still had this idea in my mind that I really wanted us to sound more like Steppenwolf and I wanted to get a keyboard player. Then Bern and I saw Darren play and it was like, "I don't want a keyboard player anymore – I want him." He was just a show-off and a fucking good player. And I needed someone to deflect the limelight from me.'

They didn't ask Darren to join straight away. Instead, they invited Sonic Tapestry to open for Powderfinger at a couple of shows at Bonaparte's Hotel in the Valley.

Unaware of any ulterior motive at play, the Tap actually thought this was their big break and, again, performed as if their lives depended on it. 'We thought we were awesome and that we blew Powderfinger off the stage,' Darren says, laughing.

Maybe they were right. The Fingers invited the Tap to play another show with them, this time at the Orient. Following that performance, Donnie, the Orient's booker, came up to the band, raving about how great they were. He immediately offered them more gigs and the Tap ended up supporting the Fingers once a week for the next month.

And that's when the Fingers put the hard word on DZ.

Hoggy invited Darren along to the Royal Exchange in Toowong for a quiet drink and a chat, and asked him if he'd be interested in coming along for a jam, with a view to formally joining Powderfinger.

Darren was conflicted. For one thing, he'd recently graduated from his TAFE course and had been offered a highly sought-after chef apprenticeship from the Hilton hotel chain – a guaranteed no-risk career path to becoming a professional chef. And then, of course, there was the matter of Sonic Tapestry.

'The Fingers were a fully committed band.'

Darren let Trav know what was happening. They called a band meeting over nachos and beers. Before anyone else said anything, Trav left no doubt as to where he stood on the issue: Darren would be mad not to join Powderfinger.

'Darren was still backing us,' says Trav. 'He said: "If you guys say you still want to do this 100 per cent, then I'll stick with you." I was in design school and I said, "I think I'll be better at that than I am as a singer – I'm going to follow that path."

'The other two guys were gutted, going, "I can't believe you said that!" And I was like, "Come on, you've got to be sensible, guys – you heard our recording, it's not scintillating. If you guys want to keep going, you can find another guitarist and another singer."'

'Trav said to me, "Mate, you should do it because there's more of a future there than there is with us,"' recalls Darren. 'I needed Trav to be okay with that at the time, even though I wanted to do it, and he knew that. It was nice of him to let go of me.'

With that, Sonic Tapestry came to an end and Darren was free to throw in his alternative career as a cook and join Powderfinger.

'And I haven't looked back since,' says DZ. 'I didn't think, "This is a good business move" – that these guys could take me to the top. I just felt like it was the right thing to do. The Fingers were a fully committed band, they were one of the better bands in Brisbane, so that was the right step for me. And they saw something in me that made them think, "Maybe we should get another guitarist." Which was, of course, the right move for them.'

CHAPTER 9

The Fifth and Sixth Fingers

POWDERFINGER MK III
JUNE 1991

IAN HAUG - GUITAR
JOHN COLLINS - BASS
STEVEN BISHOP - DRUMS
BERNARD FANNING - VOCALS/GUITAR
DARREN MIDDLETON - GUITAR

PAUL PITICCO - MANAGER

DZ's initiation into Powderfinger was, without compare, the weirdest and scariest of anyone's. Bikers, topless girls, free drugs on stage and at the bar – and that was just night one. 'I entered the world of Powderfinger among a barrage of leather and Harley-Davidsons,' says Darren.

Not his audition. That was quite stress-free and uneventful. Once everyone found their groove, it went off without a hitch.

Hoggy says as far as he's concerned, Darren's real audition took place on the table at the Wests football club, but it wasn't until a couple of months later, in the middle of 1991, that Darren made his first appearance in the 'Finger's rehearsal room above the music store in Spring Hill.

'He liked heaps of different stuff that I didn't like,' says Hoggy, 'but we bonded over AC/DC. If you don't like AC/DC, there's something wrong with you. Seriously, I still stand by that.'

DZ remembers initially feeling a bit anxious, jamming for the first time with a bunch of strangers. 'I set up and rolled a cigarette,' he says. 'I'd only just started smoking, I didn't really like it, but they all smoked, so I rolled a cigarette and got a head spin because I wasn't really used to it. I was 20, in a new group, wanting to fit in. And we went from there. It was a good fun rehearsal. We played a bit of Zeppelin, Neil Young, a couple of covers they taught me.

'It was a slightly different thing for me because I had to learn all these covers that I didn't know, and I remember the band saying, "Do you know this, you don't know this?" And I said something like, "I don't really learn covers – it clouds who I am." [Darren laughs at the memory.] It was sort of in self-defence of why I didn't know these songs, but also the fact that I liked to write songs too.'

JC was immediately impressed by the new guy. 'We used to call Hoggy "Lightning",' says JC, 'but Darren was pretty quick on the fret board, too. He was all over it. He liked all that '80s glam metal shit that I hated, but he did like Acca Dacca, so he liked good rock & roll along with the bad stuff.

'He was a really easy guy to get along with. He didn't come into the band and upset the existence of what was there – he's a guy who goes with the flow. He's pretty easy, he's a good player, he added some songs as a songwriter, and he just got better and better at that as time went on. We were definitely more rock & roll once he came in.'

The only person who felt put out by DZ's integration into Powderfinger was Bish. It took him some time to adjust to Bernie coming into the fold and now, a whole new fifth member was a bit too much to take.

'When Darren joined the band,' says Bish, 'I felt like: "Here's another person! Change! Change is difficult! What's going on?"' I had a little animosity. I think I was nice to him but I felt things had changed without my consent. But I got used to it.'

Certainly, Darren was oblivious to any tension in the band room, but Bish's increasingly peculiar demeanour wasn't going unnoticed by the other Fingers.

There wasn't any time to faff around – shows were booked, the band had to get on with it. After only a couple of weeks' worth of rehearsals, DZ was ready, or at least half-ready, for his debut appearance with Powderfinger. Like Bernie before him, it would be a tiered introduction, a few songs at first, increasing gig by gig as he learned all the material.

The band's part-time agent, Rod McLean, offered the guys a novel show. Really well paid – $600 for a night's work. Very exclusive audience. Only catch – the venue was the clubhouse of the Brisbane chapter of the outlawed Black Uhlans motorcycle club, down south in Logan City. 'It was a pretty heavy joint,' says Rod. 'It was a straight-out bikers' do where you don't get any applause after you play a song.'

Welcome, young Darius, to the wonderful and occasionally weird world of Powderfinger.

'I only played about half the set,' says Darren. 'For the rest of it, instead of sitting at the bar, mingling, which just looked way too frightening to me, I sat at the front of the stage, like an adoring fan, not going anywhere near the bar. Because the bar contained bowls of substances and there were girls without tops on … that was good.'

'It was pretty weird,' Hoggy says, laughing. 'The door prize was a machete. They brought us a bong and a bowl and left it on the front of the stage for us to use as we pleased. I remember Darren stayed at the very front for the whole set.

'Then it was around 2 am and we were like, "Okay, let's go." And they were like, "No, you guys aren't going." We were like, "We don't know any more songs." But it was like, "Play 'em again." So we were like, "Okay!" and we played the whole set again. As we were getting into our van to go, they threw a bag of weed at us as big as a pillowcase.'

Hoggy remembers it was a tight squeeze getting out of the car park after the gig, trying to manoeuvre his dad's Kombi in between all the rows of Harleys, fearing he'd tap one and send them all toppling over like dominos in a repeat of that scene in *Pee-wee's Big Adventure*. 'They didn't make it very practical for us,' notes Hoggy. 'If I had nicked one of those bikes, it would

have been death. But Darren made it through that initiation. I don't think he realised what he'd got himself into. I don't think we knew either.'

Around this time, the 'Finger's return show at the Orient, now as a five-piece, earned the band its first-ever mention in mainstream media. On 18 July 1991, Brisbane's *Courier-Mail* wrote:

> *One of Brisbane's best emerging rock bands, Powderfinger, play at the Orient Hotel, City, tomorrow night after a month's lay off and with the addition of new guitarist Darren Middleton. Powderfinger say they are faster and funkier than ever, with hard-working originals dominating a revitalised set of 'rock, funk and boogie'. They play with the Tellers and Stella 7.*

BEHIND THE SCENES, POWDERFINGER was on the move again. They packed up their rehearsal space in Spring Hill and headed deep into the dark and seedy Valley, into the abandoned TC Beirne building overlooking the Brunswick Street Mall and backing onto Chinatown. This establishment is best remembered in music terms as the legendary Target building.

In the history of Australian music, what took place in the Target building in the early 1990s remains a true oddity. The massive, decrepit former shopping mall and office block was turned into a multi-room rehearsal space, attracting virtually every flea-bitten outfit in Brisbane's burgeoning alt-music boom. (The building has since reverted to a state-of-the-art shopping mall in the now gentrified modern-day Fortitude Valley.)

Part rabbit warren, part ear-piercing shemozzle, it would be the setting for the creation of some rock & roll mythology. When Powderfinger moved in, in mid-1991, it already housed, or was about to house, Toxic Garden Gnomes, Puzzlehouse, Screamfeeder, Custard, Brasilia and Pangaea (members of the latter two bands eventually formed Regurgitator). Herein lay the seeds of an overdue antidote to the suffocating covers movement which had all but killed off original music in the Brisbane live scene and beyond since the latter half of the 1980s. Just as grunge was about to explode on the world stage, here in the Target building in the middle of Brisbane a truly unique new music scene was unfolding.

A truly unique new music scene was unfolding.

'It was a real melting pot,' says Hoggy. 'Heaps of bands rehearsed there. We paid $30 a week to a guy who was kind of the caretaker, pretty much to stop the junkies squatting in there.'

'There were all these cool indie bands and they had the terrace studios overlooking the mall,' says Bish. 'We had this fucking little room around the back.'

With junkies in the corridors, brothels and strip clubs out the side door, the Target building would remain Powderfinger's rehearsal space for the best part of the following three years.

It wasn't just the band making a change; around the same time Hoggy left his family home in Indooroopilly and moved in with his girlfriend, Ingrid. The pair moved into a sprawling '70s-styled suburban house on the other side of Indooroopilly. Their new pad, with its backyard pool and massive open-plan living areas, became party-central for the extended Powderfinger family over the next couple of years. After almost every gig, there'd be an all-night after-party back at Hoggy's.

The place should have had a revolving door as family and friends moved in and out while Hoggy and Ingrid lived there. One housemate was arguably the biggest party animal any of them knew – a steel-selling, wannabe real estate auctioneer whom everyone came to know and love simply as Teaks/Teaksy/Piteaks.

PAUL PITICCO CAME FROM a somewhat different background to all those prissy private school boys in Powderfinger. Born on 7 March 1969 at Royal Brisbane Women's Hospital, Teaks was an only child ('Explains the fascination with myself,' he says.) and grew up in the then working class, inner-city suburb of Paddington. His dad was a self-made businessman, running his own company installing steel for high-rise constructions, while his mum worked part time but mainly stayed home looking after little Teaksy. He attended Petrie Terrace State School in Paddington, followed by Kelvin Grove High School in the neighbouring suburb.

The budding entrepreneur started working part-time in the family business from his mid-teens and, after he finished school, enrolled in a real estate degree, but he threw that in after a couple of years and went back to selling steel full-time.

Before crossing paths with the 'Finger, Teaks had already immersed himself in the Brisbane music scene. A mad Oz rock fan, he was good mates with the Toxic Garden Gnomes and at one time shared a house with some of the band members. Teaks got his first taste of the rock & roll life while hanging out with those guys – he got a feel for all the fun stuff, like loading gear in and out of a venue and making covert

poster runs around town in the middle of the night. He was soon staging his own events at places like the Orient.

Paul's girlfriend at the time was a girl named Amanda, whose best mate just happened to be Hoggy's girlfriend, Ingrid. Amanda took Teaks along to Hoggy's 21st birthday party, a barbecue at Hoggy's folks' place. Teaks brought along a present – a set of headphones. Instant brownie points.

It was at the party, in February 1991, that Teaks was introduced to the other Fingers, still a four-piece at this point. Teaks immediately recognised Bernie from a previous life – the pair had played on the same soccer team back in primary school.

'He said to me, "I know you, I used to play soccer with you,"' says Bernie. 'I'd forgotten him, then I remembered the next day. He was a handy winger and I remembered him telling me how he'd pashed some girl on the high jump mats at school and me thinking, "This guy is a hot operator."

'Then we all became mates. Teaks is cool. He was a really friendly, outgoing guy, like he still is. He loved getting wasted, big fan of that.'

Within about six months of that party, Hoggy was living in his new place with Ingrid, Amanda and Teaksy.

It didn't take long for Hoggy and Teaks to bond over their shared love of partying and rock & roll. Ian immediately felt he'd found another kindred spirit and was impressed by Paul's obvious instinctive business acumen and blue-collar work ethic. One thing that could always be said about Teaks, which still applies to this day: He parties hard, but works even harder.

'It was a fortuitous meeting,' says Hog. 'It was good fun. Everything was about sitting in the lounge room, pretty much. Lots of bucket bongs. It was trouble.'

Bernie and his first serious girlfriend, Kate, were also regular visitors. 'We were over there most of the time,' says Bernie. 'They were our best friends and we all hung out together. Hoggy was super cool, a really chilled-out guy. We had a fun time, hanging out, listening to records. The Black Crowes had a record out, and also Lenny Kravitz. The Black Crowes had a pretty big impact on everyone.'

BACK ON THE BAND FRONT, THE NEWEST FINGER was settling in comfortably. 'I felt like I fitted in quite well,' says Darren, 'but I wasn't a big pot smoker, and a few of the guys were into smoking a bit of grass [JC being the notable exception], so I definitely got into it a bit then, just to try to fit in. Not that I found it hard because I did enjoy it for a few years.' Enough to earn himself the added nickname, 'Green River'.

Perhaps it had something to do with all that dope, perhaps it was their growing obsession with the Black Crowes, perhaps it was the general global uprising of the slacker grunge

Fire exit

LOCAL BANDS USE THEIR INITIATIVE

It was inspiring to see two local bands use their initiative in organising their own gig. Powderfinger and Tripsome arranged to play at the Sherwood Aussie Rules Club on February 9th and managed to draw a crowd of nearly 250 people away form the city and into the suburbs. This number was largely due to their admirable postering campaign. there was a wide array of people in the crowd with a significant number of metal fans hoping for a "good night".

Which is certainly what they got. Powderfinger played first and though they thought they had a bit of an "off" night, they have improved dramatically since I last reviewed them. Though still playing many covers, I was impressed by their growing number of originals, including two new ones "Mercedes Eye" which seems to dabble with a heavier sound and "Manson Gun".

They also did a haunting cover of "No Quarter" which their lead singer Bernard described as "an interesting adaptation of the song for keyboards to guitar". Powderfinger are devoting this year entirely to concentrating on the bank and maybe going on the road, so hopefully we'll be able to see them playing more often as they only get better each time.

Tripsome took to the stage next. This five piece that came second in the Brisbane Battle of the Bands is predominantly a metal covers band. Actually I can't recall them playing any originals but I do know they have one called Tripsome. None the less, they were and are an incredible crowd pleaser. Drawing from Metallica, Black Sabbath and The Cult etc, they had hair flying everywhere. They're very energetic performers and the metal fans adored them, although I felt there was little variation in their song selection. It would be interesting to see them turn their abilities to something that would add contrast to their performance.

It was decidedly a very successful night and other bands should be encouraged to do some hard work on their own behalf and organise similar nights.

SARA HERALD

generation, but almost unconsciously, the members of Powderfinger started growing their hair ridiculously long. They also started wearing similar clothes, which all looked as if they came straight out of a Led Zeppelin video clip, circa-1969. In short, Powderfinger had found itself an image – a sort of long-haired, hippy, barefoot, op-shop, corduroy, leather pant (Hoggy), open vest (Bernie), Thai fisherman pants (Darius) image.

While the guys all looked a bit like '60s hippies, not an entirely uncommon fashion in Brisbane in 1991, Darren was actually pretty close to being the real thing. He and his girlfriend, Annabel, wholeheartedly embraced the alternative lifestyle. Apparently the two of them looked virtually identical when viewed from behind.

Darren went vego, started growing a lot of his own food, including kombucha mushrooms and wheatgrass. He constantly drank kombucha tea and chewed wheatgrass.

'I was into all that sort of stuff, natural living, self-subsistence,' says DZ. 'On our driving trips with the band in the early days, I would take bags of wheatgrass and chew it in the van, swallow the juice and spit the grass out. That was part of my touring pack. No one else was into that, which I thought was pretty strange.'

Even more disturbing for the road trips, which were about to become a very common aspect of life in Powderfinger, was that Darren's main source of sustenance was lentils. He'd eat them almost daily. All those lentils had a side-effect that his surfing safari mates outside the band were all-too familiar with.

'He's got the worst arse in the world,' says DZ's old mate Andrew Sands. 'Going on surf trips with him was just the worst. It was like, "Mate, one more and we're sticking your arse out the window."'

'He got another nickname for that,' adds Travers Murr. '"Lunchie" [as in 'Lunchie-poo'], which Bernie coined, because he used to fart so much. The lentil days were very smelly.'

Amid all the farts and partying, Steven Bishop wasn't having such a great time inside this new Powderfinger. He was growing increasingly anxious about the direction of the band, as well as almost everything else.

Bish couldn't put his finger on the source of his anxiety, but all the alcohol, dope, late nights and occasional acid trips certainly weren't helping matters. He felt as if the world was closing in. He was out of university, broke, working in a semi-professional band, had girlfriend issues and was hearing constant gloom and doom associated with the Gulf War and the recession. He was struggling with all of it.

What's more, he didn't like where the band seemed to be heading musically. Bish wanted to go down more of an alternative rock route, like R.E.M. or Jane's Addiction, whereas, in reality, especially since Darren's arrival, the 'Finger seemed to be moving towards a much heavier style of rock. But Bish wasn't making his thoughts clear to anyone. Indeed, he seemed to be internalising everything.

'I was sort of in a bad spot,' says Bish. 'The band is trying to get good, we're trying to get serious, and I'm dragging it along. I felt like I put an anchor in the band and I was getting pulled in a direction I didn't want to go.'

There were several episodes around this time that started seriously concerning his mates about his headspace. He'd show up to band rehearsals of a morning and start nodding off by 11 am, unable to focus or keep his eyes open.

At his own 21st birthday party, held on a cruise boat on the Brisbane River, Bish suddenly dived off into the water, swam to the bank and disappeared, leaving all the other guests panicked and confused. The party immediately stopped and everyone spread out across the city in search of him. He was found hours later, curled up on the steps of Parliament House.

On another night, at a gig, Bish showed up and just sat there, staring at his drums. When the others asked him what the hell was going on, he muttered something about having forgotten how to play. Bish wasn't wasted – just lost and pretty vacant. The rest of the band didn't know what to do with him, how to handle the situation. Bish remembers Bernie trying to counsel him, saying: 'It's mind over matter, Bish – you've got to try to snap out of it.'

It was obvious there was something seriously wrong. 'I was in a deep sort of hole,' says Bish. He finally sought some professional help and was diagnosed as clinically depressed. Seeing a psychologist helped and things got better for a while, Bish lightened up a bit and was back to playing at his best.

'There were always fights and people being kicked out.'

Out on the live front, Powderfinger's regular gigs at venues such as the Orient, Bonaparte's, the Ship Inn, Dooleys and the Pineapple were continuing to pull ever-growing crowds, but the money they were making from these shows, along with their fortnightly dole cheques, barely made ends meet. Especially now that they were looking at raising funds to make a recording.

Rod McLean, the band's part-time agent, remembers getting a fairly desperate call from Bernie, telling him the band needed to generate more work or they didn't know how much longer they could survive. Did Rod have any other gigs he could offer them? Turned out, he did.

Rod had just started looking after the entertainment for a venue in the Valley called Club ACs. It was another biker joint, this one run by members of the Odin's Warriors. Located among the sex shops and strip joints, straight across the road from the old Roxy, one of Brisbane's most famous clubs, Rod's idea was to turn ACs into a late-night, after-show venue, a place where music lovers could end up for a drink and more music after they'd already been out for the evening.

Rod offered Powderfinger four nights a week at ACs, Thursday through to Sunday, playing four half-hour sets, from midnight through to 4 am, for $400 a night. The Fingers didn't need to be asked twice.

Club ACs wasn't as hardcore a biker venue as the Black Uhlans clubhouse, but it wasn't too far off.

'That was a major gig for us,' says Bernard. 'I have two main memories of that. First one being it was fucking freezing, because all the bikies wear their leathers, so they cranked up the air-con. We would be on stage playing in jumpers and jackets and scarves, inside in Brisbane. Pretty weird.

'Then there were all the fights. It was a bit of an introduction to fight culture, which was basically bourbon and conflict. There were always fights and people being kicked out. One particular memory was of a scrag fight, where a girl dragged another girl down the stairs by the hair, which was really full on.

'But we kind of managed to navigate our way through that pretty successfully. A lot of our friends would come for the first hour and then leave. One mate used to come by himself, he was working shifts or something, but he used to come and sit down and watch the Fingers for hours, by himself. Sometimes there would be no one else in the room. Like Sunday night, honestly, we would be playing to no one except the sound guy. It was really good practice for us, that got us good a lot quicker, playing that amount of time on stage.'

This was the Beatles-in-Hamburg phase of Powderfinger's development, if we may be so bold as to draw such a comparison.

'Except the Beatles in Hamburg had big crowds,' says Hoggy. 'We were playing to empty rooms. For us, it was like a rehearsal. We were learning our shit, we were learning how to do stuff. At that time there were no smoking laws, so we probably smoked a packet of cigarettes each on stage. Whenever there was a break, you'd get free drinks. Wasn't anything fancy, you'd get a beer, that was a bonus.

'Bikers used to love us, they probably still do. Bikers like good music – they like the Rolling Stones, they like Led Zeppelin, and we knew all the standards. That is how we learned to play together. We used to do a really long version of "Dazed and Confused" by Zeppelin, that was good fun. There was some Beatles. I don't know how many of our own songs we were doing at the bikie clubs, probably a couple, they would have worked their way in.'

IT WAS WHILE THE BAND WAS IN THE MIDDLE of its extended residency at Club ACs that Hoggy asked his housemate Paul Piticco if he might be up for managing the band.

'We were driving one night to go get some booze,' says Paul, 'and Hoggy was like, "Why don't you come and see our band with a view to managing us?"'

'Teaksy had a brown Celica so I thought he was super-loaded,' Hog says with a laugh. 'I was still organising most of the band stuff, so I asked him, "Would you ever be interested in looking after a band?" And he's like, "How do you do that?"'

'The first couple of times I saw them was playing two or three sets down in the bikers' dungeon at ACs,' adds Teaks. 'It was certainly a dive bar.' But Teaks didn't need any more convincing – he was in.

Paul Piticco's first semi-official involvement with the band was at a show that everyone involved ranks among the most unforgettable events in Powderfinger's early history – the Muttaburra B&S Ball.

Muttaburra is a tiny farming township in the middle of nowhere, about a 14-hour drive northwest of Brisbane. Its self-professed claim to fame is that it's the geographical centre of Queensland.

Somehow, through a friend of a friend, Powderfinger was invited to provide the night's entertainment for the town's annual bachelors and spinsters ball. It was, by a long way, the band's biggest fee to date – $1500.

The trip didn't get off to the bes of starts. Bisho crashed his Bedford van the weekend before the show, so they had to use their soundman's rundown van, which had a top speed of 80 kilometres per hour, adding more time to an already endless trip. But once they eventually hit town, the Fingers and their entourage were treated like visiting royalty, put up in the local pub and, along with the rest of the people in the bar, shouted dinner by a passing trucker.

The band's entourage on the trip totalled two: Teaks, who handled the light show, consisting of flicking the switches on a couple of Kambrook powerboards, and Dave Wood (aka Downtown Dave), the band's sound guy from Club ACs.

The event was staged in a huge tin shearing shed. 'It was just rum-soaked,' says Teaks. 'Good people, but they were wild country folk. It was nuts.' The town's normal population was a few dozen people, but swelled to about 400 for the ball. 'Although,' adds Teaks, 'it was hard to tell how many were watching the band and how many were out rooting in their utes.'

The party trick of the night was crowd members lining up for beer bongs – a funnel and hose contraption forcing a 750 millilitre longneck of beer straight down their throats. Following ingestion, they'd chant 'Suck me dry and call me Dusty.' You could hear the chant all the way through the performance, which only added to the bizarreness of the night. The fact that many of the band members had dropped a tab of acid prior to the gig probably helped as well.

It was a long, mad, trippy night. The band played for four hours, their extended set of classic rock covers going down an absolute treat. Afterwards, they headed back to the town's only pub and stayed up all night partying with locals, trying out the beer bongs for themselves.

It was awesome ... until someone came bashing on their door at around 10 am the next morning.

'There was this *bang-bang-bang-bang-bang* on the door,' recalls Teaks. 'And we're like, "What is it? What is it?" It was one of the guys saying, "You've got to get up and play! It's the recovery!" And we said, "Are you joking? No one ever told us anything about playing a recovery!" And they're like, "Yeah, it's a B&S – everyone knows there's a recovery!"'

'We were as hungover as donkeys,' says Bernie. 'All-time hangover. We got up, had a steak sandwich and went back into the shed to play. First song, I tried to sing and this squeak came out of my mouth. I had nothing. I said, "Fellas, I can't do this." I went out the back and lay down on a concrete path. And they stayed on stage and played "Sandman" by America for 15 minutes.'

Off the stage, Teaks, as messy as the rest of them, was dealing with his own dramas. It was so hot at high-noon in the tin shed that he was sweating profusely, and the sweat was dripping onto the powerboards, causing sparks that were giving him electric shocks. It took him a while to notice that Bernie wasn't on stage. He only realised something was amiss when Bish started singing 'Sandman' for a second time.

'So I go out the back of this shearing shed,' says Teaks, 'there's a washhouse that they'd turned into an improvised bandroom and Bernard is lying on the concrete floor of this outhouse, in the foetal position, asleep, being swarmed by ants.'

The rest of the band told the crowd they were taking a break and came out and joined Teaks, standing over Bernie's limp, ant-infested body, wondering what they should do.

'I was absolute dogshit,' says Bernie. 'There was one guy who'd been up the front all the night before, real funny bastard, a jackaroo. He comes out and says, "Right, I know how to fix you: beer bong." Gives me a beer bong. Bang!'

Suck me dry and call me Dusty!

'Straight away I'm up, brushing ants off myself and, after that, I could sing like a bird, I was fine. I was still an absolute pisshead in those days,' adds Bernie. 'I didn't change my ways for quite a while, either.'

'It was pretty fucked,' says Hoggy. 'But bands need to do that shit. Bonding, totally bonding.'

The weekend made such an impression on Bish that he wrote a song about the experience called 'High Country' (which he later performed with another band, Roma). 'That was the one real happy time we had in '91,' he says.

Sadly, this was to be the last happy time Bish experienced for a long while. Almost as soon as Powderfinger got back to Brisbane, Bish entered what would turn out to be the unhappiest period of his life.

BACK IN TOWN, POWDERFINGER SET ABOUT LOCKING DOWN its arrangement with Teaks. Everyone wanted to do it right, so they brought in a lawyer to draft up a contract that formally made Paul Piticco the manager and representative agent of Powderfinger. From then on, basically everything outside the actual music making would be split six ways.

'It lapsed a long time ago, but we don't have a running contract except for the one that was initially set,' explains Hoggy. 'We always stuck to the conditions of the contract, bar a few things.

'That was a significant moment. Teaksy brought a sense of organisation, although he was probably kidding us a lot of the time. He had no fucking idea what he was doing. A couple of times he went to the casino with money we got from gigs – "Fuck, our manager is using our money to go to the casino!" – but he always paid us back,' Hoggy says.

'I had no idea what I was doing,' admits Teaks. 'And there was no one around to teach me. I just tried to follow commonsense.'

Needless to say, Teaks' business instinct and commonsense approach would serve both himself and his band very well in the years to follow.

Weekly band meetings became a concrete fixture in Powderfinger life from then on. The meeting room, like the rehearsal room, would be run as a simple, straight-up democracy, with Teaks as the non-voting chairman.

The first of these meetings sketched out a basic road map for the band's foreseeable future. Three immediate goals were set.

1. The time had come to stop being a covers act – if Powderfinger was to survive long-term and prosper, it needed to back itself and become strictly an originals band. Powderfinger would continue to drop the odd cover into their live set forever more, but the days of a 50–50 originals–covers split were over.

2. Get into a studio and record something.

3. Start touring beyond Brisbane and Queensland.

Before this brave new era could begin, Powderfinger had a couple of weeks' worth of shows to play out at Club ACs. The money from those gigs, along with the cash from Muttaburra, would just about cover the costs of recording a debut EP.

Meanwhile, their soundman Downtown Dave managed to secure some free access to the

School of Audio Engineering in Milton, the same place in which Darren's previous band, Sonic Tapestry, recorded their demo.

Powderfinger's access to the studio was limited to between students' lessons, which meant they could only get in there for two or three hours at a time. So it ended up taking a couple of weeks to put down a handful of demo tracks. These were Powderfinger's first-ever studio recordings, rough versions of songs that, all going well, would form the basis of a debut release.

The tracks included the live favourite 'Dirty Old Man', a cover version of the classic 'Knock on Wood', and another original called 'Satisfy', which was an early version of the song 'Mama Harry' which would eventually appear on the *Transfusion* EP.

These demos would be the only Powderfinger recordings to feature Steven Bishop on drums. Unfortunately, the tapes of these historic sessions have disappeared. Downtown Dave takes the blame. 'I moved house a couple of times and lost them,' he says. 'I wish I could find them, because Ian always says, "Have you got those tapes, Dave?" But they're gone.'

David's memories of the recordings are that 'the originals were really complex. Everyone wanted to show off their specialties and recording them was like, "Whoa guys – three chords is all you need. Make it simpler." A lot of guitar and lead breaks. Very Soundgarden-ish.' Certainly, Soundgarden – alongside fellow contemporary American rockers the Black Crowes – were rapidly becoming a telling influence on this early era of the 'Finger.

BACK AT CLUB ACs, IN AN INSTANT, EVERYTHING FELL OVER in a heap. The obvious improvement in Bish's recent behaviour suddenly evaporated. All the late-night sessions and the rock & roll lifestyle of recent months had taken their toll and he experienced what he describes as a full-blown mania attack.

'There's a lot of bravado and cockiness associated with it,' says Bish. 'And that spiralled into complete craziness. So I was walking around being really cocky with the band. Paul had just started and was trying to manage things on strategy and direction and I was just not cooperating. It was a hard time for the whole band.'

Everything came to a dramatic head on the band's last night at ACs. At about 3 am, following the third of the band's four sets of the morning, Bish simply disappeared. Powderfinger was left stranded without a drummer for the last set and the bikers who ran ACs were not impressed. 'They were threatening us,' says Hoggy. 'It was a bad situation.'

Bish eventually showed up again and all hell broke loose backstage. There was a scuffle between Bish, Hoggy and JC. Lots of yelling and argy-bargy with Bish trying to push the other two off him. 'It wasn't violent-violent, but there was definitely some physicality to the altercation,' says Teaks. Bernie jumped in, trying to pull everyone apart.

Bish says he can't remember exactly what happened, why he was a no-show for that last

THE ORIENT HOTEL
CNR QUEEN & ANN STS, CITY
FRI 13th JULY ~ 9pm - 2am $5
THE TELLERS
The FIVE HANKS
COME IN YOUR CRAZIEST CLOTHES
SAT 14th JULY ~ 6 pm - 2am
"The REAL THING"
STARRING
FIVE BANDS FOR $5
GOATS IN THE MACHINE
THE BATFINKS
POWDERFINGER
THE WORMS
LAST GIG FOR 6 WEEKS OF
ALOHA PUSSYCATS
SUN 15th JULY ~ 8pm-12am $4
COME EARLY AND SEE
THE RETURN TO BRISBANE OF
The BENEDICTS
HOWLIN' MOONDOGGIES
TOXIC GARDEN GNOMES

set. 'I was knackered,' he says. 'I was with my girlfriend, we were all a bit sort of out of it, and I think I just forgot to turn up. I went with my girlfriend somewhere else, to another bar. I came back and we had a bit of a fisticuffs or a bit of a tussle in the backstage area. And I said, "That's it – I'm out! I've had enough!" And, yeah, that was it.'

The idea of quitting the band had never even crossed Bish's mind before the heat of this moment. And, in reality, it was the last thing he wanted.

'It was a split-second decision,' he says. 'The mania and, I guess, the marijuana. Up to that point, the band was my world in a way, or a lot of it. That was what I wanted to do.'

The rest of the band was left utterly shell-shocked. 'I still don't really know what happened,' says Hoggy. 'We had a bit of a scuffle ... and it all fell apart.'

That wasn't the last of the dramas this bizarre morning had in store.

The band minus Bish stumbled back to Hoggy and Teaks' place in Indooroopilly at close to 5 am to find a scene of absolute chaos on the street outside their house.

'There were crashed cars everywhere, a massive stack,' says Hoggy. 'A car had smashed into Bernie's car in front of my house and it set off a chain reaction – it hit his car into my girlfriend's car, and the other guy we lived with, Rob's car. We were like, "What the fuck is going on?" It must have just happened because there was another car in the middle of the street with its doors open, but the driver was gone.'

'Turns out it was a cadet cop who was drunk,' continues Bernie. 'We came round the corner and there's this car in the middle of the road and our cars all jammed together.'

'We were standing around in the street,' says Hoggy. 'Bern wearing his fucking waistcoat, we're all going, "What the fuck's happened here? All our cars are fucked." It was pretty weird.

'So then Bish was gone after that night. A bad night, you know? It was the end of an era, a marking point.'

There was a band meeting in the days that followed in which Bish was given an opportunity to change his mind, but he was still too messed up to take it.

'When I quit, I just didn't realise the implications,' he says. 'But we had a meeting after that and they said, "Is this definitely your decision?" I think Ian and John [JC] were still shocked. Didn't see it coming: "What's going on?" And I said, "No, that's it – you had your chance."

'In broad daylight, I probably wanted them to listen to what I had to say, but I wasn't saying it. And I felt intimidated by Paul Piticco, he's got an intense presence, even back then. If I was older and wiser, I would have said give me two weeks off or something, but back then, once I made the decision, I was out of there. I went to Mackay [to his parents' house] and then I went to Sydney.'

Most distraught about this sudden turn of events was JC. He and Bish had been best mates for almost a decade, lived out of each other's pockets, made a pledge that they would always make music together. Now all that was seemingly gone overnight. 'I felt a little bit guilty that he left and I was still there,' says JC.

Although Bish was officially no longer a member of Powderfinger, it was not the last time he and JC and Hoggy would make music together. But that was much later.

After relocating to Sydney, it took Bish some time to get his life back on track. At first, he rock & rolled harder than ever. He played in a variety of outfits, including a stint performing with Alex Lloyd, but he had to hit rock bottom before he could start getting better, eventually 'landing like a crumpled plane'. After a couple of years in Sydney and another major manic episode, Bish was admitted to a psychiatric hospital, where he was diagnosed as suffering from bipolar disorder and finally correctly medicated for the condition.

With his health improving, it still took Steven Bishop a very long time to come to terms with giving up his place in Powderfinger. He moved to the United Kingdom, where he spent the remainder of the 1990s. 'No one knows who Powderfinger is over there,' he says with a half-laugh. 'That liberated me a bit and helped me when I came back to be a bit removed from it.'

Bish's departure left a massive void in Powderfinger, but there was never any question over whether the band would keep playing. They had generated so much momentum and put in too much work to stop now.

What Powderfinger needed to do was find a new drummer.

CHAPTER 10
Cogsy

Jonathan Coghill

It wasn't an act of God that set Jonathan Coghill on his path towards Powderfinger – at least not as far as he was concerned, and not as defined by the law or insurance companies.

Yet, when he was 13, Cogsy was riding his brand-new green racer home from indoor cricket one afternoon when, out of nowhere, a car turned into him at speed. It swept him off his bike and into the air, bouncing him over the car and slamming him into the road.

It all happened so fast. Jon's immediate reaction was to pick himself up, but as he got to his feet his right leg gave way and he collapsed to the ground. Then came the most excruciating shards of pain. In shock, in agony and scared, he looked up to see a middle-aged couple sitting in the car, staring at him but not moving. Jon begged them: 'Help me, help me!'

The driver got out, slowly approaching the injured teenager, but instead of reaching down and trying to assist him, this man looked down at Jon, hands in the air, and said: 'I'm a good Christian – I don't deserve this!'

A bystander eventually came to Jon's aid. An ambulance was called. By the time it arrived, Jon's natural endorphins had kicked in and his pain had settled. He remembers asking the paramedic: 'Mate, soccer sign-on is this weekend – do you think I'll be okay?' The medic looked down at Jon's leg and replied, 'Don't worry about it, mate – it's just a bruise. You'll be fine.' He was lying. Jon's leg was badly broken, the lower part of it snapped in two.

Jon never did get to soccer sign-on that year; he spent the following two weeks in hospital and months afterwards in recovery. The God-fearing couple in the car ended up paying him $2000 in accident compensation. The money was put into a trust fund that he could only access once he turned 18.

As his 18th birthday approached, Jon made plans to take off to Bali with one of his best mates on the most awesome surfing trip imaginable. They were all set to go, just about to pay for the tickets, when his mate backed out. 'Because he'd started hanging out with cooler people,' Cogsy says. 'So I didn't go and I bought a drum kit with the money. That was my first brand-new, proper kit, which I had for the next four or five years.'

JONATHAN ROBERT COGHILL – Jona to his family, Jon or Cogs or Cogsy to the rest of the world (his band mates later added Bulldog to the list of nicknames) – was born in the rural township of Warwick, Queensland's 'rose and rodeo city', about 150 kilometres south-west of Brisbane, on 26 August 1971.

Soon after his birth, the Coghills briefly moved to Brisbane, but by the time Jon was in year three, his family had relocated to Nambour, home of the Big Pineapple, just inland from the Sunshine Coast and 100 kilometres north of Brisbane. Jon worked at the Big Pineapple every Christmas holidays for years. 'Great job,' he says. 'Refilling the drink and ice-cream containers and stuffing my face.'

Cogsy's upbringing was dramatically different from that of his future musical colleagues. The final piece in the Powderfinger puzzle, Cogs would prove a perfect fit. Yet also, from beginning to end, he was always the odd Finger out. For starters, growing up in Nambour meant Cogs was never a part of any Brisbane scene or social clique. It wasn't until 1989 that he returned to Brisbane to attend university. Right up until just before joining the band, he lived his entire life in complete isolation from any of that incestuous inner-city stuff. He might as well have beamed down into the Brisbane alt-rock world from another universe.

Cogs joining Powderfinger also broke up the band's private boys' school club. Like Teaks, Cogsy was the product of the public school system, in his case Nambour State primary followed by Nambour State High School, whose other most famous alumni includes, as the rest of the Fingers enjoy constantly reminding everyone, former prime minister Kevin Rudd.

Also, unlike any of his band mates, Jon is the middle child in his family. His brother, Chris, a doctor, is 18 months older and his sister, Maria, a nurse and mum, is four years younger.

And in stark contrast to Bernard's church-focused upbringing, Cogsy was raised, heaven-forbid, an atheist; which is hardly a surprise considering his father, Graham, was a science teacher and academic. He was head of the science department at Nambour High and the author of several textbooks included in the national school curriculum. Jon's mother, Diana, was also a teacher, initially for primary school and later in Special Education. Graham and Diana brought up their kids to question everything. Jon remembers his dad saying: 'It's no use having an argument unless it's a really good argument.'

The Coghills were passionately involved in grass-roots politics and active members of the Australian Labor Party – hardly the in-thing on the Sunshine Coast in the 1970s. They regularly held ALP parties in their home, helping plot the overthrow of incumbent state and federal conservative governments. Jon remembers seeing many a political heavyweight come through the front door of their place in the late-'70s/early-'80s, including future long-serving Queensland premier Peter Beattie. He doesn't remember ever seeing Kevin Rudd in the house, but three of Rudd's nephews were school mates.

So, at the height of the ultra-conservative Bjelke-Petersen era of Queensland politics, the Coghill household was a hotbed of left-wing, free-thinking activism. 'My parents were all about social justice,' says Cogsy. 'I was going to protest marches from 12 years old. We'd go to a protest for endangered frogs in the forest behind Maleny one week, and then the next week we'd be protesting high-rises being built in Maroochydore.'

Jon embraced all of his parents' small-l liberal philosophies. 'One Christmas when I was about 14,' he recalls, 'back when Peter Garrett was in the Nuclear Disarmament Party, my brother and I were given these tie-dyed, red and orange and yellow t-shirts with a big map of Australia and a nuclear explosion that said: "One flash and you're ash." I thought it was just the best and I wore it at Christmas lunch. When my granddad saw it he said in a very sarcastic manner that it was a nice thing to wear for Christmas.'

For all the differences between Cogs and the rest of the Fingers, there was also the odd similarity in their upbringings. Cogs, like the rest of them, was an absolute sports nut. He started surfing, initially boogie-boarding, when he was 10, heading for the nearby Sunshine Coast with his mates at any given opportunity.

Like Bernie, Teaks and DZ, Cogs was into junior soccer right up until his bike accident, after which he turned to rugby league for his final few years at high school. Jon also loved his cricket. As a result, almost every break during rehearsing and recording in the first decade of Powderfinger was filled with intense three-way cricket games between Cogs, Bernie and JC in laneways, hallways, backyards or car parks – basically anywhere they could swing a bat and ball. DZ, Hoggy and Teaks occasionally joined in, along with anyone else who was around. The cricket-obsessed trio even managed to convert their American producer, Nick DiDia to the game.

However, Cogsy's musical tastes and experiences as a child bore no resemblance whatsoever to that of the other Fingers.

At school in the mid-'80s – while Hoggy was listening to his post-punk, JC to his bleak electro, Bernie to his singer/songwriters and DZ to his hair metal – Cogs was loving Michael Jackson. He and his sister Maria played MJ's *Thriller* ad nauseam. 'The start of it, where the door creaks open,' says Cogs of the album's title track, 'was amazing.' Jeff Wayne's *The War of the Worlds* musical and their dad's Jimi Hendrix records also received regular spins on the Coghill home stereo.

Cogsy's introduction to live music came courtesy of his dad's jazz band, which occasionally rehearsed in the lounge room of the family home. Cogs was entranced by the way his dad and his band mates interacted, seemingly telepathically.

Jon and Chris both took guitar lessons in their early teens but what really ended up rocking young Cogsy's musical boat, and got his groove pumping once he hit his mid-teens, was hip hop. Ol' skool Electric Boogaloo, Rock Steady Crew-style hip hop. (Hey DZ – does this make you feel any better about your teenage music tastes?)

'There was a movie called *Beat Street*, which was massive, and *Footloose* was huge too,' says Cogs without the slightest hint of his trademark sarcasm. 'There was all this stuff happening. *Footloose* was pretty cool because Nambour was a bit like the town in the movie. It was pretty stiff. We used to do dancing lessons at school and we had to do square dancing, but every now and then the teachers would say, "Put on whatever you want, some dance music or something", and all the guys would start doing those worms. And I thought, "Fuck – what's that? What's this awesome breakdancing shit?"'

His moment of true enlightenment came during the local heats of the annual Rock Eisteddfod at the Nambour Civic Centre when he was about 14. The event included a demonstration performance by a local kid made good, a guy named Carson Webb, who'd finished high school and was on his way to pursuing a career as a professional dancer.

'Out comes Carson,' recalls Cogs, 'and he was dressed like Michael Jackson, but he was a white guy, and he did this amazing breakdancing, which was a lot of doing the robot, but doing it so well. Then, about three-quarters of the way through his act, and I remember this so clearly, bang! He did the moonwalk. Everyone was gobsmacked. It was the best thing we had ever seen. That influenced me a lot as far as wanting to become a performer.'

Immediately, Cogs and lots of other guys at school got together their own breakdancing crews. Cogsy's posse was made up of him and his mates Bernard Gormley and Darren Blackman. After school, they would head down to the local pinball parlour and play a single game each because that's all they could afford. 'In the parlour was a piece of laminated wood for breakdancing,' says Cogs. 'Someone would put on the ghetto-blaster and we'd do breakdancing, pretending we were in the Rock Steady Crew.'

But that wasn't the end of the after-school entertainment. After the pinny parlour, Cogs and his homies headed across to the local library, a hangout for the town's kids because the progressive librarian encouraged socialising rather than reading in silence. 'You could hang out with girls, read books or play games. My brother and his mates were right into Dungeons & Dragons, so I used to hang out and play with them once or twice a week and it was fucking wicked. All of Chris's mates were the nerds at school and they were the most interesting guys. They were quick and clever and they all loved listening to Queen. All the nerds loved Queen. That had a massive influence on me as well: breakdancing and the Dungeons & Dragons game.

There were some cool people in Nambour, if you found them.'

Between all the surfing, breakdancing and Dungeons & Dragons, it might be hard to believe that the future Powderfinger heartthrob claims he wasn't a star with young women during his early teens. 'I didn't have any girlfriends or anything like that,' says Jon. 'Maybe for two weeks at a time, but I was too scared of girls.'

This is vehemently refuted by Matthew Goggin, one of Cogsy's best mates from Nambour High. 'All the chicks thought he was pretty good stuff,' says Matt. 'They loved him. That was part of my motivation for hanging around him, so I could run off his shoulder.'

He says Cogs was one of the most popular guys at school, which in year 12 led the pair to mount a half-hearted campaign to get him elected as school captain. 'But he was too much of a joker and didn't get the gig,' says Matt. 'We were both prefects but we never took anything too seriously. There was always some prank going on.'

Such as, for instance, a competition among classmates to see who could get away with urinating in the rubbish bin during chemistry. The winner got a calculator. Nerds with attitude.

IT WAS ANOTHER KID AT NAMBOUR HIGH, George Ward, whom Cogs credits with inadvertently turning him onto drums. Around the same time Cogs was finding his groove breakdancing, George and a bunch of other students spent their lunchtimes in the school music room, playing the same song over and over again – 'Boys Don't Cry' by the Cure.

Hearing those guys play live music sparked something in Cogs. For his 15th birthday, he asked his parents to buy him some drums and they obliged with a $120 second-hand Pearl kit. At first, Cogsy's favourite songs to bang along to were 'Easy Lover' by Phil Collins and 'What You Need' by INXS, as well as the first album from Crowded House.

After a couple of years of bashing along to songs, Cogs hit year 11 and got serious about his playing. He started studying music at school and, though he just barely passed, he began to display the sort of focus and dedication required to become a serious musician. Every afternoon, while his mates headed for the pinny parlour or were out playing sport, Cogs headed home and put in a few hours' practice on his drums.

There were no bands to join in Nambour, so Cogs put his hand up to play in the orchestra for the annual school musical, a production of *Grease*. His dad played bass in the same orchestra.

Becoming part of the musical didn't fly too well with Cogsy's mates on the school football team, especially when he missed the inter-school rugby league semi-final because it conflicted with a performance of the show. It earned him a new nickname from the jocks: Pigskin. 'I got the Jon "Pigskin" Coghill tease for ages,' he says, 'as if to say, "You should have played footy, you prick." Some of them still call me that.'

Nonetheless, performing in the musical was a life-altering experience for the young Cogs. 'I was shithouse at playing back then,' he says. 'The tempos were all over the shop. I didn't realise you had to watch the conductor, which got me in trouble – the conductor constantly bawled me out. But it was amazing.'

COGSY DID VERY WELL AT SCHOOL and was accepted into the University of Queensland to study science. He wanted to major in Human Movement Studies, with a view to working in the field of sport. Being an out-of-towner, he moved into Union College, one of the residential colleges on campus, and, like a character in some B-grade Hollywood frat movie, his academic ambitions evaporated in an instant. Presented with the option of studying or non-stop partying, Cogs made the obvious choice.

The high school prefect failed his first semester. 'I spent the first six months getting drunk,' Cogs says. 'I was at uni for three years and I didn't get a degree because I just wasn't a very good student. I was more interested in hanging out.'

And playing music.

Cogs's music tastes shifted significantly once he started taking his drumming seriously. By the start of uni he was utterly obsessed with the mainstream white-boy funk of INXS and the hardcore punk of the Dead Kennedys. Living on campus in the heart of Brisbane, he was suddenly exposed to a whole new world of rock & roll.

One of the first big concerts he experienced in Brisbane was Mötley Crüe at the Entertainment Centre on their 1990 Dr Feelgood tour. 'It's one of the best things I've ever seen in my life,' says Cogs. 'That was when Tommy Lee did his drum solo spinning in the air, upside down and side to side. It was just magical. After that I got into metal, especially soft metal like Faith No More and Guns N' Roses. But I also started listening to thrash metal.' Darius would be proud.

Every Friday afternoon, Cogs went record shopping and treated himself to a new disc. It was here he came to fall in love with Oz alt-rockers such as Radio Birdman (who he worshipped), the Celibate Rifles, Lime Spiders and Screaming Tribesmen. Virtually a crash course to prep him for meeting Hoggy and becoming a Finger.

With his new drum kit in tow – an immaculate navy-blue Pearl export set courtesy of the Christians who ran him over – Jon soon joined his first group: Thrillhammer.

Thrillhammer was a covers band made up of mates, most of them living in the Union College at university: Paul Bullpit (aka 'Fred' Bullpit) on vocals; Dave Shenfield on guitar; Chris Bosley on bass; and, of course, Cogs on the skins.

Their college building came with a ready-made rehearsal room – a disused dank and mouldy storage cellar they called the bunker. 'We'd go down into this stinking cement box that sounded like death and we'd jam,' says Chris. 'It was a lot of fun, sometimes in ankle-deep water. It was pretty dodge.'

Thrillhammer was a university party band that never managed to score a gig off campus. They performed at the university's Rec Club, at events for the uni rugby club and at various college socials. Their usual set-list was made up of covers of all of Cogsy's favourite bands: Celibate Rifles, Screaming Tribesmen, Radio Birdman and – here is where all the planets align – the Sunnyboys, Led Zeppelin and Pink Floyd. 'We were pretty shit,' says Cogs.

On one occasion in 1990, Thrillhammer entered a campus battle of the bands held at the Rec Club. Playing on the same stage on the same day was Powderfinger.

'They were great,' says Cogsy. 'All the bands were crap and then Powderfinger came on and everyone was like, "Wow", they had an aura about them. The sound gelled and it was really pure. But they didn't win the band competition – apparently one of the judges was friends with one of the other bands.

'Then I saw them play at another venue at the uni and there were only about five people there. We were really drunk and somehow we got Dave Shenfield up on stage with them to play a solo. And, of course, I'd seen them rehearsing that time I gatecrashed their rehearsal room.'

Thrillhammer didn't survive past 1990 but it served its purpose in crystallising Cogsy's resolve to be a musician. He and Chris Bosley became best mates and continued to play together after Thrillhammer folded.

But things were changing, and by the end of 1990, Cogsy was in love. He moved out of the Union College building and into an apartment with his girlfriend, Catriona (the couple would stay together for more than a decade).

Cogs and Chris no longer had the bunker to use as a rehearsal room and they struggled to find a space to replace it. As a result, they would regularly wait until late at night and then break into the rehearsal room in the student union building, the very same room Powderfinger had used.

'Rehearsals cost money and we didn't have any money,' explains Chris. 'So Jon and I would sneak into the campus rehearsal rooms. We'd wait until 11 pm when all the bands had finished practising, and we'd sneak in. There was a hole in the fence outside and you could jimmy the door a bit. We'd pass the drums over the fence, because obviously the bass drum wouldn't fit through the hole.

'We were very keen. We just wanted to play and get better and play in bands.'

With the two of them jamming intensively, just bass and drums, they spurred each other into learning more complex rhythms. The pair became intrigued by the work of highly technical artists such as the American drummer Dennis Chambers. This also coincided with the growing popularity of American acts like the Red Hot Chili Peppers and Primus, whose innovative syncopated style and proficient musicality had a defining impact on the emerging Brisbane music scene.

Around this time, Cogs and Chris briefly found themselves in a little blues boogie outfit called Deguello, whose guitarist was, believe it or not, Cameron McKenzie – Hoggy's mate from high school. And so Cogsy's indoctrination into the incestuous world of the Brisbane live music scene began.

By 1991, both Cogs and Chris were looking to join a serious band so they started auditioning around town. Chris ended up joining Brasilia, the outfit featuring another former Hoggy cohort, drummer Martin Lee. Chris would later star in Resin Dogs. Meanwhile, Cogs answered an ad to audition for one of Brisbane's emerging acts – Custard. Cogs remembers it being an awkward session – the band were set up in someone's parents' bedroom. Anyway, it didn't go too well and Custard passed on the chance to have Jonathan Coghill as its drummer.

Fortunately, later in the very same week, Cogs had another audition scheduled . . .

CHAPTER 11

Powderfinger by Powderfinger

1992

MK IV – FINAL LINE-UP
NOVEMBER 1991

IAN HAUG – GUITAR
JOHN COLLINS – BASS
BERNARD FANNING – VOCALS/GUITAR
DARREN MIDDLETON – GUITAR
JONATHAN COGHILL – DRUMS

PAUL PITICCO – MANAGER

Since the conception of their current line-up in late 1991, Powderfinger have written, rehearsed, performed and subsequently recorded a wealth of material. This has provided a catalyst for them to rise to the top of the Brisbane heap, and (they are) potentially one of the best unsigned bands in the country at present.

Press release, early 1992

With Bish gone, Powderfinger put the word out around Brisbane that they needed a new drummer. It felt like every stickman in town applied. Seven guys made the short-list and Cogs was the first to audition.

Cogs didn't know any of the Fingers personally, although his girlfriend Catriona knew Hoggy and had introduced the pair one time at university. Also, Cogs occasionally drank at the Royal Exchange in Toowong, the Fingers' regular hangout. 'I remember Hoggy and his crew,' says Cogsy. 'They were all these long-haired dudes. I always thought of them as Led Zeppelin dudes and I was anti-Led Zeppelin because where I grew up in Nambour, all the bogans listened to Zeppelin, Midnight Oil and Cold Chisel, so I used to lump them all in together.'

Ahead of his jam with the band, Cogs was given a cassette with a few songs to learn, including the Rolling Stones' 'Midnight Rambler', Aretha Franklin's 'Respect' and Powderfinger's own 'Dirty Old Man'.

Bernard remembers meeting Cogs outside the Target building on the day of the audition. In a sign of things to come, Cogs was the first to arrive. 'There was this car park and this little walkway that went over to where our building was and Cogs was standing there, waiting,' says Bernard. 'I'd spoken to him on the phone and I thought, "Yeah, this guy seems pretty cool."'

'"Dirty Old Man" was the first song we played and he started playing a completely different beat from what Bish ever had on it. And it was really good. It was like, "Wow, this guy can really play drums."'

As fate would have it, Cogs had recently taught himself to play some standard funk rhythms. 'There's a few beats you learn with funk drumming,' he says. 'When they played me "Dirty Old Man", I thought, "Oh yeah, I'll put one of those funk beats into it." And it fitted perfectly.

'I think there were three reasons I got the gig. Because I did that and they went, "Wow, that was great." And I had long hair. And because no other good drummers tried out for the auditions.'

The latter wasn't entirely true, but as with Bernie's audition a couple of years earlier, Cogs virtually had the job sewn up before the first song was over.

'So Cogs came, he left and I thought, "He's pretty good, but we can't take the first guy,"' says Hoggy. 'We did a few more auditions. A couple were alright, but some of them were really terrible. There was a guy who had hat stands as his cymbal stands, and I remember we got to the peak of whatever we were doing, I think it was "Roadhouse Blues", and he hit the cymbals and everything collapsed. I was charged with walking the unsuccessful guys back to their cars and giving them the bad news.'

Not everyone was immediately convinced that Cogs was such an obvious choice. 'I think JC had his misgivings about him in the beginning,' says Bernard. 'There was this other guy who had auditioned, who was quite good, but he had a real indie vibe and he also had red hair, which made him a non-starter as far as I was concerned.'

It didn't take long for everyone to reach a consensus. 'Cogsy was easily the best,' says Bernie. 'It was like, "This guy is it, for sure."' Hoggy gave Cogs the call with the good news.

'They rang me up,' says Cogsy, 'and said, "You've got the gig. Come over – we're having a party." It was at Hoggy and Teaks's place in Indooroopilly.'

Cogsy, like JC, was never a pot smoker – he was a drinker – so he was a bit taken aback by what confronted him at his Powderfinger welcoming party. 'They were just these pot heads who used to sit around the lounge smoking,' says Cogs. 'And Teaks was the ringleader. I remember that night he showed me this massive marijuana plant he had in the backyard. It was four metres high and two metres wide. I think Teaks was the manager of the lounge room before he was the manager of the band. Manager of the bong.'

It was a crazy party. JC found Hoggy's old racer, filled the wheel spokes with newspaper, set it alight and took it for a ride down the stairs. 'Like Evel Knievel on fire,' says Hoggy.

'I was so drunk, I could hardly stand up,' says Cogs. 'And I was smoking cigarettes, even though I don't smoke. I was trying to be cool.' Hoggy remembers feeding Cogs some hash, which he'd never had before, and it completely pushed him over the edge.

'I remember leaving because I was blind and having to sleep in my car out the front,' Cogs says. 'I had to get away. I was asleep by about 11 o'clock, because I was so wasted. That was my introduction to the band.'

WITH THE FINAL LINE-UP CAST, Powderfinger took a few months over the Christmas period to rehearse, write new material and overhaul their set-list. When they reappeared on the Brisbane live scene early in 1992, almost all the covers in the band's repertoire were gone. As Bernie explained to *Rave* magazine, one of Brisbane's leading free music papers, on 25 March 1992, Powderfinger were now performing about 95 per cent original material and had 20 of their own songs to choose from, including four brand-new ones written since Cogs joined the band.

The singer also took the opportunity to sing the praises of their newest member in the *Rave* interview. 'Jon's made a huge difference. Everything has a different feel now – we've got a lot more groove. We were getting a bit stale last year, but now we are having fun again. We've got a new lease on life. We're recording six songs on disc around Easter, then we'll hopefully get down to Sydney and Melbourne for a tour.'

Cogsy's debut shows took place at the band's familiar haunts, including Dooleys, the Orient and the Pineapple Hotel. There were other early performances at Her Majesty's Bar in the Hilton Hotel in the city, the Brunswick Hotel in New Farm and the Pump Club at the Dead Rat Hotel in the Valley. The transition from Bish to Cogs was almost seamless and, as Bernie suggested, it instantly felt as if Powderfinger was born again. Quickly, the band generated a whole new momentum, coupled with another surge in popularity.

Along with the change in sound, Cogs brought a fresh edge to the band. He looked a bit different to the rest of them. While he had the matching long hair and happily donned a corduroy jacket for photos, he wasn't into all the hippy gear, choosing to dress more like the surfer dude that he was.

Also, as much as the guys tried to play it down, there was no denying Cogs's presence upped the band's spunk factor. There were always lots of girls at 'Finger shows, but with Cogsy's arrival there was an undeniable indie heartthrob vibe creeping in.

'They would have so many girls at the gigs,' says producer Magoo. 'And all the guys would go to the gigs not really to see the band, but because the girls were there.'

'Everything has a different feel now – we've got a lot more groove.'

With Cogs well and truly bedded in, Powderfinger could finally return to the agenda they had sketched out with Teaks prior to Bish's departure. Having already fulfilled step one by ridding their set of most covers, the time had come to make a proper studio recording.

No one was really sure where to start, although one thing was obvious, it wasn't cheap to make a record in 1992. Teaks set the band a budget of between $3000 and $4000, which included pressing 1000 copies of the recording onto compact disc – an almost unheard of extravagance when most independent bands in Brisbane were still only releasing their music to the public on cassette tape.

Powderfinger didn't have $4000. Their savings had disappeared while they were off the road between drummers, so they had to find the money elsewhere. Encouragingly, there was no shortage of benefactors willing to make up the shortfall.

Geoff Viner and Michael Carter, two of Hoggy and JC's old mates from Brisbane Grammar, who also played alongside Bernie at the Wests Cricket Club, stepped up to invest in the recording. And Darren's parents offered to cover the lion's share of the costs. 'It was very generous of my folks to do that, it was a great show of support and faith in me, which I'll never forget,' says DZ. 'I don't know if we ever paid them back.'

With the budget sorted, Powderfinger went in search of a suitable studio. 'I remember driving around with Teaksy and Bernard,' says Hoggy. 'We looked at heaps of studios in Brisbane. None of us really knew anything about studios, but we were reticent to use the new digital stuff.'

They finally decided on Broken Toys, a tiny independent studio near the Story Bridge in Kangaroo Point, run by a guy named Leroy Bath. The studio had recently acquired a new 24-track, one-inch analogue tape machine, which sealed the deal for the 'Finger.

Broken Toys had produced recordings for a bunch of Brisbane indie acts, including the Lost Boys and the Apprentice Dentists, and Leroy Bath had just completed work on the debut album for another local indie act, Fear of Falling, when he got a call from Bernie. Leroy had heard the name Powderfinger but didn't know anything about them, so he made a few enquiries. 'I asked around and everyone was going, "This is the next big band out of Brisbane,"' he says.

Within the week, Leroy sat in on a band rehearsal at the Target building, saw them perform a gig and instantly appreciated what all the fuss was about. 'It was obvious they were going to be great. They had all the right personalities, the songwriting capabilities. I could tell there was going to be something special about them. I wanted to make sure I captured the feel of the whole band.'

Leroy asked Ian Taylor, his partner in Broken Toys, to get involved. A well-established audio engineer, Ian had just finished up a high-profile gig as the live sound producer – ie: the front-of-house guy – for Oz rock legends the Angels. Ian, in turn, asked the drummer from Fear of Falling, a budding sound engineer named Mark McElligott, who was hanging around the studio, if he'd also like to work on the Powderfinger project. Mark's reaction was straight to the point: 'No way in hell – I can't stand that band!'

'I didn't like them at all,' says Mark. 'I thought they were just boring old '70s rock, like Led Zep and the Rolling Stones, which they all loved and I hated.'

The irony is that by the end of 1995, Mark McElligott – Marky, as everyone knows him – became Powderfinger's personal front-of-house man and would remain so right through to the band's last-ever show in 2010. 'The Fingers all think it's hilarious that I used to hate them,' says Marky. 'But I was a complete indie snob, with the '80s hair-do and paisley shirts.'

In April 1992, Powderfinger spent a handful of days at Broken Toys studio recording their eponymous debut EP, which would come to be known as the 'Blue' EP or 'Blue' album or simply 'Bluey', courtesy of its distinctive monochrome artwork designed by JC. The band recorded seven songs, most written since Cogsy's arrival in the bandroom, and all were used on the final cut of the EP.

'It was a magic recording, as far as I was concerned,' says Leroy. 'They were all dedicated to getting the best of everything in the studio. One of the most professional bands I've ever worked with.'

'When we did it, we thought we were the greatest band in the world, obviously,' says Bernard.

Of the songs on *Powderfinger*, the singer says he remembers writing the base of 'Freedom' on the old piano at his parents' house – the first time he ever wrote a song on piano. 'Take a Light' started with lyrics and a verse that Hoggy brought to a rehearsal.

'Hoggy was the main songwriter in the very beginning,' says Bernie. 'Then I joined and I started writing a few songs. Then he would have a song and I would write lyrics and melody to it. Darren still wasn't doing a lot of writing then; he was writing parts, not songs.' (Although, early on, DZ infamously brought in a medieval-flavoured track called 'Log Down a River', which no one ever lets him forget:

'Time drifts by like a log down a river/ Day turns to night as I lay on my quiver/ ... Goodbye, goodbye, goodbye to the one I love'

'Everyone put in their five cents worth all the way along,' continues Bernard. 'It was the very beginning of how it ended up flowering into a five-way scenario, the full blooming of five ideas at once – every idea was going into every song, which is why it ended up being such a mishmash.

'We were purely focused on trying to write good rock songs. I was really limited as a guitar player in those days, so my ideas were always getting fleshed out, which continued to the end anyway. It was all pretty self-centred. They're all songs of yearning and loss. There was a fair bit of navel-gazing going on then.'

At the time, the band described its style as 'hard groove rock' and most of the songs on the debut EP were heavy on twin-guitar riffery. While the rocking opener 'Take a Light' featuring local singer Anne Dellar on back-up vocals wouldn't have been too out of place on *Vulture Street*, it was in the mellower moments that Powderfinger's future trademark style was most evident – namely 'Freedom', the introduction to 'Sacrifice' and the ballad 'Save Your Skin' (which the band would re-record for its debut album).

'It's got some pretty wicked guitar shredding on it,' says Darren. 'It was fun. It was our first studio experience and we wanted it to be good and loud. It sort of reflects the time – a young band that had shitty gear, and that's how it sounds.

'The most noticeable change to me is Bern's voice – you can really hear that it's nasally and squeaky and he's just screaming back then. It really matures over the years. The change in his voice is incredible.'

WITH THE RECORDING IN THE CAN but its release still some months away, the band and a bunch of mates headed down to Byron Bay over the Easter long weekend for the annual Blues Festival.

'There were 10 or 15 of us camping there, including all the Fingers,' says Bernie. 'We were all stoned out of our brains for the whole period. Well, Hoggy and I were, at least.'

On the evening of Good Friday, the guys were drinking in the packed backroom of the Byron Bay Services Club. Hoggy went up to the bar to get a round and met a couple of girls who were buying themselves a tray full of B-52 shots (a potent mix of Kahlua, Baileys and amaretto liqueurs). Hoggy, in his inimitable style, grabbed one of their drinks and skolled it. Before the girls could protest, he bought them a replacement. Everyone went back to their tables and, as it happened, the girls and their friends were sitting right next to the Powderfinger gang. They got to talking and before long they all started shooting trays' worth of B-52s together.

One of these girls was Jessica Ducrou, Powderfinger's future booking agent. This chance meeting was the beginning of one of the most significant and enduring relationships in Powderfinger's history.

At the time, Jess was working in the accounts department of *Australian Rolling Stone* magazine in Sydney, but within months she took over the band booking duties at the Lansdowne Hotel, one of the premier independent live music venues in Sydney in the early '90s.

'We got shit-faced, absolutely trashed,' Jess says of that first night. 'I can't really remember what happened but we went back to the camp grounds, woke up the next day and this Kombi van goes past and it was Powderfinger – they were staying at the same camp ground. We went back to the services club, they were there and we all got drunk all over again and became mates.'

Such was the instantaneous bond, Jess and a couple of her friends went up and spent a week – a 'massive mute fest', as she describes it – at Hoggy and Ingrid's place in Brisbane. (Teaks had moved out of the shared house by this stage.) Jess's car broke down, so she had to return a few weeks later to collect it and it was on this second trip that she had her first proper interaction with her soon-to-be lifelong business partner, Paul Piticco.

Although they had briefly met in Byron – right next to the site where a decade later they would stage their hugely successful joint music festival, Splendour in the Grass – the pair didn't recognise each other when they met again in a nightclub in Brisbane. ('Paul hates this story,' warns Jess. 'He won't let it in the book.')

Jess went up to the bar to buy a drink. Teaks was standing there and introduced himself and told her he managed Powderfinger. Jess said, 'Oh, that's cool,' to which Teaks replied, 'Oh no, it's not really cool.' Jess replied, 'What do you mean?' And Teaks spun her a story: 'Well, I've been struggling for a long time … I've got AIDS. Yeah, I don't know if I have much time left …'

Jess was obviously shocked and offered her condolences. Later that night, at yet another party at Hoggy's, Jess was talking to Bernard and told him how sorry she was to hear about their manager. Bernard set her straight: 'Oh Jess, the guy's having you on.'

'That was my first experience with Paul and it probably defines our relationship from then on,' says Jess. 'He's a pretty funny guy. He hates that story because he thinks it doesn't make him look like such a great person. But it's so Paul Piticco. He has such a droll, dry sense of humour. Where does that come from – where do you even think about telling someone you've got AIDS? And he's done that to me a few times over the years … just reels me in.'

BACK IN BRISBANE, THE BAND GOT STRAIGHT TO WORK. One of their gigs was at the Orient, supporting an up-and-coming Sydney rock band on their first trip north of the border – Baby Sugar Loud. This was the beginning of another lifelong friendship.

'We played first,' recalls Bernie, 'and they were on the bill – we had no idea who they were – and we were like, "These guys are amazing!" During their set, they said, "You know what – it's Jimi Hendrix's birthday and we're gonna play a song in his memory," and they played this really shit-hot version of "Crosstown Traffic". I was like, "God, how good are these guys?"'

'So we went back to their hotel and got on the booze with them. They were staying at the Dockside, which is where all the bands stayed when they came to Brisbane. Because we lived in Brisbane we never went there or knew anyone who went there, but we headed back to their room and had a massive party. And I go, "You guys, that's pretty awesome that it's Hendrix's birthday and you can just pull out a Hendrix song." They were like, "Oh no, it's not Hendrix's birthday, we say that every night." It was a fucking great lesson in how to get a crowd going. So showbiz.'

'I remember it was us, the Dalai Lama and the New South Wales State of Origin team staying in this hotel,' says Ben Quinn, the singer in Baby Sugar Loud. 'We got on so well with the Fingers and we've never looked back.'

It was these new friendships with Jessica Ducrou and Baby Sugar Loud that would provide Powderfinger with an entrée into a career beyond inner-city Brisbane. But not just yet.

POWDERFINGER'S EVER-GROWING REPUTATION as a live force saw Teaks begin to field offers for support slots on Queensland shows by visiting high-profile interstate rock acts.

The first of these big gigs was at the beginning of July, opening for the Baby Animals, the biggest new rock band in the land back in 1992. It was a one-off at Stewarts Hotel up the coast in Alexandria Headland, just near Cogsy's old neck of the woods. It was Powderfinger's first experience working alongside a commercial mainstream act, giving them a behind-the-scenes view of how a fully professional band puts on a show. And they loved it.

'It was an awesome gig,' says JC. 'There were about 1500 people and it was the first time we ever got real applause and genuine love from another band's crowd. And the band was so great to us, like, "Come and have a beer, come and chat." And they were massive at that time.'

Making the experience even sweeter was the fact that the Baby Animals had just played a bunch of shows with Powderfinger's idols, the Black Crowes. The Fingers had all gone to see the Black Crowes perform at Brisbane's Festival Hall just a few weeks earlier.

'There were only about 500 people there but it was amazing,' says Cogsy. The only downer that night was hearing the Black Crowes perform their latest hit, 'Remedy', which sounded like a virtual cover version – or vice versa – of one of Powderfinger's brand-new songs, 'Let It Grow'. It was for this reason that 'Let It Grow', which all the Fingers believed was their strongest song to date, would never get released.

Invites...to

The Orient Hotel

to celebrate their

CD Launch.

Friday 21st August

With Lolita Carbine supporting
$5.00 entry, cheap drinks ($1.00 spirits, throwdowns, wines)
Starting at 8pm Open Till Late

If I find the road back home
Will it lead me to your door?
The more I learn it seems the less I know
Can you teach me anymore?

The next major date on Powderfinger's calendar in 1992 was 21 August, the official launch of their debut EP at the Orient Hotel.

From beginning to end, the *Powderfinger* EP had been a genuine DIY project. The guys held mini working bees to personally assemble the CDs. 'I remember putting it all together at Hoggy's house,' says JC. 'Put the CD in, put the case together, put the sleeve in, all done by hand. Like that story of Joy Division putting together *Unknown Pleasures*.'

There was an accompanying DIY public relations blitz. 'We sent out invites, stuck up posters,' says Hoggy. 'This was pre-texting, pre-Facebook, pre-internet. It was true word of mouth.'

Andrea Smith from the Orient remembers seeing a couple of the guys out on the streets in the city handing out flyers for the show. 'They were talking to people, trying to get them to the gig,' she says. 'I think that's partially what set them apart from some of the other acts, being willing to put in the hard yards. After shows as well, they'd talk to people and acknowledge that they had taken the time to come along.'

'We all did the mail outs and poster runs,' adds Bernard. 'You could stick up posters in Brisbane in those days, it wasn't totally illegal, but then they shut it down. JC and Teaks got busted by the lord mayor for putting up posters on some backstreet in Kangaroo Point.'

The net result of all this effort? The CD launch at the Orient was a sell-out. In fact, it was more than a sell-out. 'The place probably held about 400 people,' says Teaks, 'and we sold about 600 tickets. There were people who couldn't get in, there were people on the sidewalk and it was obvious that something was happening here.'

The band didn't disappoint, putting on the show of their lives. They played all the tracks from the EP, as well as a couple of covers – 'Misty Mountain Hop' by Led Zep and 'What's the Buzz?' from the soundtrack of *Jesus Christ Superstar*.

'That was great fun,' says Darren. 'What band wouldn't be happy filling out a venue for the launch of their first EP of original material? It was a big thing in Brisbane at the time. We were pretty proud.'

'It was the best gig we had ever done in our lives,' says JC. 'It was absolutely packed. We had the windows open, another 100 to 200 people were out in the street watching – people were passing them beers out the window. It was fantastic, the best night ever in terms of band stuff. It doesn't happen very often, but when it happens to you, it's hot.'

In the aftermath, the band wrote an open letter to its fans via *Rave* magazine:

> *Powderfinger would like to thank everyone who came to the Orient Hotel for the CD launch on Friday night. It was an amazing turn out. We hope everyone had as good a time as we did.*
>
> *Mostly though, we apologise to those who did not make it through the door. If we had any idea how many people would come, we would have had it somewhere bigger.*
>
> *Once again, thank you.*
> *Powderfinger*

Apologetic, but the spectacle had the desired effect. Within a few weeks, *Rave* put Powderfinger on its front cover. Inside was an accompanying article and glowing review of the EP: 'These are great songs performed with pride and passion and, most importantly, a very real subtlety,' wrote P.D. Davies.

On the same day, *Time Off*, Brisbane's other main music street paper, heralded the arrival of Powderfinger as a major new recording act. 'A tasteful and sonically stimulating debut from one of Brisbane's finest live bands,' wrote reviewer David Waugh. 'In essence, Powderfinger have redefined the perceptions of Australian rock … *Powderfinger* is first class.'

Perhaps the only negative in the whole 'Bluey' chapter was that someone broke into Paul Piticco's house around this time, making off with a bunch of his CDs, including boxes filled with stock of the debut EP – about 200 copies of the disc, minus the artwork, which JC still has stored away. Those copies have never resurfaced. Something of a lost treasure considering what a collector's item it's become: In recent years, single copies of the *Powderfinger* EP have resold for more than $500.

Teaks would like to take this opportunity to conclusively reject the conspiracy theory – perpetuated by the likes of Hoggy and JC – that he had anything more than a passive involvement in the disappearance of those CDs. 'I've heard those theories,' says Teaks. 'That I was thinking ahead to my retirement plan. But no, you can put that story to rest.'

All jokes aside, the release of the EP gave everyone a glimpse of Powderfinger's true potential. 'We'd been garnering fans all along,' says Teaks, 'but this was the first real sense that something bigger could happen.'

RAVE

Issue #56 November 4th - 10th 1992 KNOW YOUR PRODUCT

POWDERFINGER: On The Trigger

COMPLETE A-Z LISTING OF LOCAL BANDS

RF BRAHM: Fishy Rumblings

0055: Info Line Now Open

CHAPTER 12

Transfusion
1993

A week after the inner-city love-in that was the EP launch, Powderfinger found themselves back in eerily familiar surrounds, out in the middle of nowhere, playing to a crowd of hardcore, hard-arse bikers.

It was the end of August 1992 and the band was booked as the opening act for Aratula '92, a non-stop 30-hour festival of music, booze, bikes and boobs, staged by the Rebels Motorcycle Club on farmland 100 kilometres southwest of Brisbane. It was supposed to kick off at 10 pm on the Friday night, but the Fingers didn't take to the stage until after 1 am.

The band's old mate Rod McLean got them the gig. He sorted out all the music for the event, as well as compering the show. It was just like being back in the dungeon at Club ACs, only on a much larger scale.

'It was an eye-opener,' says Cogs. 'Here was us, a whole lot of hippies in our Kombi van, and there were bikers walking around with their Nazi helmets on, some of them had girls on dog leashes. In between bands, it was either strippers or wet t-shirt competitions made up of girls from the audience. They were let off their leashes to come up and get all their gear off.'

It was Cogsy's first and last experience playing to a crowd like this. Aratula was Powderfinger's final biker show, the end of that era.

It wasn't as if anything drastically changed overnight for Powderfinger after releasing the 'Blue' EP. None of its songs got played on radio anywhere, aside from the odd spot on Triple Zed's homegrown shows. It was certainly too low-key a release to get noticed by Triple J, the Sydney-based national youth network that began broadcasting into Brisbane at the end of 1990.

Initially, all it really meant was that Powderfinger had a compact disc of original songs for punters to buy at shows. Outside the gigs, the CD was only available in a couple of independent record stores around Brisbane. Still, reports of the launch party filtered through to the major record labels in Sydney and Melbourne via their local Brisbane branch offices, putting them on that radar for the first time.

Many of Powderfinger's hometown contemporaries were also in the throes of releasing debut recordings. Bands like Dreamkillers, Pangaea, Brasilia, Custard and Screamfeeder simultaneously garnered interest from out of state.

This was the tipping point, the height of the international grunge movement – alternative acts like Nirvana, Pearl Jam and Soundgarden were suddenly the best-selling music artists in the world. It was inevitable that the major record labels in Australia would start paying attention to the homegrown indie music revolution festering up north.

Alongside the Target building, another focal point of this early '90s Brisbane scene was the weekly Rock Against Work concerts, staged on Friday afternoons, first at Bertie's Tavern and then at the considerably larger Metropolis Tavern in the basement of the Myer Centre shopping mall in the city.

The idea was simple. Free concerts staged in the middle of the day, cheap beer and lots of live music from local acts, followed by an indie/alternative dance night. At their peak, the shows drew up to 1000 music fans and began featuring interstate bands as well. Every indie muso and dole bludger in the greater Brisbane area, including the Fingers, would be there almost every week, either playing or just hanging out.

With all this action happening on the home front, Powderfinger prepared to initiate the third and final part of their masterplan – to perform outside Queensland.

The band's ever-growing profile had brought them to the attention of the Harbour Agency (Sydney) and Premier Artists (Melbourne), the leading booking agents for rock gigs around the country, both part of the Mushroom music empire of local impresario Michael Gudinski. These agencies organised the touring schedules for most mainstream local artists dating back to the 1970s. They offered to set up a bunch of shows for the band in Sydney.

So, in September 1992, Powderfinger packed the Kombi and set off in convoy, squeezed into Teaksy's Celica and a second car headed south.

Aside from family holidays as kids and the Blues Festival in Byron Bay, most of the guys had never travelled outside Queensland. Bernard remembers arriving in Sydney for the first time and walking through the city. 'I was smiling at people and getting blank looks back,' he says. 'Real yokel cliché. I was like, "What is this place?" Dorothy was in from Kansas.'

The Fingers weren't complete strangers in town. They knew the guys from Baby Sugar Loud, as well as Jessica and her mate Mel and the other girls they met in Byron. All these new friends (and others in the future) kindly opened up their homes to the band. For the first few visits to Sydney, the Fingers and their entourage—Teaks, Darren Aitcheson (their sound guy from the Orient) and Scott Coleman (on lights)—slept on their new mates' floors and couches. Darren and Scott took turns sleeping in the Kombi so no one would make off with all their gear.

'I used to live above a music store on Parramatta Road in Sydney called the Bass Player,' says Baby Sugar Loud's Ben Quinn. 'It was a horrible place, rat-infested, but Bern and Hog used to stay when they came to Sydney. I used to charge Bernard one version of (the Beatles') "Rocky Raccoon", make him sing that as his rent. We used to play guitar all the time, smoke quite a lot of pot and just make up songs and keep singing them around and around and around.'

Ben was one of the handful of people on hand to witness Powderfinger's debut Sydney performance at the Forest Lodge Hotel in the backstreets of inner-city Glebe. Also there on the night were Teaks (playing door bitch); Bernard's old mate Sean Fogarty; Stuart Miller (Baby Sugar Loud's drummer); a couple of young female music fans; as well as Ben's flatmate, a young aspiring singer and future chart-topper named Alex Lloyd. And that was it.

'There was no one else in the bar at all,' says Alex Lloyd. 'But, fuck, it was an awesome gig.

I was pretty blown away. I was inspired by them and I had a lot of respect for them. The first EP, we played to death – we played it all the time.'

Powderfinger performed four shows in five days on that first Sydney visit, including Max's at Petersham and the legendary Annandale Hotel, which became a regular fixture on subsequent visits for years to follow.

The band also made its debut appearance at the infamous Kings Cross venue, Springfields. At the time, Denis Sheahan, the band's future tour manager, was working out of Melbourne, taking care of acts like Roxus, Frente, Jo Beth Taylor and Indecent Obsession. His advice to Bernard was to forget about all the poncy indie crap – hit the old-style pub rock joints like Springfields.

Springfields was the antithesis of the indie cool of the Annandale. A seedy all-night music venue, it was a hangover from the pre-grunge, big hair, leather-pant-wearing, corporate pub rock scene of the 1980s. Powderfinger, of course, still had some leather pants of their own, so didn't feel entirely out of place. 'We had a hot time,' says JC. 'It had the best PA system and it was all set up for us.'

The band performed there half a dozen times during their initial trips to Sydney, playing alongside classic pub rock acts like the Choirboys, the Poor Boys and Horsehead. 'To me, that epitomises what we did in those days,' Cogs says. 'That was a big gig for us. There was still that Oz rock element to music in Australia and Springfields had a following in Sydney. It was seedy and always really late, a venue you played and then walked out of at 5 am off your face.'

'It was more the traditional old pub rock style place,' says Bernard. 'The Springfields scene was starting to die and we saw them turn the lights out there. Back then, the indie scene, especially in Sydney, was full of confidence – Ratcat had just happened.' (Sydney alternative trio Ratcat became an unexpected mainstream pop phenomenon in 1991 with their single 'Don't Go Now'.)

Bernard says his one clear memory of those Springfield nights was seeing JC perform an act of virtual magic. The two of them were in the process of lugging gear down the back stairs of the venue out to the Kombi. ('The others will say it's one of the few times that I was actually loading out,' Bernard notes with a grin, 'but I had important business to conduct, networking for the band.') JC was carrying half his heavy bass amp in one hand and a beer in the other. He slipped, went arse over head, dropped the amp, but somehow managed to save his beer. 'He didn't spill a drop,' says Bernie.

It wasn't a fluke. Bernie witnessed JC pull off a similar gravity-defying feat a few years later at a Big Day Out after-party in Melbourne, an incident the singer rates as his favourite JC moment of all time. 'It was a situation where it was all strangers and JC was smashed. He somehow managed to walk into the club, fall on a table, which was marble, break it, smash every drink that was on it, of which there were about 15, hold onto his own and not spill a drop, and then go around to everyone sitting on the couch, shaking their hands and saying, "G'day, I'm JC."'

The drive back to Brisbane basically killed off both the Kombi, which was costing more to refill with oil than petrol, as well as Paul's Celica. But the Fingers had got their first taste of life on the road and they loved it. 'We really just want to keep touring,' Bernard told *Rave* magazine's Janie Fitzgerald when the band arrived home. 'It's not only necessary, it's bloody fun.'

Bernard also added:

> *We'd love to get a big record deal. We've had some interest but we don't want to sign something that's going to be a total gip. We just have to wait until the right one comes along.*
>
> *If you can keep learning, you can keep improving. That's the idea, unless you play for 20 years and just pump out the same old boring fart music. If you learn new things, then you've got to write new things, as long as you utilise what you learn.*

IN NOVEMBER, POWDERFINGER WAS ONE of the bands invited to represent Brisbane on Australian Music Day, sharing the bill at the Metropolis with Pangaea, the Tellers, Puzzlehouse, the Genes, Solar Baby and other up-and-comers.

Powderfinger were back to playing their regular shows around Brisbane, but the Premier/Harbour agents offered them a big gig for late December, as opening act on a round of regional Queensland shows with Oz rock legends, the Angels.

The aging Angels were still a major drawcard in 1992 and shared a manager with the Baby Animals (John Woodruff), who the Fingers had had such a great time supporting earlier in the year. No one in the Fingers' camp was necessarily a fan of the Angels, but how bad could it be supporting one of the biggest bands in the country for a few shows?

'It was hideous,' says JC.

'The first gig we played was the Burpengary Tavern near Deception Bay (40 kilometres north of Brisbane),' says Cogsy, 'and we came on to a chant of "Fuck off! Fuck off! Angels! Angels!"'

The chants only got louder throughout their set, so the Fingers ingeniously decided not to leave any gaps between songs, in an effort to drown out the crowd. This meant they finished a few minutes early. They walked off stage and were greeted by the Angels' tour manager who yelled at them: 'You've still got three fuckin' minutes – get the fuck back on stage!' Which they did. During the main act, the Fingers watched on from backstage as singer Doc Neeson popped off during guitar solos to suck on an oxygen mask.

It was Powderfinger's first experience with the ways of old time rock & roll. Part of the tradition was the 'two-in, two-out' rule: support bands supplied manpower, at least two guys, to help lug the headliners' equipment in and out of the venue. Darius stepped up to do his bit but the lentil-eating hippy wasn't wearing any shoes. This earned another verbal scolding from the rough Angels' roadies.

'Every band should do a tour with the Angels,' JC says. 'Learn how to show up and do your thing.' There were five shows in all. 'There was nothing wrong with those guys. We had a beer with them on the Gold Coast, they were fine. It was just the tough crew.'

'They weren't exactly lovely to us,' adds Ian, 'but that's sort of what was expected then. It was a different world. It was the first time I ever saw a mobile phone. Their road manager had one, this massive thing. We were like: "Wanker!"'

On the eve of the Angels' shows, the Fingers had splashed out on a new van for themselves, $1800 for a second-hand, 1980 Ford Econovan. They christened it the Econodog and it would prove a most loyal dog indeed.

In the first few weeks of 1993, Powderfinger headed south to Sydney again. There wasn't enough room in the new van for everyone, so Darren and JC caught a train. Their second visit saw the band return to Springfields and the Annandale, as well as performing their first show at the Lansdowne Hotel, the venue where Jess Ducrou booked the bands. Teaks had asked Jess to help them sort out some more shows and Jess put them on a bill supporting the Hellmenn, skater-punk darlings of the Sydney live scene at the time.

Soon afterwards, Jess left her job at the Lansdowne to become a full-time agent with the Sydney-based APA Agency and Powderfinger asked her to become their personal booking agent. Jess, in conjunction with Paul, booked every Powderfinger show in Australia from then on, right through to the last tour. 'Paul has always had faith in my ability as their agent, and that started a long history of working together,' says Jess. 'I was aware from the start they had the potential to become a stadium band. Very aware. I'm not surprised by where they got to. If anything, I'm surprised they weren't bigger.'

Jess says that during the band's first few visits to Sydney, the crowds grew with each performance. 'They had the ability to impress a crowd so that when they came back, the crowd had doubled in size. And it was purely based on their live show. There was something very raw and pub rock about it, unique compared to what else was going on. Bernie was a freer frontman back then, more a show pony. And they were five good-looking guys. The girls loved Powderfinger.'

Back in Brisbane, some of the guys were still playing the odd additional gig outside the confines of Powderfinger. Cogsy played a couple of shows with a sideband called Gland, which included his best mate at the time, the 'Finger's lights man Scott Coleman. They played mostly high-energy Nirvana and Mudhoney covers, plus a couple of originals.

Bernard was also still performing the occasional solo set. Andy Mac (nee McDonell), a stalwart of the Brisbane indie music scene and a close mate of the band,

hosted a weekly Tuesday night get-together at Her Majesty's Bar called Drink & Play, where anyone could get up and play a song and receive a jug of beer. Bernie briefly took over the emceeing role ('Got paid about 100 bucks, which was big in those days,' he says), as well as occasionally performing alongside Andy at the Victory Hotel in the city on a Sunday afternoon. Bernie also made a couple of solo appearances back at the Gap Tavern, where he played his first solo show a few years earlier. None of these extracurricular activities would carry on for too much longer.

Come March 1993, the band headed back down the Pacific Highway, this time all the way to Victoria. Powderfinger's first experiences in Melbourne came with none of the culture shock associated with their first Sydney trip. It immediately felt like a second home. They stayed on the outskirts of St Kilda and easily adapted to the city's cosmopolitan pub and club culture. Musically, the band was instantly enveloped into the town's bustling and eclectic live music scene.

Their first Melbourne gig was in the small front room of St Kilda's famed Esplanade Hotel, the Espy, but it didn't take many trips to graduate to that venue's considerably larger and more opulent backroom, the Gershwin Room. They also played a gig across town at the Central Club in Richmond, performing on a tiny B-stage while v.Spy v.Spy played the main stage.

'This was the start of our driving odyssey across eastern Australia,' Darren says. 'Down to Melbourne and up to Cairns. We'd play wherever we could, sometimes to five people, and gradually those numbers would increase, because we spent as much time as we could driving around.'

The plan was to visit Sydney and Melbourne every couple of months and play as many stops along the way as possible: Gold Coast, Byron Bay, Newcastle, Canberra, Albury. When heading north of Brisbane, it was the Sunshine Coast, Rockhampton, Mackay, Townsville and Cairns. Tens of thousands of kilometres, all in the Econodog. It was still several years before the band could afford the luxury of flying anywhere.

'Every six weeks we'd go away for a couple of weeks, then come back and then go away again,' says Darren Aitcheson, Powderfinger's first full-time front-of-house man. 'It was a never-ending cycle.' This is what old time rock & rollers called paying your dues.

Between all the travelling, there were more shows in and around Brisbane, where the Fingers were now routinely playing to hundreds. Mainstream media picked up on the buzz. *Sunday Mail*'s pop columnist Jacqueline Nunan described Powderfinger as 'one of the hottest drawcards on the Brisbane live scene' and 'the most innovative originals band on the live circuit'.

The spunk factor was duly noted too.

Mention the word 'girls' and they start to squirm. Being the hottest spunk act for miles tends to erode rock cred somewhat.

'That's just not true, we get equally as many guys in our audiences, they're just not as visible,' drummer Jon Coghill protested. 'The girls dance up the front and come closer to the stage while the guys stay cool down the back. No one could call us just a girls' band.'

For a multitude of reasons, all this girl talk sat most uncomfortably with the band members, first and foremost because they were all in serious relationships. With other men. No, only kidding. They all had long-term girlfriends. Indeed, JC had recently started dating a young woman named Tara (who in time became his wife and mum of their three kids, twins Grace and Rosie and their youngest, Scarlett).

THROUGH EVERYTHING THAT WAS GOING ON, Powderfinger recorded a new EP. Initially it had the working title of *Slave* but was ultimately called *Transfusion*. The recording was made at Red Zeds, the same rooms where Bernard briefly worked as a nightwatchman and the four-piece version of Powderfinger rehearsed.

The EP was recorded by Jeff Lovejoy, a young Brisbane indie music producer who was making a name for himself producing EPs for thrash punks the Dreamkillers. Following the release of the 'Blue' EP, Jeff stalked the Fingers, begging them to let him produce their next EP. He got his way, co-producing the disc with the band. There was an initial session as early as December 1992, followed by five days recording and mixing in May 1993.

Again, the whole project was self-financed, this time straight out of Powderfinger's own coffers. The recording budget for *Transfusion*, not including the manufacturing of CDs, was $2000. It was double Jeff's previous biggest recording budget for any project. Jeff says they didn't master the EP because no one knew such a thing as mastering even existed back then.

Also in the studio, credited as the engineer on the sessions, even though he says he didn't merit the title, was Magoo. 'I didn't really do anything,' he says. 'I recorded bongos on one song ('Blind To Reason') and the rest of the time my job was to keep the band out of the studio because it was so tiny. I kept them entertained playing cricket in the hallway.'

There was no lack of material for the disc. The Fingers had started writing songs even before the 'Blue' EP was officially released. The band's sound was changing quickly, the new songs notably heavier.

'We wrote "Reap What You Sow" and "Change the Tide",' says Bernard, 'and with both of them we were like, "Oh, these are pretty fucking good!" And then there was "Blind To Reason" and "Rise Up" and "Mama Harry", and we knew we had made a pretty big step.'

There were several other live favourites that didn't make the cut. 'That's when the songs "Silverline", "Let It Grow" and "Dirty Old Man" were around but they never made it on to that EP,' adds Bernard. 'The labels had decided EPs had to have a single and four whatevers. So "Reap What You Sow" was the single.'

Inexperienced in the studio, the Fingers made up their own language to describe the sounds they wanted. More 'dunny' meant more reverb, the sound akin to singing in a bathroom. Background sounds were called 'dinner party', because if you noticed them you would talk about them at a dinner party. Their favourite aural adjectives were 'pure' and 'purity', as in 'Yeah, that's pure – that's purity!' They even rechristened Jeff as 'Chumps', because, as Cogs explains, 'He's so cherry, he's chumpy – he was all about big guitar solos.'

Aside from the five songs that ended up on *Transfusion*, the band also recorded versions of 'Silverline' and 'Let It Grow'. Jeff remembers all the actual recording was done in the first three days. 'They were long sessions but it was recorded pretty much live, with vocals added later,' says Jeff. Particular attention was given to getting 'Reap What You Sow' right. The first two days ran from midday through to 3 am. On the third day, the session stretched until 6 am with Hoggy spending three hours adding countless layers of guitar on the unused version of 'Let It Grow'.

The final two days in the studio were dedicated to mixing the music. Here, Powderfinger's already infallible five-way democracy was on full display. There were endless discussions about what sounds should be loudest in the mix. 'Each of them didn't like it unless they were the loudest,' says Jeff.

He worked out a cunning way to make them all happy. He invited each band member into the control room separately to work on their parts. As each came in, Jeff made their instruments the loudest, then balanced it back down once they left. That way, everyone won.

'There was probably a feeling of being on the verge of something,' Bernard says. 'We knew it was the best recording we had done so far and it was all very exciting. With Magoo and Jeff, they were our mates and that made it even more fun. We were all stony broke, classic poor dudes making sausage rolls do for tea, and scrounging up enough money for a carton of beer between us. Just fun.'

Sonically, *Transfusion* was a monumental leap from *Powderfinger*. There was a sharpness and loudness to the new recording. The meandering bluesy song structures from the first EP were replaced with tighter, punchier and rockier grooves and riffs. And Bernard's voice was already sounding bigger and stronger. You could hear the experience gained from the touring and extra playing in the CD's mix of three straight-out rockers and two more open, mellower tracks ('Change The Tide' and 'Blind To Reason').

And in 'Reap What You Sow', they had produced an exciting single, a contemporary cut capturing all of Powderfinger's skill and potential in five and a half minutes, with a big singalong chorus.

For Paul Piticco, it was the perfect lure to dangle in front of potential record company suitors.

TEAKS ALREADY KNEW A LOT OF PEOPLE IN THE BRISBANE branch offices of the major record labels. He had delivered them copies of the 'Blue' EP, started building a contact base and almost everyone in the music business in Brisbane had seen Powderfinger perform by then.

There was general curiosity from record company types for a while, but the first serious expression of interest came from Imago Records, a Sydney-based independent label set up by John Woodruff, manager of the Baby Animals and the Angels.

Michael Parisi, Imago's general manager and A&R scout, travelled to Brisbane to check out a bunch of bands, in particular Pangaea, Brasilia and Powderfinger. Shortly afterwards, Teaks and the band went to a meeting at the Imago offices in Sydney and not long after Parisi took Woodruff to see a show at Dooleys in Brisbane. 'I remember we played like shit,' says JC, 'so that didn't last long.' Indeed, Imago's interest evaporated following that gig. (Parisi didn't end up signing any of those three bands although a couple of years later, when he moved over to Warner Music, he signed Regurgitator.)

There was fleeting interest from Michael Gudinski's Mushroom Records. MDS (Mushroom Distribution Services) looked after the distribution of the 'Blue' EP into selected independent record stores around the country. Jo Corbett, one of Mushroom's PR and A&R reps in Sydney, had fallen in love with the disc and pushed her bosses to sign the band, but they passed. 'They thought they were a little bit too Black Crowes,' says Jo. (That wasn't the end of Jo's personal involvement with Powderfinger. She and her friends were at the first Forest Lodge show in Sydney and she became part of the Powderfinger network, members of the band would crash at her house for years to come.)

The most serious offer prior to the release of the *Transfusion* EP came from Sony Music Australia. Jo Grogan, one of the label's Brisbane reps (and future personal manager of Delta Goodrem), had brought the band to the attention of the company's Sydney headquarters and they were ultra keen. Denis Handlin, Sony's chairman, personally flew to Brisbane in an effort to entice the 'Finger to sign with them.

A fancy restaurant was booked for dinner and the chairman and his entourage offered the band the world, including a brand-new shiny Tarago van for touring. Handlin thought he had the deal stitched up, especially since he was an ex-Terrace boy, just like Bernard. But he was wrong – Sony's approach freaked the band out. They represented everything the Fingers feared a corporate major label would be like. 'Halfway through the meeting,' says Ian, 'we went to the bathroom and it was like, "This is fucked – let's just order the lobster and go." We didn't connect at all.'

In the meantime, Tim Prescott, the head of Australian music at the Melbourne-based Polydor Records, was receiving constant missives from his Queensland representatives. Steve Widdicombe, the company's Queensland state manager, and Tony McKenny, the state head of promotion, wanted Tim to take a serious look at Powderfinger.

'They said, "There's something happening with this band in Brisbane and lots of people are seeing them live,"' recalls Tim. '"Everyone's really passionate about this band – Brisbane is where it's at."'

Polydor was on a hot streak. The label's investment in Australian alternative music, pre-dating the grunge movement, was paying dividends with critics and on the charts. They had just released *The Honeymoon Is Over* by the Cruel Sea (in partnership with the boutique Sydney label, Red Eye Records). It was a defining Australian alternative recording of the era with crossover commercial success. Polydor's roster also included Clouds, the Fauves, Beasts of Bourbon and later Spiderbait and Tumbleweed.

In late July 1993, Tim flew up to Brisbane to see for himself what all the fuss was about. On a Friday night, Steve Widdicombe and Tony McKenny took him to see Powderfinger play at Metropolis. Tim was an instant convert.

'I remember being blown away,' says Tim, 'because this club was quite big and there were a lot of people there – there would have easily been three or four hundred kids in the room. I was used to seeing little bands that we had worked with at Polydor with 20 people in the room. The first time I saw the Cruel Sea, there were literally 20 people in a pub in Melbourne.

'I really, really enjoyed the show, loved the show. Bernard's voice just cut through straight away – that was the first thing that hit me. Then the next thing was the energy that was being driven in the band, and it was coming from Cogsy at the back. The rhythm section was just fantastic and the two guitarists either side could really play. For a new act, they looked great, I thought they had great songs, and Bernard was a star.'

After the gig, Teaks asked Tim and the Polydor guys if they wanted to come back to a party at Bernie's place at Indooroopilly. 'I was like, "Absolutely – we're going!"' says Tim. 'And off we went. And I met the guys at this shared house and we were standing around the kitchen cracking XXXXs. It was like being back at university.'

Tim talked to all the guys about music and the

Brisbane scene. JC remembers telling him he thought they'd played a fairly average show. Tim reassured him: 'I didn't come up to see a good show, I came to see if you're a good band or not.'

'He spent all night with us,' says Bernard. 'He loved us.'

And the feeling was absolutely mutual. 'We really, really liked Tim Prescott,' says Teaks. They gave Tim a tape cassette of the unreleased *Transfusion* EP. 'I left that evening knowing this was an act we should sign,' says Tim.

The following week, Powderfinger opened the highly publicised Boggo Road Gaol concert on 31 July 1993. It was another glimpse into ye olde world of Oz rock for the band, sharing a stage with the likes of Rose Tattoo, Divinyls and Billy Thorpe and the Aztecs, who were performing together for the first time in 20 years. Powderfinger was the first of nine acts. They were on so early in the day that there was hardly anyone in the venue to watch them play and the Fingers packed up and left long before any of the headliners performed. Still, on page two of the *Sunday Mail* newspaper the next day, right next to a photo of Billy Thorpe was a photograph of Bernard.

Back in Melbourne, Tim wrote a memo to his boss, Paul Dickson, cc-ing Tim Read, the head of Polydor's parent company, Polygram Australia.

POWDERFINGER

INVITES ______________________________

TO THE "*TRANSFUSION*" EP LAUNCH

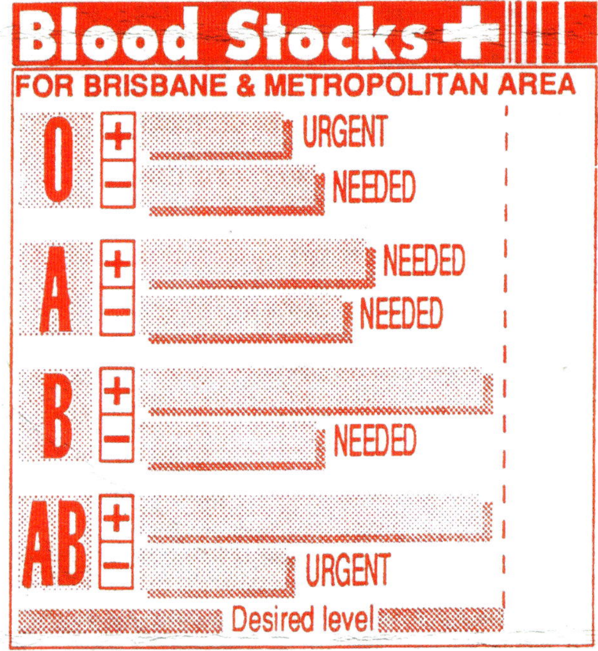

Your type is Urgently Required at

METROPOLIS TAVERN
FRIDAY OCTOBER 1ST

Transfusion Assistants - Doctor BULLDOZER

- Nurse DEVOID

- Matron BUCKET

invitation's required NOT
I.E. THIS IS A PUBLIC FUNCTION
AND INVITATIONS
ARE NOT REQUIRED

5 August 1993

POWDERFINGER

I saw this band in Brisbane two weeks ago and I can now understand the excitement they are generating. As you've heard, they've got a very good front man and have a retro/Black Crowes kind of sound, combined with a real cred from a lot of playing. I would like to put out their next single on a P&D (packaging and distribution) deal to test the water.

Tim's plan was for his label to release the *Transfusion* EP on the band's behalf, to take care of the manufacture, marketing and distribution of the disc on a no-risk, no-commitment basis. 'They needed a certain amount of romancing, but it was more about their ethic of not liking big record companies,' says Tim. 'They didn't want to be with a big record company, they didn't want it to feel like a big record company. But I knew in my gut once I met the guys that despite their independent ethic, they wanted to be successful. So our whole strategy to sign them was: we are independent thinkers and we're on your wavelength. We don't want to sign you to change you.

'We had to prove ourselves with that *Transfusion* EP. We hadn't signed them when we put that out. What we said to them and Piticco was: "We'll put it out without a contract and we'll show you what we can do. We understand you guys want to be independent but we are going to provide you with the resources to help you get the success you want." We believed it.'

WITH AN OFFICIAL RELEASE DATE for the *Transfusion* EP set for 27 September 1993, the band and their new mates at Polydor went about preparing a launch show at Metropolis on 1 October to outdo the 'Blue' launch.

In the lead-up to the EP's release, Ian and Bernard gave an insightful interview to *Rave* magazine's John Mullen, articulating their current state of mind. 'We didn't really get any airplay from the first disc, which is sort of a blessing because it sucks compared to this one,' said Bernard.

The pair revealed their growing frustration at being written off by some as a Led Zeppelin cover band or 'Brisbane's Black Crowes', calling such descriptions 'uninformed and out-of-date'. 'Maybe it's because we're a five-piece band as well and we've got two guitarists who play similar sorts of sounds,' Bernie surmised, 'but the actual music is nothing like theirs. I mean, sure, we like the Rolling Stones and Lep Zep too, but we also like Soundgarden and Alice in Chains and that's starting to creep more into our music. Thanks to our drummer more than anyone. He's never satisfied and he's a really good songwriter.'

The interview concluded with Bernard being asked how he thought the band would handle success when it inevitably came their way. 'We're all pretty down to earth and the whole idea of rock & roll stardom is a total toss as far as I'm concerned,' Bernie explained. 'It's just like being a butcher except you play guitar and write songs. It's not you that puts you in that position but the people who watch you that put you in that elevated position. I just hope that we're treated as the good blokes that we are,' he concluded with a grin.

As with the 'Blue' launch, the band personally invited everyone they knew to the *Transfusion* launch show but this time, with the backing of Polydor, there was also a high-profile advertising campaign in the free music street press around the country letting everyone know about the imminent release of the EP.

The gig was a sell-out, with 1300 friends and fans crammed into the Metropolis Tavern. The band had planned an unforgettable night of entertainment, with three support bands – Bulldozer, Devoid and Bucket – plus a performance piece featuring three of the Fingers' mates, musos-cum-actors Andy Mac, Paddy Dempsey and Andy Forbes.

'They made a rock & roll monster,' says Hoggy. 'It was a crazy piece, with a grinder, sparks flying, blood, pigs' hearts. It was disgusting. There was squashed pig's heart all over the stage. We had to pay to replace girls' dresses and guys' shirts because they threw blood at the crowd. Pushing the boundaries. After that, we learned not to give people free rein. You don't want to get sued.'

Cogsy's mate Chris Bosley was stage manager on the night. 'It went bad,' he says. 'Everyone was yelling and the crowd was throwing drinks. I had to keep the stage clear and it was filling with bottles and Andy Mac had enough and got all these offal bits and goes, "Ah, fuck ya!" and threw them into the audience. And the audience threw them back. I was bending down running across the stage, trying to clear this ocean of bottles and cans as the actors left the stage. Someone threw a billiard ball and it hit the kickdrum – *boom!* – and I thought, "I'm getting off this stage." It descended into chaos for a while, got a bit hairy, but it was pretty funny. Then Powderfinger came out and just kicked it.'

Powderfinger's performance brought the house down. The show received rave reviews. 'These longhairs appreciate the value of silence, acoustic axes, pace change,' wrote *Time Off*'s Richard Kwong. 'In short, it's all there.'

Even more praise was showered on the EP. 'This sounds more perfect, more powerful, more Powderfinger than they've ever played,' wrote *Time Off*'s editor Simon McKenzie. 'It quite simply kicks substantial ass. "Reap What You Sow" has to be the loudest and most momentous recorded moment to come out of this town – or this country – in years. This is more than just confirmation of how good they are, it's proof that they're better than anyone might have suspected. This calls for fucking champagne.'

'It gave us a massive confidence boost,' Bernard says.

Confidence is one thing. What happened next blew everyone away.

KODAK 160VC
43
KODAK 160VC
44
KODAK 160VC
45
2
3
4
47
KODAK 160VC
48
KODAK 160VC
49
KODAK 160VC
6
7
KODAK 160VC
51
KODAK 160VC
52
KODAK 160V
9
10

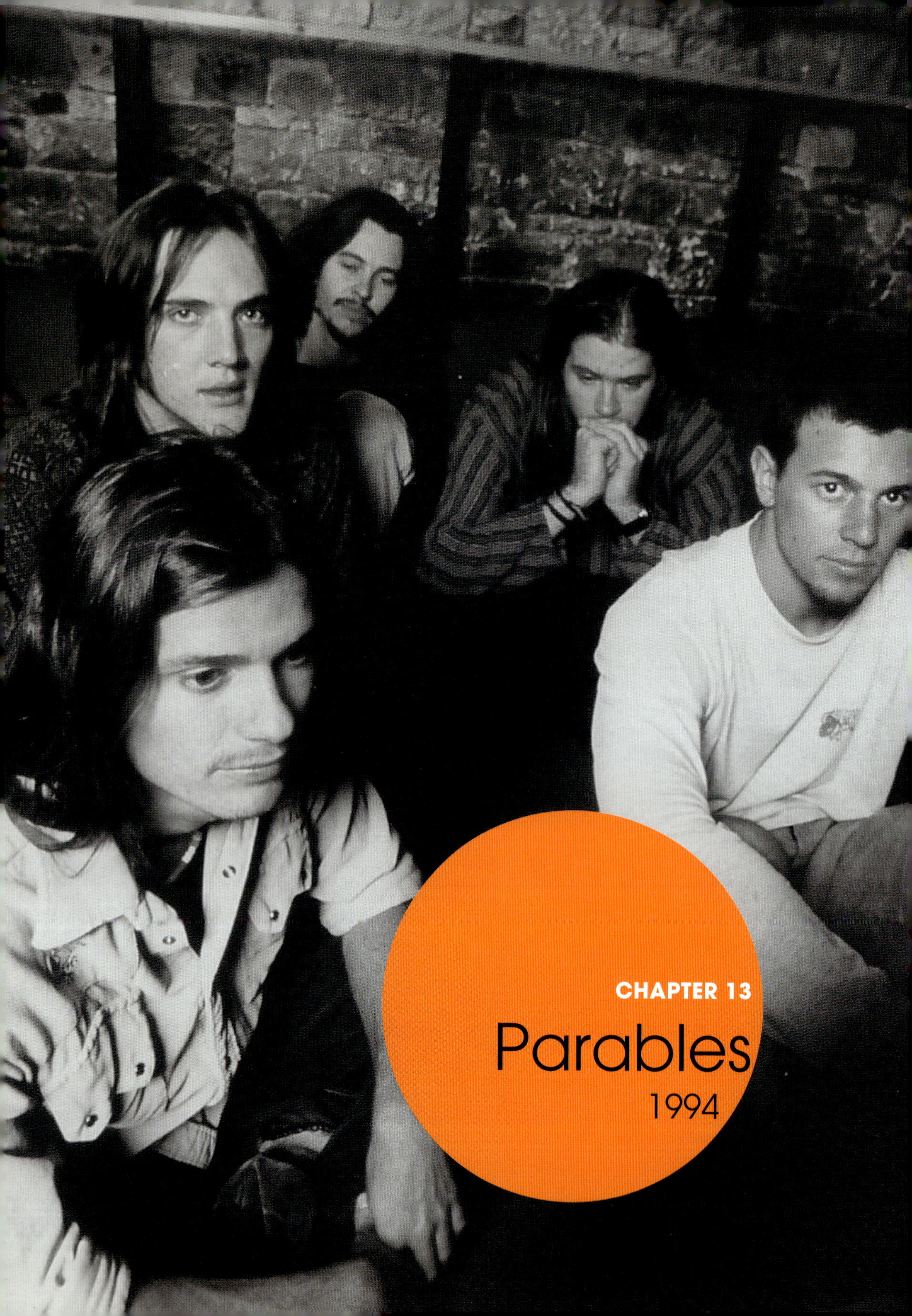

CHAPTER 13

Parables

1994

In the days following the *Transfusion* launch, Powderfinger were shooting scenes for the 'Reap What You Sow' film clip, their first-ever music video, in an old quarry at Kangaroo Point under the Story Bridge, when Paul Piticco arrived on set with a case of beer and some extraordinary news. *Transfusion* had debuted on top of the national ARIA alternative chart, knocking off Nirvana's 'Heart-Shaped Box'. It was an unfathomable concept that the Fingers had never even contemplated before it happened.

'Reap What You Sow' was receiving regular plays on Triple J, which meant people as far away as Perth were hearing Powderfinger for the first time. It was more coverage than the song got on Brisbane's fiercely indie Triple Zed. 'They hated us,' Bernard says. 'We were commercial private school boys.'

Even before they'd signed them up Polydor gave the band $7000 to produce a video clip for the track – over three times what it had cost to make the EP. The Fingers hired a young Queensland College of Art graduate named David Barker to direct the clip. Hoggy and JC had met him only a few weeks earlier when they were at the printers making copies of the flyer for the *Transfusion* launch. David walked in with Paul Curtis, Regurgitator's manager, to print off copies of their fanzine *Scorch*. They all got talking and ended up at David's place watching the wannabe filmmaker's show reel.

Suddenly, they were making a big-budget music video together. It would be the first of nine film clips that David would produce for Powderfinger, a relationship that would continue through to *Odyssey Number Five* in 2000.

After capturing the scenes of the band performing in the quarry, David took the Fingers down to a natural waterhole on the Gold Coast, near Burleigh Heads, to film some additional atmospheric, 'hippy-style' shots. He wanted the guys to strip down and jump into the water. It took some persuading to get them to agree, helped along by one of the crew members pulling out a spliff. Some of the footage from this 'Norsca' session, as the guys dubbed it, made it into the clip – dreamy vision of the guys lying on rocks, water rushing over their semi-naked bodies. ('You've got to watch it,' insists Teaks, laughing his head off at the memory.) One trippy scene, with all five of the guys frolicking in the water together, well, that was just too much and the band made David pull it from his original edit.

Watch the 'Reap What You Sow' clip
www.powderfinger.com/footprints

Meanwhile, having delivered on everything they'd promised so far, Polydor's Tim Prescott and managing director, Paul Dickson, made a formal offer to the band. 'I remember having a meeting not long after *Transfusion* came out,' says JC. 'Paul told us the record company wanted to offer a five-record deal.'

This was uncharted territory for a contemporary Brisbane rock outfit. And for Teaks. He had no experience in signing a record deal, let alone one of this magnitude, and there was no one around to ask for advice, so he hired a couple of heavyweight Sydney-based entertainment lawyers to help out.

'I loved Paul Piticco,' says Paul Dickson. 'He was just this enthusiastic kid who knew absolutely nothing about the business. But he never misrepresented the band. In all our dealings we knew that what he was telling us was what the band was really feeling, so there was a great trust from the band to him and from us to him. He was a fantastic conduit and he learnt on the job. In the end, he was one of the best managers I ever dealt with.'

The negotiations lasted for over a month and finally, in the middle of November 1993, Polydor and Powderfinger agreed on the terms of a five-album deal. Bernard remembers being a bit spun out by the idea. 'I was like, "Do you guys really want to be doing this when you're 35, standing around playing 'Reap What You Sow?'" I very clearly remember Hoggy saying, "Fuck yeah!"'

Prescott and Dickson flew up to Brisbane and took the band out to lunch to celebrate at the Pier Nine restaurant, one of Brisbane's fanciest eateries at the time. Everyone kept drinking and, next thing, it was late at night. A few of the guys wanted to keep partying. It was a weeknight, so there weren't many options and they headed to the Hellfire Club, a gimmicky bondage-themed nightclub in Fortitude Valley.

'We were watching these fat blokes in their underwear being thrashed by women in leather,' says Paul Dickson. 'After five minutes, we got bored and started playing pool.'

After a few games, the Polydor guys called it a night, leaving Bernie, Teaks, Hoggy and JC behind. Bernard went up to some guy at the bar and asked for a light. He picked the wrong guy to ask. Suddenly, it was on – pushing, shoving, people grabbing at each other's shirts. The bouncers stepped in and threw a bunch of guys out the side door of the club, including JC, who'd had nothing to do with the kerfuffle.

'Paul told us the record company wanted to offer a five-record deal.'

'I got kicked out with this guy,' JC says, 'and I said to him, "I didn't even do anything." He just walked up and clobbered me in the face. I went up to the bouncer and said, "Let me back in – this guy is going to kill me!" I wasn't being aggressive at all so the bouncer said, "Okay, I'll take you through the other way."'

Not long after the Fingers all left together through the front of the club and hailed a taxi. As they were about to get in, a car swung around the corner and the guy who'd whacked JC jumped out, along with a couple of other guys wielding pool cues. JC's attacker gave him another sucker punch to the face. Hoggy grabbed the guy in a headlock and pulled him to the ground. Fists and pool cues started flying everywhere. Then Hoggy shouted, 'Bernie, he's biting me! He's biting me!' Bernard tried to help, throwing out a haymaker. 'It was a disastrous punch,' Bernard admits now. 'No one knows who it landed on, it could have been Hoggy. The fight got broken up. JC had his lip split open and so we went to the hospital and sat there all night.' JC needed stitches and Ian got a tetanus shot. 'It was full on,' Bernie says.

The official signing took place a few days later, on 27 November 1993, which was, coincidentally, Australian Music Day. Tim flew up to Brisbane again with all the paperwork and took the guys out for an incident-free brunch at the Eiffel Tower Café in the Valley. And that was it. Done deal.

Afterwards, the band threw a party at their local, the Royal Exchange in Toowong. 'All of our mates came,' says Bernard. 'It felt really massive,' JC says. 'No one from Brisbane had signed a five-record deal in a long time ... all our friends and family dropped in to have a beer and celebrate. It was a really awesome day – the start of something. We now knew we were going somewhere. We could go make a record and someone would put it out.'

THE FINGERS WERE HAVING THE TIME OF THEIR LIVES. The group could not have been tighter or have spent more time together. If they weren't on stage, on the road or in the bandroom, then they were out drinking together at parties or at each other's homes. They were a band of brothers, thick as thieves, a rock & roll band in the truest sense of the term.

They had a record deal, they were touring non-stop. This was it. The dream becoming a reality. Except they were all still dead broke and on the dole, and would remain so for several years yet. For all *Transfusion*'s relative success, it only peaked at 118 on the mainstream ARIA national chart, so that was hardly going to make them rich overnight, either. 'The band was making money, but only enough to sustain paying for the accommodation and the petrol to get between towns,' says Ian. 'We got paid $20 a day, to buy cigarettes, a couple of beers and a bowl of noodles. That didn't worry us because we got to drink the rider at shows and play some rock & roll.'

Already by this stage, the band had made the decision to stay based in Brisbane, breaking a long-standing tradition of local bands with record deals moving to either Sydney or Melbourne or overseas. 'We think you can do it from Brisbane if you really want to,' Bernard told *Rave* magazine at the time. 'If you're dedicated enough and prepared to sit on your arse in a van for 24 hours every six weeks. It's just a day out of your life.'

A key element in their decision was the escalating potency of the national Triple J radio network. For the first time ever, alternative Brisbane bands could get their music played across Australia without leaving home.

'Triple J in the 1990s was just glorious for Australian music,' Paul Piticco says. 'So many bands from all over the country got a leg up. No matter where you were from, you could be heard nationally. A pivotal time, I think. And another reason to not leave Brisbane.'

Still, the band's new record label was gently suggesting it would be best for everyone if they stuck with tradition and considered moving south. Polydor itself had recently relocated from Melbourne to Sydney.

'But we all railed against it,' says Teaks. 'We liked Brisbane, we grew up there, there was a lot of Brisbane pride. And there were a few other bands with the same philosophy at the time, like Screamfeeder and Regurgitator. The community of bands were sticking to Brisbane.'

'We always said we'd rather spend an extra day in a car than move,' adds JC. 'That was our mentality. Also rent was much cheaper in Brisbane. We couldn't afford to do what we did if we lived in Sydney because we were broke.'

All the same, the band was now spending a lot of its time in the southern cities, and loving it. Especially in Sydney – it felt like one long summer holiday away with mates.

'They were the best times,' Cogsy says. 'Beautiful sunny days, playing gigs at night. We were loving each other back then. It was the idyllic life. We had no money so we used to while away the hours. We'd wake up at 10.30 or 11, we'd play cards or play chess or some stupid game all day, then we'd go to soundcheck.'

'We had a ball on the road,' Bernard adds. 'We were so broke, none of us had spare money, but we would get 10 beers a night at the show, or at somewhere like Springfields where we got better riders, maybe a carton. Every show we played we would be there from soundcheck until the lights went out, just hanging around, meeting people, having fun getting on the piss, playing pool, playing pinnies, all the stuff that entertains adolescents.'

Following the first few trips to Sydney, the band finally upgraded from sleeping on friends' floors and couches to the relative luxury of the Glebe Point Backpackers in inner-city Glebe, which would remain their home away from home for the next few years. 'I really enjoyed the backpackers,' says Darren. 'Roughing it when you're in your early twenties is good fun. It's how you meet people and gain a bit of character. It was a great social scene. We'd go to trivia night on Tuesday nights at the local pub.'

'We spent so much time in nightclubs, drinking, talking shit with people, hanging out,' says Cogs. 'On our nights off, we would go out with some of the backpackers, or they would come to the gigs and get drunk and we'd end up in their room talking crap.'

It was around this time that Bernard had to deal with his first heartbreak, after splitting with Kate Blackburn, his girlfriend of three years. Ben Quinn remembers dropping by the house the couple had shared in Indooroopilly to find the singer alone, drowning his sorrows in red wine, guitar in hand, composing odes to love lost. 'She became a mystical figure,' says Ben. 'There were a lot of good songs about her.'

But there was no time for heartache in Sydney. The boys were always out to play – boys being boys. Their regular gang included Alex Lloyd; members of Sydney band Juice, who had also just signed with Polydor; as well as their mates from Baby Sugar Loud.

'We spent so much time playing cricket with those guys,' says Cogs. 'Or with a goon bag [a wine cask bladder] hung up on a Hills Hoist, playing drinking games. I remember one night I was hanging out with Ben and Stewie from Baby Sugar Loud and Lucius [Borich], the drummer from Juice, and we were all in love with our bands so we decided to walk around Balmain [a neighbouring suburb to Glebe] with aerosol paint cans, spraying the names Powderfinger, Baby Sugar Loud and Juice all over the road.

'We got to the middle of Balmain, near the big town hall, and Lucius saw these temporary caravans so he ran over and started writing "Juice" on one of them. The rest of us were hiding behind a shop and all of a sudden the curtain opens on the caravan and a cop looks out – it was a temporary police station. We're shouting, "Lucius, watch out!" He rubbed the paint off and the cop let him off with just a talking-to.'

On another balmy evening in Balmain, a large gang of the guys converged on the Town Hall Hotel, which became their local in Sydney. The publican, Annie, an attractive woman in her early fifties, always looked after the boys with a couple of free beers.

Once a week, the pub held a karaoke competition with a prize of $100. Each week it was inevitable that Alex Lloyd would take out the prize money and share it amongst his mates.

'We got really drunk, had a massive night, got up and sang a few songs on the karaoke machine,' Alex says. 'It was quite a busy bar on a Sunday night. Annie was quite vivacious, she kicked us out, but she kept Bernie in there – "You can stay for one more drink."' Cogs snuck a peek through the window and sprung the pair having a pash.

'I never actually saw anything happen,' Alex says, 'but Bernie came out with a half grin on his face and a half look that said, "What did I just do?" We paid him out about it. It was pretty funny.'

The fun didn't stop when they travelled further south to Melbourne. They played all over town, as far out as Frankston, as well as at all the coolest inner-city hubs, including the Esplanade, the Evelyn Hotel and the Punters Club, and the Fingers made lots of new mates wherever they went.

It was at the Punters Club in Fitzroy that they first supported You Am I, fronted by the ever-effusive Tim Rogers, just as the then-trio was about to be declared the hottest new act in Australian rock. The two bands immediately bonded over a shared passion for beer, the Black Crowes, the Rolling Stones, Neil Young and Soundgarden.

'We were both hairy and lairy and rifforama,' says Tim Rogers. 'We were like cousins more than brothers. We all just wanted to get loaded and enjoy each other's company and play in front of more and more people each night.

'They were far more together than we ever were,' Tim adds. 'They were the first band I saw where their guitarist had an effects rack. Their equipment was light years ahead of ours. We'd make pedal boards out of wood and nails, they had professionally made ones and it was like, "Oh, we better step up." Darren would be taking his gear off stage in two hands and it would be quite ergonomically correct, while ours would have tacks and Velcro falling off. That was a bit of an eye-opener. It was like, "Shit – who's headlining here?"'

In between the playing and partying, all this touring meant endless hours on the road for the Fingers. Darren decided to give up drinking during this time, so luckily for the other guys there was always a designated driver on hand. 'Most of our travelling during that time we'd rotate driving shifts,' DZ says. 'Although Bernard would rarely drive – he somehow managed to get out of that.'

It was not uncommon in these early years for the band to take their rickety Econodog from Melbourne to Cairns in one go, a road trip in excess of 4000 kilometres. All this without air-conditioning or even a cassette player. 'What were we thinking?' says JC. 'Couldn't we put some money towards a stereo? We used to listen to the potato report.'

No stereo, but they did have a cellular telephone. Teaks had got himself one of those brand-new brick-like mobiles and he'd lend it to the band when they were out on the road without him, to be used in case of an emergency.

The band did have a couple of close calls in the early days. On one occasion, driving along the Hume Highway in the middle of the night, the van suddenly spluttered out of petrol. Hog was at the wheel and he pulled over in the darkness and pitched the van into a ditch. The rest of the band had to wait for hours while he hitchhiked to get fuel.

On another occasion, in broad daylight, the band was cruising along the highway between Brisbane and Sydney. DZ was driving, JC was next to him in the passenger seat, Hog and Bernard were in a car behind, when suddenly the dog lost a wheel.

'We'd just had the tyres done on the van,' says Darren. 'Retreads because that's all we could afford at the time. We assume the guy didn't screw one of the wheels back on properly. I was driving and we were doing about 100 down the highway when the back end just dropped and the van started snaking left and right and started to swerve.'

JC was freaking out, yelling 'Hold it! Hold it!'

'Somehow we got out of that okay,' says Darren. 'The tyre bounced past the Econovan a few minutes later, continuing its journey southward.'

The Fingers are eternally thankful to have survived all that treacherous travel on the rough country roads of the early 1990s but the bouncing wheel incident made a lasting impression on JC. 'That could have happened at night on any highway and we would have been gone,' he says. 'I hated driving around the country. I spent most of the time in the car shitting myself that we were going to die. That's why I started driving most of the time. I couldn't sleep in the van. I was paranoid. Probably because where I grew up, so many people died on the road between my town and Brisbane.'

JC remembers playing the Roxy in Brisbane on New Year's Eve at the end of 1993 and watching Wollongong band Tumbleweed rock up to play a show across the road in their brand-new Tarago.

'We were like, "Look at that, that's awesome, lucky bastards",' says JC. 'We had a bit of car envy because we were still struggling in our shitbox. And they'd flown up for the show on a plane. If we wanted to play a gig in Wollongong we had to drive down and sleep in the back of our van. And I just thought, "At some stage, we have to get to that level because I probably can't sustain driving around the country." But all good things come to those who wait.'

BACK HOME IN BRISBANE AT THE END OF 1993, Powderfinger's focus turned to their debut album, but there was plenty of other action going on at the same time.

The band was invited to perform its first Big Day Out shows in January, sharing the bill with the likes of the Smashing Pumpkins, the Ramones, Björk and their favourite contemporary band, Soundgarden. They were locked in to play the festival's smallest stage on the Gold Coast and in Melbourne.

This booking, along with the performance of *Transfusion* on the alternative charts, was enough to bring Powderfinger to the attention of *Rolling Stone Australia* for the first time. The magazine wanted to know what it felt like to be bigger than Nirvana. The Fingers' natural instinct was to smack down any scent of hype.

'It just made us realise how small the market is, and how easy it is to get to number one,' was Bernard's unadorned assessment of their chart success, pointing out that they had only sold about 1000 copies of the EP. 'All it did was make us aware of how few people buy records.'

It was also towards the end of 1993 that the band moved out of its rehearsal room in the Target building. The place had been robbed, with lots of the resident bands losing a load of gear. But not the eternally blessed Fingers – they were touring at the time, so they had all their gear with them. The only thing they'd left behind was a PA, which the thieves didn't bother taking.

The Fingers found themselves a new rehearsal space right in the middle of town, on Adelaide Street, across the road from Brisbane's City Hall. When they weren't out on tour you'd find them here. The band still jammed religiously, almost daily. Cogsy usually arrived a few hours ahead of everyone else to slot in some extra drum practice.

'You could hear the music from our room all across the city – it was so loud,' says Ian. 'But you couldn't tell where it was coming from. It echoed all through the streets so we never got hassled about it.'

Powderfinger already had more than enough tracks for their record by the time they moved into Adelaide Street. There were the leftovers from the *Transfusion* sessions – 'Silverline', 'Let It Grow' and 'Dirty Old Man' – and they had written a bunch of new songs too. They'd demoed an album's worth of material with Jeff Lovejoy and Magoo and the tentative tracklist included new titles such as 'Lemon Tree', 'Over The Water', 'Smiling Eyes' and 'Dream Free'.

And then, suddenly, only a couple of months out from the start of recording, Powderfinger made a monumental change in direction and style. No one knows exactly why. But even though the band may have left the Target building behind, their time there proved to be the defining influence on the shape of their debut album.

'It happened really late, towards the deadline,' JC says. 'We had all these other songs but we basically forced ourselves to write almost a concept album in this two- or three-month period. I don't think we even knew we were doing that.'

There was no doubt Powderfinger's sound was growing ever heavier in recent times. People had started comparing them more to Soundgarden rather than the Black Crowes. The Fingers had performed a ton of shows with the likes of Pangaea and Brasilia and rehearsed alongside both of them for over a year. They were mates. 'We thought they were the best bands ever,' says Cogsy. And their edgy, punky approach rubbed off on all the Fingers.

Cogsy was particularly enamoured with this more aggressive, sophisticated, almost mathematical approach to producing music. It wasn't too far removed from what he was playing back in university with his mate Chris Bosley, who was the bass player of Brasilia. Marked by complicated time signatures and virtuosic playing, it was cutting-edge music, making the 'Finger's traditional blues rock sound pretty basic by comparison.

It wasn't just Cogs who was into it, though. 'For some reason,' says JC, 'the guitarists got into some heavy music. Cogs and I started listening to a bit of [US band] Tool because we were trying to connect, and we just fell off the Powderfinger truck. We had a really good record sitting there ready to go and we moved away from it.'

Perhaps, subconsciously, the band felt obliged to play a part in the Brisbane new wave movement, to show that they too could play their instruments just as well and be as cutting-edge as their contemporaries. 'Techo and conservatorium shit,' as Bernard now describes it.

'We were trying to be pretty tough,' says Darren. 'We'd had bands next door to us [at the Target building] who were doing the heaviest music we'd ever heard, so we tried to be heavy like them, but that wasn't really our genetic make-up so we didn't do a very good job of it. We were just easily influenced.'

With a creative red mist clouding their better judgement and their new record label promising them complete creative freedom, Powderfinger were slated to head to Melbourne in

The magazine wanted to know what it felt like to be bigger than Nirvana.

February 1994 to begin work on their debut album. But first, in late January 1994, they experienced playing the huge Big Day Out festivals in Queensland and Victoria. And, even better, in what had all the potential of being the highlight of their career so far, Soundgarden invited the Fingers to open for them at a one-off sideshow at the Palace in Melbourne.

The Fingers were one of the early acts at the BDO Gold Coast show, playing at 11 am on a tiny stage far away from the main stages. 'It was awesome,' Bernard says. 'Being exposed to that festival environment, how professional it was. It was an amazing situation for local bands to be in.' Unfortunately, they couldn't hang around and enjoy the rest of the day because they had to jump straight in their van and drive to Melbourne in time to play the Soundgarden show the next night. After driving for almost 24 hours, the Fingers made it only to have their support slot cancelled because of some issue with Soundgarden's gear not arriving in time.

They were shattered, but the Soundgarden guys invited them backstage for drinks. The Fingers were already well lubricated before the offer, having started drinking as soon as they realised they had the night off. 'We got to meet Chris Cornell and Kim Thayil and the guys, who were really nice blokes,' says JC. 'We'd had a few. I went to the toilet, had a vomit, came back out and kept chatting. The next day was the Big Day Out in Melbourne. We didn't really set the world on fire that year.' Hangover aside, the band played in a massive tin shed at the Melbourne show that sounded more like an echo chamber.

A few nights later, Powderfinger scored another high-profile international support for their troubles, invited to open for Urge Overkill at a memorable gig at the Phoenician Club in Sydney. And there would be brighter Big Day Outs ahead. Plenty of them.

COMPARED WITH TODAY, IT WAS A VERY DIFFERENT MUSIC business back in the mid-1990s as Powderfinger entered the studio to record their debut album. It was pre-internet, pre-music files, pre-piracy: the compact disc had just hit critical mass and alternative and mainstream music were now one. It wasn't quite the pop and rock heyday of the '60s, '70s or '80s, but the major labels were still capable of tapping into 'rivers of gold', as Teaks describes it.

Polydor's Tim Prescott and Paul Dickson had a lot of faith in Powderfinger's potential as a credible, crossover mainstream act. When the pair had worked together at Sony over a decade earlier (then CBS Records Group), they played a crucial role in discovering international hit-makers Men At Work. They believed that in Powderfinger, they might just have found a new Midnight Oil – an earnest, unique, brilliant rock band with a conscience. And they were willing to invest some serious money to back up this belief, advancing the Fingers a $70,000 budget to record their debut album. It wasn't an exorbitant amount compared to some of the other Australian albums being made at the time, with budgets in excess of $500,000, but this was a lot of money considering it was only nine months since Powderfinger recorded their *Transfusion* EP for $2000.

Craig Kamber, Polydor's A&R wunderkind at the time, was assigned to the project. But really, at this stage, the band was simply given the best tools available and left to its own devices.

A month's worth of studio time was booked at one of Australia's best and priciest state-of-the-art recording facilities, Melbourne's Metropolis Studios. And the band was provided with the undisputed hottest record producer in the country at the time: the legendary Tony Cohen.

Throughout the 1980s, Tony Cohen's guttural, demonic-sounding recordings for the likes of Nick Cave's Birthday Party and Tex Perkins's Beasts of Bourbon made him a genuine idol of the underground music scene. In the 1990s, his considerably more refined work with Nick Cave & the Bad Seeds and Perkins's latest outfit, the Cruel Sea, had Cohen being hailed as a genius mainstream producer. He was proof solid of the convergence of the alternative and mainstream music worlds.

Powderfinger walked through the door of Metropolis Studios on 20 February 1994. They brought Jeff Lovejoy along to help out and let him experience what it was like to work in a major studio with a professional producer. Jeff acted as engineer, alongside the studio's in-house engineer, Andy Baldwin.

Metropolis Studios is located in Albert Park and the band, Teaks and Jeff stayed at the Barclay Apartments, in nearby St Kilda. Between recording sessions, Bernie, JC, Ian and Cogs – and occasionally DZ – could be found playing cricket in the apartments' car park. The band always had a bat and taped-up tennis ball in the back of the Econodog for any quiet moment. 'Bernie and I would just try to hurt JC while we played,' says Cogsy. 'That was pretty much our MO. We hit him in the balls so many times. In-swingers to the nuts, we'd call it. He had to build himself a protective box out of cardboard.'

The Barclay Apartments would be the band's regular Melbourne home for many years to follow. They normally crammed three into each apartment, with one lucky Finger sleeping on the couch. During this trip, the band also had the record company fly Ben Quinn down from Sydney, with the excuse of having him sing back-up vocals on the new version of 'Save Your Skin'.

Jeff Lovejoy remembers the night before recording began, there was a meeting to lock down the list of songs to record. Jeff was pushing for the guys to seriously consider recording 'Let It Grow', which the band had already demoed twice and which Jeff still believed was their best track. But the band wouldn't entertain the idea – they believed they had moved way beyond that song.

'The vibe I got from the conversation,' Jeff says, 'was that if they did "Let It Grow", the record company would want to release that as a single, and then they'd be pigeonholed into that Black Crowes thing. It was such a strong song that if it was released, it would have done well and, dare I say it, become a hit. It's almost as if they didn't want to have a hit single on their first album, so that they didn't risk being a one-hit wonder.'

Similarly, the record company suggested the band include a version of their recent minor hit,

‘Reap What You Sow’ on the album, a common practice for a debut record. ‘They didn’t want to know about it,’ Tim Prescott says. ‘And in the end, we respected that.’

‘They [Polydor] heard “Reap What You Sow”,’ says Bernard, ‘and must have rubbed their hands going, “Alright, let’s have a big glam rock, Noiseworks meets Guns N’ Roses record”, and that’s nothing like what they got.’

The band settled on a final selection of 15 tracks to work on in the studio, several of which were only weeks old. They were so fresh, Bernard was still penning lyrics for them in the van and in the studio.

When recording finally started, one thing quickly became apparent – for all his indie cachet, Tony Cohen was not the greatest choice to produce Powderfinger’s debut album. ‘With my way of working,’ Tony Cohen says, ‘you present me with your songs and play them as well as you can and I’ll try to make it sound good. There are other producers who come in and say, “Try playing this chord, try changing this to that.” It’s a different way of working and I think they [the Fingers] really started to get their wings when they got some education from people like that. But I’ve always worked with people like Nick Cave and if I dared say to him, “No Nick, that chorus is too long – halve it,” I’d get punched in the nose.’ (Which literally did happen on one occasion.)

Putting the Fingers in the studio with Tony Cohen was ‘a mismatch in personalities’ according to Paul Piticco. ‘Oil and water, a mistake,’ concedes Tim Prescott. For starters, Tony was very obviously not in the best of health. He had recently been diagnosed diabetic – he regularly sent his girlfriend, Astrid, out on ice-cream runs – and, as a result, his energy and mood fluctuated wildly. He also bore the scars of a hard living, rock & roll lifestyle. Some scars more obvious than others. On his forehead was an indent in the shape of a knob from a sound desk, the result of passing out and hitting the control panel after several nights without sleep while mixing the Cruel Sea’s *The Honeymoon Is Over.*

‘Tony was a lovable larrikin, but messed up,’ offers Cogs. The producer’s behaviour was certainly eccentric. One of his many

quirks was to bring a variety of toys into the control room. One day he lined up little plastic soldiers all over the mixing desk. Another day he brought in a spud gun with which to shoot the soldiers off the desk. Yet another day he had a tiny effects recorder and recorded himself saying 'Hey, fuck you!' and then randomly dialled numbers on the intercom and played the recording to whoever picked up. He was also obsessed by the studio's Addams Family pinball machine, constantly playing it and shouting out 'Mamushka!' along with the machine.

'He was a bit of a fruit loop,' says JC. 'Lovely, but a bit of a mad scientist, all over the shop. It was a bit daunting for us. I don't think we knew how to handle a producer.'

'The actual experience of being there, just going to a studio like that was incredible,' Bernard says. 'A massive room, a massive desk – we'd never seen anything like it.'

The singer remembers being starstruck at the sight of Paul Kelly walking through the corridors. 'I was really pumped that he was there and thought, "Oh my God – how am I going to talk to Paul Kelly?" So I asked him the cricket score. He was looking at me like, "I don't know if I really want to talk to this bloke – I can't tell if he really wants to know the cricket score or if he's just a punter." He wasn't rude to me or anything – I was just a little afraid of him. He was a massive artist – he would have been the biggest Australian male artist in the early '90s.'

Back in the control room, Bernard says he felt Tony Cohen was very encouraging of what the band was trying to achieve. He had a peculiar saying whenever he loved a song, that it would help 'egg the nest', a saying the Fingers later appropriated for their own ends. 'He was really into it, he was saying "This is really great shit that you're doing here", and that maybe fed into the gloominess of it as well, because that's where he was from, the kind of dark room sounds that he created.'

'I loved them immediately,' says Tony. 'I just thought, "Here's a really talented, raw band that are going somewhere." I knew that. Back in those days, they were pretty simple lads, green musicians with lots of stinky socks, basically living out of their van, which I respected a lot.'

However, Ian recalls Tony being notably uncomfortable with the lyrical content of one of the songs, 'Grave Concern', and its deathly themes. 'He didn't want to be singing that,' says Hog. 'He figured out that he could sing [the Bee Gees's] "Stayin' Alive" over it, kind of the opposite to "Grave Concern", so he kept singing "stayin' alive".'

No one's well-being in the studio sessions was aided by the fact that everyone except Cogsy chain-smoked. One of Tony Cohen's first acts as producer was to string a cigarette lighter up over the control desk. There was a permanent smoke haze in the room. 'I don't know how Cogs put up with it,' JC says.

After the first few days, Tony's presence became increasingly intermittent. He'd either arrive hours late, disappear after lunch or regularly take excessively long toilet breaks. 'Tony would disappear from the sessions,' says Jeff, 'which was fine with us. We just keep ploughing on with it. The album says "produced by Tony Cohen, engineered by Jeff Lovejoy and Andy Baldwin". But I would say it was more the opposite of that.'

When Tony *was* present, his recording style was unorthodox. He didn't seem too interested in extracting the best performance out of the players, more in capturing the raw energy of a first or second take. The levels on the mixing desk were constantly peaking into the red zone, so Jeff and Andy would routinely turn them down whenever Tony looked away.

It was during the final mixing stage of the recording, once all the music was captured on tape, that Tony assumed total control. Unlike Jeff during the mixing of *Transfusion*, Tony had no interest in buying into the Fingers' band democracy and refused to enter into any discussion about what sound should be where or how loud.

'He was like, "I'm mixing it – I'm doing my thing",' says Jeff. '"If you want something different, I can't do that, but I can give you the phone number of someone who will." The relationship between Tony and the band broke down. It became a bit of a stand-off. I remember JC wasn't happy with a bass part and wanted an effect on it and Tony was like, "Nah! This is how it is."

'On the very last day we were sitting out in the lounge area and Tony came out with his bag and his jacket on, ready to go. He said, "See ya, Jeff – see you at mastering next week." And he just walked out. He literally did not say goodbye to the band at all.'

IT TOOK JUST OVER A MONTH FOR POWDERFINGER to record and mix their debut album, the cumbersomely entitled *Parables For Wooden Ears*.

The name was meant as a joke. The band had toyed with calling it *Songs For The Deaf* but thought that was too obvious. (That album title would get used years later by US rockers Queens of the Stone Age.) So instead, the Fingers borrowed a line from 'Walking Stick', the opening song on *Parables For Wooden Ears*.

Dogs and children lift their legs
To tattoo a teenage mother's breasts
Widows of precocious days
Wear slogans resurrected late
Parables for wooden ears
Steer vehicles of wisdom

What the hell does any of it mean? It might help to understand Bernard's state of mind at the time he penned those words. 'I remember going to Triple Zed Market Day in Albert Park and taking acid with Hoggy and a few other people,' he explains. 'There were these trips called Red Dragon, which were really full on, and I didn't have much experience with any of that stuff. I remember freaking out and I climbed a tree, and just sat there watching for a couple of hours. I had my dillybag, which I always carried with me back then, and I had a notebook, so I sat there and wrote all this stuff down.

'It was a real Jim Rose Circus kind of scene, everyone had tatts and kids and dogs. It was quite aggressive, it wasn't all soft and lovey-dovey – it was hardcore. They were ferals, tough guys with tribal tatts and dreads. We were all pretty cynical about that whole scene. So "Walking Stick" – that's Triple Zed Market Day.' See – it all makes perfect sense.

There was a lot of stream of consciousness at play in the *Parables* lyrics. 'Whenever I've looked at it again, it all seems quite paranoid and conspiratorial,' Bernard says. 'A bit Orwellian, Catholic guilt, universal power-is-out-of-my-hands kind of crap. "Tail" [the first single to be lifted from *Parables*] was the chief protagonist of paranoia: *Here I stand with my tail between my legs, set to confess to these sins I didn't commit.* Pretty bad, but it's how I felt, breaking away from the Catholic world, finally having the guts to say it out loud, not just in my heart and my mind, to no longer be Catholic.' (The two extra tracks the band recorded during the sessions, 'May Morning' and 'Slip', appeared as b-sides on the single version of 'Tail'.)

Of the songs on *Parables*, Bernard says he's proudest of the lyric for the slower 'Hurried Bloom', written late one night while on the road in the back of the Econodog. 'I do think they are nice lyrics, more poetic rather than just doom and gloom, actually describing the night sky. I was pretty interested in writing in different ways, trying to work out what I was good at.'

Cogsy is credited as co-lyricist on two of the album's other mid-tempo tracks, 'This Syrup to Exchange' and 'Father's Pyramid', the band's first overt display of social conscience, a song about human rights, as they described it to the media upon the album's release.

When the band eventually packed up and left Melbourne for the long drive home, they still weren't entirely sure of what they had caught on tape. 'As we were doing it, we thought it was fucking great,' says Ian. 'We thought we'd created this complicated opus. I remember getting home to Brisbane, cranking it up on the car stereo and thinking, "Wow, we've made a beast."'

'We were all really into it,' says Bernard. 'It's partly enthusiasm that made the songs as structurally complicated as they were. Everyone just had lots of ideas.'

It wouldn't take long before Powderfinger knew exactly what everyone else thought about their debut album, and it would be the most jarring reality check of their lives.

PUBLICLY, THE INITIAL REACTION TO THE NEW Powderfinger material appeared quite positive. The single 'Tail' was released on 14 June 1994 and it was the heaviest recording the 'Finger had offered up so far and featured Bernard's most aggressive vocal of all time. It was accompanied by another David Barker video clip. No communal bathing this time, just the band rocking hard in a desolate industrial setting and lots of shots of Bernard scowling.

Watch the video for 'Tail'
www.powderfinger.com/footprints

Brisbane's *Rave* magazine wrote that the single 'exceeds all expectations (and they were high to begin with) by kicking harder than the majority of American bands attempting similar power and dynamics ... Well, they passed the first test pretty damned easy.' Triple J gave the song a few spins, but it wasn't embraced as enthusiastically as 'Reap What You Sow'.

The release of 'Tail' was preceded by Powderfinger's most extensive Australian tour to date. With financial backing from Polydor, the band spent five straight weeks on the road, playing all along the east coast, as well as inland regional centres, supported most of the way by Canberra band Sidewinder. This tour took them as far southwest as Adelaide for the very first time. Playing at the legendary Lennies was quite an unforgettable introduction to the 'city of churches', particularly for JC. He copped a faceful of road rage on the way to the venue. Then, while on stage, someone in the crowd flung a glass at him that just missed as it flew between him and Bernard. At the end of the gig, JC went to put his instrument away only to find someone had thrown up inside his guitar case. Good night, Adelaide!

There were a few more madcap rock & roll adventures on that tour, a couple involving some of those potent Red Dragons. The morning following a show in Ballarat with Wretched Child, several of the Fingers and their crew decided to drop acid as they headed towards Victoria's picturesque Great Ocean Road. It was the first time Cogsy had ever tried anything like this. He remembers being in the car with the rest of the band and Teaks, all of them giggling uncontrollably, annoying the crap out of the driver, a very sober JC.

Once they hit the ocean's edge in Warrnambool, JC pulled over to let the trippers take in the scenery and become one with nature. Cogsy went off into the bushes for a pee and the group could hear him shouting at his penis, 'I've got to kill it!' Later, on the deck of their accommodation at Lorne, Teaks was somewhat overcome when he spotted a possum on the handrail. He approached the small, furry creature with some fruit and it almost seemed to be trying to communicate with him. He was able to get close enough to pat his new friend. At which point the terrified possum leapt up, clawed ferociously at Teaks's face and darted off into the trees.

At the end of the tour, the Fingers scored an all-expenses-paid gig on Hamilton Island, including a couple of free days at the island's resort. During one of those days, they took a trip and headed for Whitehaven Beach. 'These corduroy-wearing rock guys tripping on acid on the same beach with all these Japanese tourists. It was hilarious,' Darren Aitcheson recalls.

On their return to the main island, Ian and DZ had a loud jam on the stage where all the band's gear was set up. 'It was all very beautiful,' says Hog. 'But then I got super depressed when

I watched these four dolphins trapped in a tiny swimming pool. I was communicating with them, just going, "I'm so sorry you're in here." I had ideas of breaking them out. Everyone had their own little trip that night. But it was good fun.'

Back in Brisbane and back to business, Powderfinger played a sold-out launch show for 'Tail' at the Site, did another quick lap of regional Queensland and then, on 18 July 1994, they unleashed their beast.

The release of *Parables For Wooden Ears* was supported by a national street press campaign, including a cover story in Sydney's major free music magazine, *On The Street*.

Keeping up with tradition, the band put on another memorable launch show in Brisbane, this time at the Roxy, backed by Screamfeeder and Webster. Once again, there was a bit of theatre to open the show – fire-breathers and a guy juggling chainsaws. These were Darren's new housemates, a troupe of street performers who shared a place together in the bohemian end of town.

'I needed somewhere to live and I pulled a flyer off one of the bulletin boards in a vegie shop in West End, saying "flatmate needed",' says DZ. 'I walked around the corner and met these crazy out-there guys who lived in this household thriving with artistic people. It was really cheap rent, $25 a week. I took up residence with them for two years, and they were a couple of the best years of my life, involving some of the most creative experiences I've ever had. We partied a lot, played around with all sorts of mind-altering experiences. It was awesome.'

Fun times for all ... until the reviews for *Parables* started coming in.

The band's hometown press was polite more than celebratory. 'The album moves through a spectrum of sounds that, despite similarities with a particular Seattle band, displays impressive individuality. Well done, boys,' wrote *Time Off*'s Andrew Burton. 'Confident and convincing, Powderfinger have delivered an album to be proud of,' added *Rave*. No one seemed to be calling for champagne this time around.

Rolling Stone was in two minds. Reviewer Jack Marx described the album as being in part 'a certified jerk-off', but added: '"Tail" is tangled and inert and teeters precariously on the brink of disappearing up its own arsehole, but a determined listener will find its hooks more infecting with each spin. That's the secret to enjoying Powderfinger – determination. I have to be magnanimous and say I like this album and have no reason to do so. Call it instinct. Isn't that what it's all about?'

The only facet of the music media to genuinely hail *Parables* was the hard rock fraternity. *Hot Metal* magazine said: 'Ambitious and very large, *Parables* is a swirl of steaming thunder rock, gentle acoustics, jazz breaks and punk 'n' funk flows.' Darryl Mason, writing for *On the Street*, described it as 'very awesome, a stunning collection of brilliantly crafted songs. This is an album rich with explorations of guitar-driven rock. And Fanning indeed doth possess one of the most fragile, frighteningly powerful rock voices spawned of this country in this decade. Glorious stuff.'

In the offices of Polydor, they were more aligned with *Rolling Stone*'s assessment.

'We were gutted when we heard the record,' says Tim Prescott. 'There wasn't a song you could get a grip of. What started out as a song ended up in a different place, a completely different song. There was nothing for radio. It really put us in a difficult place to market it. Then we thought, "Maybe the kids will all get this and we don't".'

On top of the $70,000 recording budget, Polydor spent nearly $100,000 on the manufacturing, distribution and marketing of *Parables*. Ultimately, there was no saving the project. Commercially, *Parables* was an abject failure. It was by no means the worst-selling record of all time, but nor did it leave an enduring mark on the Australian musical landscape.

Parables For Wooden Ears peaked at number seven on the Queensland music charts, but only number 51 on the national ARIA chart, and went into freefall from there. The record only sold about 3000 copies in the months following its release, reaching about 7000 copies within the first year. 'Tail' didn't fare much better, reaching number 26 in Queensland and 118 nationally. Two more singles were eventually lifted off the album, 'Grave Concern' and 'Save Your Skin', after which Polydor decided to cut its losses – ie: Powderfinger's losses – and move on.

PARADOXICALLY, DESPITE *PARABLES'* LACK OF SUCCESS, Powderfinger's reputation as a performing powerhouse was spreading and their audiences around the country continued to grow. Alongside the relentless touring through clubs, the band was getting invited to play some very cool shows. In October, they performed at Brisbane's esteemed Livid festival, sharing the bill with international headliners the Beastie Boys and Frank Black (aka Black Francis, former frontman for the Pixies), along with the cream of the local alternative scene: Tumbleweed, Dave Graney, Dirty Three, Pangaea, Dreamkillers, Spiderbait and more. The Livid performance saw Magoo take over from Darren Aitcheson as the band's regular front-of-house man. In the same month, Triple J offered the band a prized Live At The Wireless slot, allowing them to perform three songs to the nation: 'Walking Stick', 'Father's Pyramid' and 'Tail'.

At the same time, the Fingers were also getting invited to play plenty of other gigs. Teaks and Jessica Ducrou endlessly strategised about where and how to position the band, especially now that there was such a great divide between the old and new rock worlds. They turned down an offer for a support role on an extensive national tour with the Screaming Jets. They probably should have also turned down the offer to open for American hardcore heavy metal band Pantera, but the lure of playing Brisbane's Festival Hall for the first time was too great. It was a decision everyone would regret – Pantera made the Angels look like angels.

'We were like, "Awesome – Festival Hall!"' Bernard recalls. 'And Cogsy was like, "Do you guys even know who Pantera is?" I knew they were American metal dudes, but I didn't know anything about them.'

It didn't take long to work out what Pantera and their fans were all about. On stage in Brisbane, the Fingers were greeted with sustained booing and chants of 'Pan-te-ra! Pan-te-ra!' that drowned out much of their set. At one point, there was a huge cheer from the crowd; while the Fingers were playing, a member of Pantera snuck up behind them carrying a huge prosthetic penis shooting fluid into the air.

Once Pantera hit the stage, Bernard remembers being genuinely repulsed. 'Seeing the way they played, the way they operated and how they treated their audience, it was horrible. Phil Anselmo [the lead singer] picked up a girl from the audience, licked her face, threw her back down and spat on her.'

The Brisbane audience was relatively polite compared to what confronted the Fingers further down south. At the Newcastle Entertainment Centre a couple of nights later, there was another band on the bill, a local trio of 14-year-olds calling themselves Silverchair, who had just scored the number one single in the country with their debut song, 'Tomorrow'. It was the 'Chair's first big show and they were shown no mercy from their hometown crowd. The Fingers were backstage to offer a shoulder or two to lean on. 'They were avuncular figures who after the show said, "Don't worry about it – they hate us too",' says Daniel Johns, Silverchair's enigmatic frontman. 'From that moment on, we've always got on well.'

'It was a bizarre tour,' Ian says. 'The only good thing to come out of it was meeting Silverchair. The Pantera band and roadies were bullies and not nice people. A lot of the other bands we worked with, even though we weren't treated well, we didn't hate them as people. We *hated* the Pantera people. We had no respect for them. It was a really bad vibe.'

At the Sydney Entertainment Centre show in Sydney, Cogsy sought to extract some revenge in his own inimitable way. A backstage guest of the Fingers, Finny, was roughed up by Pantera's security for innocently filming too close to the stars' dressing-room. So Cogsy, along with Magoo, decided they would infiltrate Pantera's bandroom.

'Cogs and I were quite drunk,' Magoo says, 'and we waited until one of the security guards stepped away from the door and then we snuck in. There was all this gym equipment and a few girls who looked like hookers. We got in there and went, "Hi!!!" Phil Anselmo goes, "Oh, hey man," and looks straight at the three security guys inside the room and they rapidly escorted us out. I thought we were going to get our heads smashed in.'

Cogsy decided he'd have the last laugh by selling his backstage laminate to a hardcore Pantera fan. He got sprung by their stage manager, a legendary and intimidating local roadie called Spider, who threatened to destroy Cogs and made him a promise: 'You'll never work in this town again!'

'Perhaps the whole thing was a good wake-up call for us,' says DZ. 'Did we really want to play this heavy music?'

MOVING INTO 1995, POWDERFINGER WERE RAPIDLY approaching a crossroad in their career. It was three years since they'd released the 'Blue' EP, three years of driving up and down the east coast building their name, reputation and crowds. Yet, for all their success so far, in the aftermath of *Parables* it felt as if their growth was plateauing.

Whilst they could pretty much sell out any room they played in Brisbane, the constant touring through New South Wales and Victoria appeared to be hitting its limits. Yes, they could occasionally play two Annandale Hotel shows instead of one, but there was a huge leap needed to get to the next level. There were also some within Polydor beginning to question the band's mainstream potential.

The Fingers recorded a bunch of new demos with Magoo at the end of 1994. A decision was taken by the label that they should record an EP rather than dive into a new full-length album. This meant it would be at least another year before Powderfinger would get the chance to rectify the misstep of *Parables*.

Meanwhile, the band members themselves began to second-guess whether they were on the right musical path. 'Playing those songs live was painful,' says JC. 'Getting it wrong all the time, trying to find the groove that doesn't exist.'

JC remembers a particular gig at the Patch in Coolangatta where it all went horribly wrong. 'I'd had one light beer before going on stage. "Walking Stick" was the first song, and I scunged it. The whole gig, I just missed everything. It was hell and I hated every second of it. It was one of those nights when nothing goes right. And it was because the music was shit. It was also my fault. So embarrassing. People walked out during that gig. It was just a really shit day at the office.'

With time, all the band members would distance themselves ever further from *Parables For Wooden Ears* to the point where, in latter years, it got turned into the butt of endless jokes. All the songs from the record were slowly weeded out of Powderfinger's live set so that it became a genuine rarity to ever hear them perform anything from *Parables* in their final decade together.

It should be duly noted, however, that there is a small, albeit very vocal, minority of fans who still swear it was the 'Finger's best album ever. These are the same people shouting out requests for the band to play 'Tail' right up to the end.

'My only real gripe with *Parables* is that it doesn't hang together as an album,' Bernard says. 'It was an overextension. But thankfully that didn't last too long.'

'I still think that the songs we did on "Blue" and *Transfusion* and also those five or six songs that we never released are better than the songs on *Parables*,' says Hog. 'We lost our head up our own arse, as a journalist said at the time. I accept that comment. We were experimenting.'

While Darren has always felt it was musically the right thing to do at the time ('They were all stepping stones as far as I'm concerned,' he says), Cogsy takes it further, saying he believes the failure of *Parables* paved the way for Powderfinger's longevity and future success.

'We used to have this set of great blues rock songs that were like the Black Crowes,' Cogs surmises. 'And then grunge happened just as we got signed to Polydor, and we went away, sat in the bandroom for however many months, and we came out with an album that was completely inspired by, or completely ripped off, Soundgarden and all those techo bands in Brisbane who we thought were the best bands ever.

'So we came out with this album that sounded like grunge mixed with technical funk-metal, whereas we had all these great songs that we probably should have used on our first album. Then again, if we had done that, we probably would have died a quick death, because we may have had a hit or two with this blues rock sound and got lumped in with the old Oz rock thing. Instead, we wrote this pretty dodgy album and then we changed, we met what was happening in music, we embraced it, which was good. Juice got signed at the same time as us and they also did that blues rock thing. When their album came out and dudded, they got dropped. When our album came out and dudded, we kept on going.'

For a long time, JC believed he had a solution to the whole *Parables* issue. He reckons they should have gone in and recorded all those songs originally intended for the debut album and release them, call it *Powderfinger's Shoulda-Been First Album*.

During the Sunsets tour, backstage in Tamworth the band decided to pull out *Parables* and give it a spin for old time's sake. Even after all those years, it was unbearable. 'It was like, "Oh no, fast forward it! Where's the beat?"' says JC with a laugh. '*Parables* just never felt good, not even in Adelaide Street.'

Back in 1995, however, it was no laughing matter.

'There was a feeling in the air that we'd make another record,' says Teaks, 'but if it didn't work, forget about it.'

The Fingers needed a change of direction.

CHAPTER 14

Double Allergic

1996

Exactly how close did Powderfinger come to getting dropped by Polydor in the aftermath of *Parables For Wooden Ears*? Pretty close. Contractually, the label had the option to walk away after the first album. Whether it should was the topic of heated discussions within the offices of the label's parent company, PolyGram. 'Everyone really liked them but it was one of the first bigger investments the label had made that hadn't gone to plan,' says Craig 'Kambo' Kamber, the band's A&R manager at Polydor.

Two of the 'Finger's biggest supporters at PolyGram were Graham 'Asho' Ashton and John Zucco, mates of the band from the early days in Brisbane who had worked their way up the company ladder. 'Despite all the love that the band had in the industry,' Asho says, 'with the label and the agents, everyone started to go, "Well, maybe we were wrong. This isn't connecting." I remember very clearly being in meetings where there was talk about dropping the band.'

'There was this great debate about keeping them and developing them or cutting our losses,' adds Zucco. 'It was a pretty impassioned debate. There was a minority wanting to get rid of them, the majority wanted to keep them. On reflection, Paul [Dickson] and Tim [Prescott] were always going to go forward. The forces against lost the argument and, you could say, some of those negative forces later claimed credit for the band's success.'

As far as Tim was concerned, there was no walking away, not yet. He felt there were enough positive signs amongst the rubble of *Parables* that reinforced his belief in the band's potential. 'I never had a sense that it was out of our control,' he says. 'After *Parables*, there were definitely people saying, "This band want to be Soundgarden but they don't know how to do it." But I believed Polydor had the strength as a label that we could continue on and wanted to continue on with that band.'

Ultimately, the decision came down to Polydor's managing director and, in spite of pressure from the penny-pinchers, Paul Dickson was still a fan. 'To Paul's credit,' says Teaks, 'it was his call to back it, and he did.'

'There was never any thought in my mind other than to hang in there with the band,' says Dickson. 'This was all organically grown and we weren't in too deep. We lost money on *Parables*, but we had already made some nice money from putting *Transfusion* out – it ticked over really nicely. The band had an unrecouped balance of about $50,000, so it wasn't stinging, it wasn't really hurting us. And the belief in the band was still absolutely there from the live gigs.'

Meanwhile, on the band front, it was status quo. Word of mouth meant crowds were still growing, albeit incrementally, and the band was popular with venue bookers so they could play as many shows a week as they wanted. 'That's the thing that sustained us,' says Bernard. 'For those small rooms, we used to play our songs pretty well. We weren't an unreliable live band, so that always helped.'

One thing did change around this time – the band members were able to get off the dole. Teaks signed them on to the federal government's New Enterprise Incentive Scheme (NEIS), a program for groups of unemployed folk to come together and create a business. Powderfinger Incorporated probably wasn't what the government had in mind when they came up with the scheme, but it meant the Fingers no longer had to hand in dole forms or pretend to apply for jobs.

'It got to the stage where I would just open the phone book and point at something and write down a random workplace,' Ian says. 'One time I opened it at a hot-air balloon company and I thought, "They'll probably check that," so I phoned them and asked, "Can I have a job?" And they said, "Sure, come on down." So I was a hot-air balloon roadie for a few days, chasing balloons around.'

'We knew the DSSs [Department of Social Security offices, pre-Centrelink] all around the country,' says Bernard. 'There were five of us all needing to put in forms at different times, wherever we were. That happened a lot on road trips, we'd have to stop and go to the DSS to lodge our forms. Getting on NEIS meant that we could put that concern to the side; we knew we were getting an income for the next six or 12 months.'

Yet the cost of touring and day-to-day living meant they were still broke, doing odd jobs where possible for extra cash. Bernard occasionally got out the old lawn mower. Darren would make sushi rolls and sell them at the local West End street fair, as much for love as money. JC had a mate at the Department of Transport who for several years threw him as much casual work as he could, generally involving counting cars and documenting traffic flow. JC shared the work out among his bandmates. 'It was good – $10 an hour,' JC says. 'Darren used to cheat,' reveals Ian. 'He'd just sit at home or in the bandroom. I used to do it legitimately.' None of them could afford their own car and either caught public transport or rode their bicycles to rehearsals.

Around this time, Teaks began expanding his business interests beyond Powderfinger. These were the humble beginnings of a future music empire. His company, Valhalla Artists Management, later rechristened Secret Service, took on a couple more bands, co-managing Brisbane outfits Webster and Turtlebox (and later Sydney's four-piece guitar band Big Heavy Stuff) in collaboration with Bernard's brother, Paul, who had just returned from three years in the UK. Paul also took over road-managing duties for the 'Finger during this period.

In January 1995, there was no return appearance on the Big Day Out bill, but the Fingers played twice in two days at the Byron Bay Arts and Music Festival, held at Belongil Fields. Then, in April, they were invited to tour with the Alternative Nation festival. Set up as a competitor to the BDO, the first and only Alternative Nation event featured the likes of Nine Inch Nails, Tool, Faith No More, Lou Reed, Ween, Primus, Ice-T's Body Count, Violent Femmes, Pop Will Eat Itself, the Flaming Lips and the Tea Party. The 'Finger and fellow local acts, including Regurgitator and Spiderbait, didn't rate too highly on the bill, relegated to playing a tiny sidestage.

The festival was great fun: Cogs had never seen such luscious backstage catering; JC got to meet Ice-T; Bernie had lunch with ex-Wall of Voodoo singer Andy Prieboy. 'He was a really decent guy,' Bernard says. 'It was a good example of how you can influence people when you are older by just purely being kind to them, even for a few minutes. We were always keen to promote that idea. We weren't hanging out with bands every night, but when we came across people we made an effort to be friends, no matter what their music was like.'

At the conclusion of the three-city tour in Melbourne, the band headed straight back into Metropolis Studios to record their new EP, *Mr Kneebone*. It was over a year since they'd made *Parables* in the same room and not a huge amount had changed.

'I remember sitting in the bandroom,' says Magoo, who produced the sessions, 'and they played me the songs and I said, "There's too much going on." Before Bernie even sang a note, there were all these riffs coming from everywhere. I was just like, "You guys have got to give Bernie a bit more space. Let him put on his words and then fill in the gaps."'

The end result was edgy and bristling and unquestionably musically adept, but still overly complex. The five-track EP had its fans ('I think "Stitches" off *Mr Kneebone* is one of their finest rock moments,' offers Paul Fanning) and, again, there were signs of what the future held in store, but these were still not the sorts of songs Polydor wanted to be hearing from Powderfinger. And nor did the record-buying public.

When it was released on 24 July 1995, *Mr Kneebone* was the band's highest national charting disc to date, but it only peaked at number 83 on the ARIA singles chart and number 11 in Queensland. The disc was launched with another sold-out show at the Roxy on 28 July, the Fingers ending the gig with a cover of Flock of Seagulls' classic '80s electro hit, 'I Ran'.

'Nothing happened with *Mr Kneebone*,' Bernard says. 'We were still in *Parables* production mode. Everything was wet, blasting. But there were actually a couple of good ideas on there. "Swollen Tongue" was an okay song. It was a really formulative time for us, because clearly our music wasn't together, but we were kind of starting to know our way around things. There's a song on there, "Drongo", which was probably the very beginning of us going, "Okay, we can make these things melodic and get real satisfaction out of them."'

'Drongo' wasn't enough, however, to alleviate the pressure within Polydor. Even before *Mr Kneebone* was released to the public, the executive team at the label decided it was time to have a quiet word to the band.

Tim Prescott and Paul Dickson flew up to meet with the guys in Brisbane. 'We had agreed we would kick on with a new album but we had to say something,' says Tim. 'It's the only time we really gave them a bit of a lecture. We delivered this spiel: "Guys, we love you, the company loves you, but if you're going to keep on, you're going to have to get back to what you're great at, and make a record that has songs we can play on the radio. That means no more songs that go off in all directions and basically alienate the fans you were starting to build."

'We tried to explain they were not selling out by doing this – they'd capture more people. That night was, to my mind, a key turning point in the band's career. Not because of what we said, but because they knew it already. We just crystallised what they were thinking, that they had great songwriting skills, they had an amazing frontman with a great voice. All they had to do was keep it simple and write what they felt. Try to write and play songs that could be loved by the fans *and* by media.'

Reaction to the 'talk' within the 'Finger camp was mixed. Naturally, the initial response from some, even though they didn't say it aloud, was, 'Don't tell us what to fucking write!' ('Which was very naïve and ignorant,' says Ian), but others immediately took the advice to heart.

'It was one of the best record company band meetings that I went to,' Cogs says. 'They were saying, "Get smart. Get rid of all the bullshit and write some songs that get to listeners straight away. Write some songs that actually appeal to radio. You've got a message, why do you confuse it so much? Why do you have to get so clever, try to be so credible?"

'I was sitting there at first thinking, "I don't know what they're talking about. We *are* writing great songs." So I just said, "What do you mean?" They said: "Here's a good example, 'Swollen Tongue', the start is just white noise that goes for about a minute. It might sound good and different to your ears, but it's boring." I thought, "This is great – these guys aren't beating around the bush." As much as we didn't like it, at least they made us start thinking a bit.'

The undesired fallout from this meeting was that, in the minds of a couple of members, it fuelled festering doubts about the long-term prospects for the band. What if this was as good as it got? There were many acts in the history of Oz rock that merrily eked out a career without ever scoring a hit record. Bands that travelled from one show to the next, journeymen rockers like, say, the Radiators, playing gig after gig, town after town, year after year. Powderfinger had spent almost five years on the road; there was no reason why they couldn't carry on like this for another 20 or 30 years if they wanted to.

The thought of this filled JC with dread. There was a level of exhaustion setting in from all the endless travel and associated playing and partying. The band still had no roadies at this point – they had to carry all their amplifiers and instruments in and out of venues themselves at every show. Except for Bernard, of course. '"I'm the singer – I'll just carry my microphone down,"' says Ian, impersonating the frontman.

'. . . there were times when it was pretty shitty.'

All of it, for all the fun, was for no discernible fiscal reward. Add to that all those endless terrifying hours on the road in the Econodog and a certain weariness was settling over some members of the band. 'It got fairly tough around '95 and I remember thinking, "Oh well, we tried",' says JC. 'There was that feeling creeping in. A little self-doubt. I know Darren felt the same because I spoke to him about it at one stage. It was a bit like, "Oh well, maybe we should do something else." This coincided with a lot of our friends graduating out of uni and getting jobs. The excitement was drained after getting signed and having a huge launch. Then nothing much happened, there was just the hard work touring, every six weeks doing a road trip. Even after *Kneebone*, the excitement didn't get back up. So it was a matter of just hanging in there. It was pretty hard.'

'I think everyone felt a bit like that,' Hog says. 'I always had this mentality that expectations lead to disappointment, so don't expect too much. Just do the best you can, keep going. While I was enjoying it and wanted to keep doing it, there were times when it was pretty shitty.'

'We were in our mid-20s by that stage and needed to consider the future financially and that sort of stuff,' says Darren. 'I definitely had that sort of concern, thinking if this doesn't work for us, maybe I need to reconsider cooking or something.'

It wasn't a fear shared by absolutely everyone. 'I never felt like that,' says Cogs. 'I was always driven by the feeling that I get when I play. Even when we were playing shit songs, I still got that feeling. It's like being addicted to a drug.

'I don't remember ever having the conversation with anyone that if this doesn't work, I'm going to have to go do something else. I remember talking to Mum and Dad about that. Someone asked them, "Did you ever say to Jona are you thinking about giving it away and trying something else?" And they told them they never had that conversation with me. You'd think your parents might say something. I reckon Bernie was like that too. Bernie and I the whole time wouldn't even think about doing anything else at all.'

Regardless of how they all felt, the simple fact was that if Powderfinger's next record didn't work, they would be dropped by Polydor. And if that happened, it would in all likelihood spell the end of the band.

POLYDOR GAVE THE GO AHEAD FOR POWDERFINGER to start work on album number two, but with conditions. The label wanted a greater say in the shape of the record, starting with the song selection, and the budget would be nowhere near as generous as the debut. In fact, it was halved; about $35,000 for recording costs, $65,000 overall.

Kambo, the band's bespectacled, red-topped A&R rep, was charged with overseeing the project. He had the unenviable task of imposing his opinion on the band's inner workings, on its creativity and its art, which led to constant friction between him and Paul Piticco, whose job it was to buffer the band from such external intrusion.

As far as Kambo was concerned, there were two key ingredients necessary to give the new record a shot at success. This time, they had to find the right producer, someone who could work in harmony with the band and act as a guiding hand to help edit and structure songs and arrangements.

But first and foremost, before the band went anywhere near a recording studio again, they needed the right songs. In particular, they needed a potential breakthrough single, an instantly recognisable signature track. Not necessarily a smash hit, but a song that would get regular airplay, namely on Triple J. They needed a single that would introduce the band to a record-buying market beyond the relatively small community of live music fans old enough to attend shows in licensed venues. Three or four potential singles would be even better.

'I suppose the band may at times have got frustrated with me,' Kambo says, 'because what they kept hearing over a period of time was "No". My thing was we had one chance, and if we didn't get it right, it was all over. To the band's credit, and Paul's credit as well, they really rolled their sleeves up and they worked really hard.'

But Powderfinger's transformation had already started before Craig Kamber made his presence felt. It began even prior to putting out *Mr Kneebone*. Powderfinger had changed rehearsal rooms and, once again, it was a move that seemed to instantly alter everything. They'd packed up their bandroom in Adelaide Street, which burnt down soon after their departure, and moved out of town, across the river into East Brisbane and into the lower level of Hoggy's new house.

Ian had recently split from Ingrid Neilson, the girl he'd been with since he was 14, and he'd rented a new place on Stanley Street, up the road from The Gabba, Brisbane's iconic cricket ground. It was during this relocation that the loyal Econodog met an untimely demise – the handbrake failed and it rolled, almost running over Hog before crashing and ripping its door off. Tragically, there was no resurrection for the faithful dog and it was put to rest, replaced by a Toyata HiAce dubbed the 'Ferrari'.

Ian's new house came with its own sound-proofed rehearsal space and he installed a studio, quite the luxury in the days before digital ProTools technology made home studios widely accessible. Initially partnering with his old mate Cameron McKenzie and Chris Neehause, this was the birth of Ian's Airlock Studios, which would grow to become one of Queensland's premier boutique recording facilities. 'An endless money pit,' Ian says. 'Although it's definitely fun being able to make a racket at two in the morning if you want to.'

The new work space brought about a dramatic change in the way Powderfinger functioned. There was an entirely different mood hanging out at Hoggy's place compared with hanging around an old office building in the middle of town. 'It was a really relaxed vibe, as opposed to being in the city,' says Ian.

'It was the best set-up,' Cogs says. 'We would get there at 10 am or 10.30, jam for a few hours, try to write something. Then we would have a game of cricket in the backyard for 45 minutes. We'd talk about the music almost like it was a dream: "Oh yeah, we're gonna do this or we're gonna do that." And as we played cricket we'd all talk about it. I think that's why we got along so well back then. We had a lot of energy.'

Most importantly, the band had the facilities to record their jams and song ideas at will. They quickly settled into a very comfortable, productive routine. 'Powderfinger rehearsal has always started with a cup of tea, a bit of mucking around, then we would jam for a few hours,' says Bernard. 'Then a bit of cricket in the yard, have a smoke because we didn't smoke in the studio, it was a small space. Then after lunch, we'd start recording.' Darren had also bought himself a small four-track recorder that allowed him to work on further instrumentation in his spare time. 'It was a healthy period for songwriting,' says DZ. 'We went back to writing songs that were a little less complicated.'

The result of this new-found work practice was a proliferation of new material. Every few weeks, Kambo would receive a cassette tape in the mail with another four or five songs.

Cogsy believes the pivotal moment in these early sessions for the new record came when the Fingers started working on a laconic track about the emergence of the café latte set in Brisbane. 'We wrote "Skinny Jean" and it had a different groove to what we were used to,' Cogs says, 'and everyone got goosebumps. I remember being in the bandroom when we wrote it and everyone was like, "What the hell is that? What's that feeling?" We'd never had that feeling before. We'd always done this techo thing or this bluesy thing, but this was something new. We became more in tune with our emotional side and how to express it, rather than trying to express music in technical terms. We all got a little addicted to that feeling.'

'Skinny Jean' would eventually end up as the opening track of Powderfinger's second album. Indeed, by the time the Fingers went out on a 10-week national tour to promote *Mr Kneebone* at the end of July 1995, they had already written over a dozen new songs, several of which would hang around long enough to earn a place on the next album, which was still over a year away from release. This earliest batch also included 'Take Me In', 'Turtle's Head', 'Give' and DZ's epic 'Oipic' (originally entitled 'Flickin' Oipic').

'We're simplifying things now, both structure-wise and time-wise,' Bernard told Brisbane's *Sunday Mail* at the time. 'We're trying to make the song the most important thing.' The next song to come along was born of this ethos and would turn out to be *the* song, the one that would cut through and connect more widely.

Since recording *Parables*, Bernard had developed a relationship with a new girlfriend, Phillippa Sison, who would remain his partner for the next decade. She was on his mind as the Fingers and their support band, Turtlebox, arrived in Canberra in mid-August during the *Mr Kneebone* tour for a show at the Asylum. 'There were lots of issues back then with being away all the time,' Bernard explains. 'We were away a lot, so having a relationship, you had to deal with that.

'I remember standing in a phone box near the 7-Eleven store on Barclay Street [in St Kilda, Melbourne, while recording *Parables*], feeding coins into the phone, and only having $1.80. I'd have a few minutes conversation and then that'd be it for the day. It made things pretty hard on the relationship, not being able to afford to even speak on the phone. We used to write letters to each other when we were recording, send each other things, that's how long we were away from each other.'

Bernard knew Phillippa was having a bad day at home in Brisbane. He was over a thousand kilometres away, sitting in his room at the Lyneham Motor Inn in Canberra, strumming away on his guitar, and 'Pick You Up' simply fell out of him. The bones of the song took about half an hour to write.

When you are set to throw in your hand
When you are far from home
When what you believe is buried in your hands
When you feel outgrown

I'll be the one to pick you up again
When you decide you've had enough of it
I'll be the one
I'll be the one

'It was a song of support, but made vague enough to apply to anything,' Bernard says. 'I think that was the big turning point lyrically for me. You can have a vagueness and a non-specific thing that a song is about, but still make it very coherent and, if you get it right, even more widely appealing. When you write lyrics where people are able to write themselves into the song, that's when a song becomes really powerful.'

Bernard played the basic version of the song to his bandmates before the show that night and it was immediately obvious to everyone that here was the seed of something different, something special. The Fingers gave it a run-through at sound check a few days later at the Peninsula Hotel at Manly Vale in Sydney. 'We played it full blast for the first time,' Bernard says, 'and we were like, "Bloody hell – we wrote this song!"'

Within a week, Powderfinger had performed 'Pick You Up' in public for the first time. 'We played it at Lismore RSL,' JC recalls, 'and it had an immediate effect on people in the crowd. From that moment we thought, "Actually, this is really good." You got the feeling it rocked in the right parts. It had everything we were looking for.'

'The place just went nuts,' Bernard adds. 'It really did. People were going crazy for the song by the end of it. We'd never had a response like that before.

'"Pick You Up' definitely had the biggest influence on our direction. We came to the realisation that there were always going to be bands that were certainly much more powerful in the heavy rock thing than us, and also bands that were much more accomplished musicians. But one of the strengths that we had was simplicity. When we did something simply, it was really powerful. It was the emotional power that actually carried it – it had nothing to do with distortion. It was more about dynamics. That's how we got ourselves to work.'

BACK AT POLYDOR, CRAIG KAMBER SET HIS SIGHTS ON finding a producer who would be the 'Finger's perfect match. He wanted someone who could help the band structure and arrange its songs in the studio, but who was overtly aware how sensitive an issue this might be. The label had promised the band creative freedom yet it had already butted in on song selection – there was no way Teaks and the band would let the label impose its choice of producer. Neither was that Kambo's intention.

Kambo thought the best approach might be to bring in a producer who was also a musician and songwriter in their own right, an artist the guys already admired and whose opinions they would instantly respect. He was thinking along the lines of maybe Dave Faulkner from the Hoodoo Gurus or Brett Myers from Died Pretty or Jim Moginie from Midnight Oil. The band was into the concept and the first person they should approach, everyone agreed, was Neil Finn of Crowded House.

Kamber put together a package of rough demos of the band's latest songs and sent them off to Crowded House's manager, Grant Thomas. The response was prompt and positive. 'Neil Finn was actually really interested,' he says. 'But it was a major problem from a scheduling point of view; it just didn't work. But the album came very close to being produced by Neil Finn.'

While the search for a producer was going on, Kambo wanted to get the band into a studio to record some proper demos of their new songs. He asked his friend and celebrated indie producer, Tim Whitten, to work on these. Tim's credits at the time included the Underground Lovers, who Craig Kamber managed, and Clouds.

In October, two days were booked at Smash Studios in Sydney for the band to lay down 10 demos. As soon as they began work with Tim, the Fingers knew they had found their producer.

'He's just the loveliest guy,' says Cogs.

'He was really good,' says Darren. 'His personality was really calm but encouraging. He had knowledge of songwriting so he was helpful, but he let us do what we wanted to do at the same time.'

Tim's influence on helping structure and edit the songs was spontaneous and subtle. On 'Pick You Up', he suggested the band cut eight bars from the second verse, and maybe add an additional guitar line, which Darren did. It was exactly what the track needed.

'There have been a handful of times in my career when I've been really, really fucking excited . . . This was one of them. I was playing it over and over in the car.'

'We've never had a producer before who's said, "Nah, just ditch that part – try this,"' Bernard told *Rave* magazine immediately following the sessions. 'It's good when someone comes in, someone we'd never met before, we didn't know anything about him. He's such a casual guy and he's got so much experience.'

Tim Prescott dropped by the studio and was blown away by what he heard, particularly 'Pick You Up'. 'It had already been recorded and they gave me a cassette of the track,' Tim says. 'I remember driving from the studio back to the office. There have been a handful of times in my career when I've been really, really fucking excited, so excited. This was one of them. I was playing it over and over in the car. And I rang Paul [Dickson] and said, "You've got to come and hear this – in my car!" So he listened to it and we both go, "Finally, we've got it – we've got the track that is going to unlock this band's career." And it absolutely was.'

It was one of Tim's last personal dealings with the band's career as he was soon promoted to the role of Polygram's commercial director. But he did have a final bit of advice for his protégés. 'I do remember when we were doing the demos,' Bernard says, 'Tim comes in and goes: "Fellas, I've only got one thing to tell ya – guitar solos are back in!" And we'd just decided that guitar solos were out the week before.'

AS SOON AS THEY GOT BACK HOME TO BRISBANE, the Fingers hit the road. They hooked up again with Sidewinder, along with Fur, a teenage band from the Gold Coast, for the month-long Truckstop tour up and down the east coast.

Powderfinger didn't play the Livid festival in November, but Bernie and DZ did, accompanied by cellist Dave Sills and singer Tylea Croucher, both of whom also performed with Powderfinger at different points. Tylea and Darren briefly shared a house, which is how the Fingers' mate Magoo met Tylea, his future wife; yet another intertwined branch of the 1990s Brisbane music scene family tree.

Around this time, a few of the Fingers had side projects on the go. Ian was gigging in the duo Hog and Skritch, while Bernard and Darren had a couple of other things happening. One was called Hott, a covers band that also included members of Pangaea; and another was an originals trio named Bum Part, featuring Bernie on guitar, DZ on bass and Rick Forsyth from Webster on drums. 'We only ever did one show,' says Bernie. 'We had this song called "Quango", a ridiculous song, nothing like Powderfinger. It was brought up as a joke quite a few times over the years in the bandroom: "It's got a bit of the 'Quangos' about it." But Darren and I always stood by it as a work of genius.'

It was a particularly creative and experimental time for Darius. He had other side projects with his freaky friends from the West End, including Khufu's Guru, a group featuring only flute, nylon string guitar and congas. Every few weeks there would be an open jam at DZ's house, people would come from all around and the night would often slide into the next day with the sounds of music and laughter. For parties, he and his housemates would completely cover rooms in aluminium foil to add to the ambience.

Teaks remembers waiting in a queue in a bank one morning when he noticed some guy ahead of him dressed as a wizard. 'He had this brown hessian cape with a rope belt and he was carrying a six-foot wooden staff,' Teaks says. 'And I thought, "Man, that guy is a fruitcake." The guy stepped up to the teller window and I realised it was Darren dressed in full medieval regalia. He was off to some medieval fair to watch the jousting. He used to get around the cafes in West End in that get-up. It started out as a costume and slowly morphed into his daywear.'

Meanwhile, back on planet Earth, the Fingers welcomed in 1996 with another milestone show, at Belongil Fields in Byron Bay: the inaugural Homebake music festival. Their booking agent, Jessica Ducrou, had gone out on her own, looking after a roster that included Spiderbait, Crow and Fur. (Jess continued to build her reputation and would launch her Village Sounds agency in 1999.) She also forged a partnership with the enigmatic Guiseppi 'Joe' Segreto, the boss of International Music Concepts (IMC), one of the country's leading independent booking agents. Together, Jessica and Joe launched Homebake, the all Australian and New Zealand annual festival that Powderfinger would play countless times in years to come. This debut event on 3 January 1996 – headlined by You Am I, Silverchair and Tumbleweed – is affectionately remembered as 'Mudbake' due to the relentless torrential rain.

'It was a lot of fun,' says Hog. 'It was particularly muddy and if there was a clean person walking through the crowd, they would get tackled by the mud people.'

A few weeks later, the band made a couple of spot appearances at the 1996 Big Day Out festival, playing the Gold Coast and Melbourne shows. The Fingers again performed on a tiny sidestage and were virtually drowned out, playing up against Rage Against the Machine on the main stage at the same time.

Finally, in February 1996, Powderfinger entered the studio to begin work on their second album – *Double Allergic*. Although they had a limited budget to work with, the first week of recording took place in one of Australia's most expensive recording facilities, Q Studios in Sydney. Formerly known as Rhinoceros Studios, it was the same room where former owners INXS had recorded some of Cogsy's favourite childhood albums, including *Kick* and *Listen Like*

Thieves. It was such a big room that during breaks in recording, the Fingers and their producer Tim Whitten played cricket inside.

Tim felt the band had learned its lessons from the *Parables* experience and came into *Double Allergic* with a completely revised attitude on how to make an album. 'It was a different record and everyone was in a different headspace as well,' he says. 'I think for *Parables* they were being very democratic – everyone had a say on everyone else's parts. When they came to do *Double Allergic*, they seemed to have a different approach. If Darren had a song, then he would say what was happening with it; if Ian had a song, then he would say, "This is how I see it". Everyone was more easygoing with everyone's ideas.

'Also, they had nothing to lose at this point. When a band goes, "Oh, we'll see what happens", people tend to run off their subconscious a bit more. They're more relaxed than if they feel something is on the line. Every record after that would have been really difficult because they had attained a certain level of success. This session wasn't about any kind of success. Everyone was pretty chilled.'

The first track they worked on was the proper recording of 'Pick You Up'. Polydor was ultra-keen to have the single ready to go out ahead of the rest of the album. Teaks remembers Roger Grierson, the head of PolyGram Publishing, calling him up after he heard the song for the first time and saying: 'Whatever you're getting paid for gigs, in six months you'll be adding a zero to it.' Which turned out to be true. The remainder of the week in Sydney was focused primarily on recording drums and rhythm tracks before the band packed up and moved into the considerably cosier and cheaper Sunshine Studios in Brisbane to record the rest of the album.

It was a liberating experience for the Fingers. Experimental and exciting. 'It felt freer and a lot more fun compared to *Parables*,' says JC.

Sonically and metaphorically, this album was never going to be a one-hit wonder. There was an abundance of material for the band to work on. Another key track emerged from a circular riff that had been swirling in Darren's head for ages, one that took only a few minutes to write. 'D.A.F.' – named after the guitar chords in the song itself – was earmarked by the Fingers as the album's second single. While the lyrics took aim at the contemporary fascination with all things *X-Files*, the opening of the song was an example of the experimentation taking place in the studio: the light clinking sounds in the intro came from recording Darren's plectrum striking the guitar strings.

Sitar, symphonic strings, inventive guitar sounds – Powderfinger played around with everything and everyone played their part in expanding the album's scope. As Cogs and JC reinvented their rhythmic approach, Ian spent hours with Tim Whitten perfecting the guitar sounds going down on tape. Darren worked on string arrangements for tracks like the intentionally overblown 'Oipic'. Bernard referenced Ben Harper for the vocal sound and he also got to play electric guitar on a recording for the first time, playing rhythm on 'Pick You

Up'. (The guitar he used was his trademark red Maton Flamingo, which his mum had picked up at a garage sale for $15. He originally thought it was an Ibis guitar, hence the name of the song 'Ibis', which appeared as a b-side on the 'D.A.F.' single.)

After three weeks in the Brisbane studio, the basic recording was complete and the team returned to Sydney for mixing. In a continued effort to keep costs down, Tim Whitten used the tiny Mirage Studios at the School of Audio Engineering, mixing a song a day.

There would be a total of 15 songs on *Double Allergic*, including three unlisted 'hidden' tracks at the end of the disc: 'Vladimir' (loosely based on an evening the guys spent in a transvestite bar in Melbourne with their mates from Baby Sugar Loud, where they saw a Russian dwarf making out with an Aboriginal trany); 'SS' (in honour of the cricket bat, Stuart Surridge); and 'Come Away'. Each single also came with at least three bonus tracks, several of which were recorded at Ian's Airlock Studios. Before Tim had even finished mixing the album, 'Pick You Up' hit the airwaves. And, quite simply, nothing would ever be the same again.

'PICK YOU UP' WAS OFFICIALLY RELEASED ON 13 MAY 1996 and the song instantly entranced all who heard it. Suddenly, mainstream media across the country all wanted to know about Powderfinger. Interviews with the band appeared in major newspapers and magazines around the country to coincide with the release. Soon, commercial radio stations also took an interest in the band, with the Triple M and 2Day networks adding the song to their nationwide playlists.

Before anyone else, however, Triple J was all over the song. This was the breakthrough the band, and their label, had been dreaming of. The single was given a humungous boost when Helen Razer, one of the station's highest profile announcers, declared it her favourite song of the year. It was an endorsement that carried enormous cachet.

'Helen Razer was our number one cheerleader,' Bernard says. 'She had quite a bit of influence. She was the station star, alongside her [on-air] partner Mikey Robins.'

'It was with a monumental sense of relief that my ears greeted this single,' says Helen today. 'I recall the consensus at Triple J being, "At last!" We'd been waiting for this band to get it right for years. Clearly, the song had merits all of its own; it was a big, masterfully sappy ballad that tapped right in to the gentle self-loathing of the time. We Gen X-ers lapped up a lyric that offered, "I'll be here, watching your anxiety attack."

'It was the perfect accessory for the era and, really, just a shit-hot song for radio. There was a very real feeling among my peers that the lads had finally delivered the work they'd been promising.'

Once the recording and mixing of the rest of the album was all done, JC was back on the Gold Coast, counting cars again. He was listening to Triple J when Bernie, DZ and Cogs came on air. As usual the democratic Fingers had split the promotional duties and the trio were in Sydney to appear on Helen and Mikey's breakfast show, in a special live-to-air broadcast from Sydney University to give an acoustic performance of 'Pick You Up'. Polydor's John Zucco had promised JC that once that song came out and gained momentum, his days of counting cars would be over. And he was right.

The band's most loyal media supporters back home in Brisbane felt vindicated for the faith they had shown the band all along. '"Pick You Up" sounds gloriously different to anything the 'Finger have ever done,' wrote *Rave* in its review of the single. 'Centred on a verse that finally gives us a chance to hear Bernard Fanning's smoky vocal brilliance, in which he plays the chivalrous saviour rescuing us from our emotional nadir with superb understatement, the band stylishly develops a sense of unease and uncertainty, and then the chorus kicks in, to pick us up. We could very well be listening to the (ARIA) Best Australian Single Of 1996.' The magazine's guest reviewers for the week, Quan Yeomans and Ben Ely of Regurgitator, who themselves had just released their critically acclaimed debut album *Tu-Plang*, added their opinion. 'I think it sounds pretty, it's not what I expected from them,' Quan said. 'I like their approach on this,' added Ben. 'It's not very masculine, much more feminine. Nice vocals, nice minimalist guitar parts, it sounds like they're not trying as hard but getting better ideas.'

Listen to 'Pick You Up'
www.powderfinger.com/footprints

But the overpowering magic of 'Pick You Up' was most evident at the 'Finger's live shows. Paul Dempsey's band, Something For Kate, was only about a dozen shows old when it got the opportunity to open for Powderfinger at the Corner Hotel in Melbourne the week after the single's release.

'The Corner Hotel was packed out and it was a crazy atmosphere,' says Paul. 'They [the Fingers] appeared to be very excited and a little bewildered. There was clearly this rollercoaster atmosphere building around them. The buzz was well and truly upon them and everyone knew it.

'It was that thing when a band is just breaking and things are going really ballistic on the radio. I saw it happen to Silverchair [Something For Kate's label mates]. I've been around a few bands at the precise moment that it's growing exponentially. It is very exciting.

'I remember talking to Darren and he was a bit bewildered by the number of people hanging around the back of the venue when the show was over. There were people at the back door wanting autographs and leaving messages under the windscreen-wipers on their van. I got the sense that they were a bit spun out by it all.'

'Pick You Up' debuted at number two on the ARIA alternative charts, just behind Soundgarden's latest single 'Pretty Noose', but moved to number one the following week. It came in at number six on the Queensland chart and peaked at number 23 on the national ARIA singles chart.

Double Allergic was originally scheduled for a July release, but was pushed back to allow the momentum to continue to build. The Fingers were out playing shows with Big Heavy Stuff, Webster and Bluebottle Kiss. There was an undeniable difference between building an audience through years of word of mouth and suddenly having countless fans pouring in through the door thanks to one alternative hit single getting flogged on the radio. They played a show at the Metro in Sydney and almost sold out the 1000-plus venue in their own right. The next time the Fingers played the Corner Hotel in Melbourne, they sold out three shows.

'That whole time was amazing,' says Bernard. 'Suddenly, our shows were a lot bigger,' notes Darren. 'We had a lot of people turning up and a real momentum was starting.'

On 5 August 'D.A.F' was released as the follow-up single. 'Now, "Pick You Up" was/is a good taste of what they're about, but this is probably even a step beyond that,' wrote Sydney's *Drum Media*. 'This just flows so effortlessly, with this barely restrained real muscle just waiting to bust through … Mighty impressive, just quietly.' That weekend, the Fingers made their first ever live television appearance, performing both 'D.A.F' and 'Pick You Up' on *Recovery*, the ABC's Saturday morning youth culture program.

'D.A.F' reached number 39 on the ARIA singles chart and, like its predecessor, was immediately embraced by both Triple J and commercial radio stations. The b-side of the single included a cover of the Warumpi Band's 'Blackfella/Whitefella', a charged socio-political commentary that marked the Fingers' intention to explore themes in their music beyond matters of the heart. The song would become a mainstay of the band's live set. 'We don't set out to preach or give social commentary,' Bernard told *Semper*, the University of Queensland student newspaper. 'But we do have the opportunity to put forward an opinion. We chose to record "Blackfella/Whitefella" because it's a topic that we feel strongly about and because it has the perfect lyrics to reflect that opinion. It just says it.'

On 2 September 1996, *Double Allergic* was finally released to widespread critical approval. '"Pick You Up", the smouldering first single from Brisbane band Powderfinger's second album, *Double Allergic*, has already burnt itself into the collective pop consciousness,' wrote reviewer Shaun Carney in *The Age* in Melbourne. 'No mean feat for an act that has excited only marginal interest since the release of its first album, the too-heavy, too-clever *Parables for Wooden Ears*. The surefootedness of that single and its even more impressive follow-up, "D.A.F.", is evident throughout *Double Allergic*, a seamless, confident exercise in hard-rock dynamics and melody. This deserves to be one of the big albums of 1996.'

'Powderfinger's debut was bloated, overproduced and overwritten heavy rock that did no justice to the band's justified live rep,' offered *Rolling Stone*'s Andrew Stafford. 'This time, however, Powderfinger are out to prove they can write songs, not just play – and they succeed handsomely. Full of quietly assured performances and some memorable tunes, *Double Allergic* leaves an impression of size and stature rather than mere bluster … It's still a little po-faced, but Powderfinger are on the move now.'

On the day of release, Brisbane's *Courier-Mail* wrote: 'After cracking day-time radio airplay – formerly considered a near impossibility for a Brisbane band – they've since heard the song ("Pick You Up") playing in a supermarket, on racing channel 4TAB and on QANTAS in-flight entertainment. All of which is music to their ears. The concept of a fiftysomething punter mixing with their younger fans presents no problems to singer Bernard Fanning. "It's awesome – it's what we've worked towards – being a band and playing our music to as many people as possible. We don't care if the people who come to our gigs are from the West End or Inala, just as long as they come with the right frame of mind that they are there to enjoy music."'

Double Allergic debuted at number seven on the ARIA album chart and eventually climbed to number four. 'We were very confident the album would debut top 10,' Craig Kamber says. 'Our mantra was "keep it top 10 for 10 weeks", which we achieved.'

Unlike the band's previous releases, which were launched with memorable sold-out hometown performances, *Double Allergic* was unveiled relatively quietly with a cruise on Sydney Harbour organised by PolyGram and attended primarily by media. The public got its chance to celebrate with the band a week later, when the Fingers set off on their biggest tour to date, supporting their musical cousins You Am I on the massive Uptight Express national tour.

'They were our heroes at that time on the Australian music scene,' says DZ. 'They were great to us,' JC adds. 'The first time we got to hang out with them, they were like, "Here's our rider". I think that was indicative of what was going on in the industry – it had gone from the old days of the Angels where it was like "You're just the fucking support band" to "This is one big show, everyone's putting it on".'

The tour included a record-breaking seven sold-out nights at Sydney's Metro (of which the 'Finger played five) and it carried the band as far west as Perth and as far south as Hobart for the first time.

'That was a really important tour, in terms of learning how to put on a show,' says Ian. In fact, almost overnight, Powderfinger went from a semi-professional outfit travelling around the country in a van with only a soundman and tour manager, and loading their own gear in and out of venues, to procuring a professional core crew to help them stage shows at a whole new level.

Several of the key personnel that Powderfinger took on at this point would stay with the band for the rest of their career, including Mark McElligott, who took over as the band's front-of-house engineer when Magoo left to produce Regurgitator's *Tu-Plang*.

'We loved touring with You Am I,' says Bernard. 'They were great mates. Really good times on that tour, one of the most fun we ever did, I reckon. The main thing I remember is that we got gin on our rider. We'd do the gigs, and they were awesome, and we'd come off stage really pumped and get right on it straight away. The bottle of gin would be gone in about half an hour. We got into this thing of calling it "bad gin" and we used to smack the bottle. No one ever had tears, we had an absolute blast.'

Anyone there will never forget the sight of Tim Rogers, celebrating his beloved North Melbourne reaching the AFL grand final by beating the Fingers' Brisbane Bears (before they became the Brisbane Lions) with a lap of the bands' hotel in Perth wearing nothing but his footy team scarf.

But the main thing Tim Rogers remembers of the tour was the precocious support act trying to steal the limelight from the headliners. 'You Am I were at their most successful and they were supporting us,' says Tim. 'Every night when they played "Pick You Up", you'd notice when the first guitar line came in the whole crowd just sinking: "*Ooooh!*" I think about a third of the way into the tour we thought, "Oh shit – the takeover begins!" It was very obvious. Those nights we were at the Metro, every time they played a song off *Double Allergic* you'd notice the crowd – *voomp!* – look straight towards the stage. Three-and-a-half-minute songs that had gravitas to them and that people would sing along to. You could see something was going on.'

The night following the last show of the tour, the two bands were reunited at the 10th annual ARIA awards, staged at the Convention Centre in Sydney's Darling Harbour. You Am I were the stars of the night, picking up five awards, including Best Group and Album of the Year for their recent chart-topper, *Hourly, Daily*.

Powderfinger received their first ARIA nominations that year, in the categories of Single and Song of the Year for 'Pick You Up', putting them in direct competition with tour mates You Am I, and the likes of Tina Arena, the Finn brothers and Nick Cave & Kylie Minogue, the latter taking out both awards for their duet 'Where The Wild Roses Grow'.

It was a night of mixed emotions for the band, which had nothing to do with missing out on winning the awards. Powderfinger had been invited to perform 'Pick You Up' during the ceremony and the lead-up was a nerve-racking affair.

'The performance was good,' says Teaks. 'Very stressful but very cool. It was just so exciting. It was back in the days when the ARIAs had a million people watching, so it was a big moment. I look back on it fondly now, but at the time I was nervously sick.'

'... we were never the sort of people to thrive on celebrity.'

No one's nerves were alleviated by the attitude of the event's organisers. 'They were really dismissive of us, telling us what to do,' says Ian. 'It was very difficult to get them to let us play live rather than mime. We never mimed any TV performances or shows.'

Bernard, in particular, felt ill at ease. 'It was total old school,' says the singer. 'There were no dressing-rooms so I asked one of the production heads, this guy with a grey ponytail, if there was somewhere I could go to warm up before I went on. I've never done scales or anything like that, I just sing a couple of songs. And he goes: "Don't take yourself too seriously, mate – get over yourself and do your job." Fuckwit.'

The Fingers felt completely out of their element. 'It was an eye-opener,' says Cogs. 'Like, look at all these legends – INXS were there and Neneh Cherry, who I was really into at the time. I didn't think we fit.'

'The whole red carpet thing – we were never the sort of people to thrive on celebrity,' says Hog.

'The music industry is a seedy place to hang around,' Bernard told Melbourne's *Beat* magazine after the event. 'We played at the ARIAs and it was the biggest wankathon. I wasn't ready for that. There's the ceremony, then the dinner afterwards and then the big coke-snorting party after that, but I had to give the coke-snorting party a miss because there were too many hand-shaking, back-slapping wankers there.'

With time, Powderfinger would grow accustomed to attending awards ceremonies, and would go on to win more than a few awards (not for a while yet, though) and ultimately they'd have the luxury of getting involved in these events on their own terms.

THE WEEKEND FOLLOWING THE ARIAS, THE FINGERS were back in Brisbane performing on their preferred side of the music industry, again playing the Livid festival in Davies Park in West End. They still weren't offered a spot on the main stage, but they drew a large chunk of the 30,000-strong crowd over to stage two to watch their set. It was the biggest audience of their career ... so far.

Another national tour followed through October and November. This time they were headlining their own Allergy Free tour, supported by Sydney's Pollyanna and Geelong's

Automatic. This was by far the band's biggest self-promoted tour to date, including two shows each at the Tivoli in Adelaide, the Planet Nightclub in Perth and the Metro in Sydney.

A third single from *Double Allergic* was released to coincide with the tour. The anthemic 'Living Type' sounded as if Bernard was again exploring religious themes but it was actually inspired by a Charles Manson documentary he had seen on TV. Its b-side featured some of the most peculiar and experimental music Powderfinger ever produced. Recorded at Airlock, the tracks, entitled 'Entrée-Mains-Dessert', ranged from soundscape to hip hop beats to punk.

When the tour hit Victoria, a most unexpected calamity occurred just before the last of the band's three shows at the Corner Hotel in Melbourne on 9 November.

Backstage, just before the start of Powderfinger's set, Darren collapsed. 'We'd done soundcheck and I had a niggling pain in my shoulder, down the left side of my back,' DZ remembers. 'Getting closer to the gig, I was hunched over and I was saying, "Something is wrong with me." And Baz [Anthony Barrett, their lighting man] was like, "Let me give you a little massage, it'll help things." And it made it worse.'

Darren started turning grey and was having trouble breathing. His lung had collapsed. He'd suffered what is medically described as a spontaneous pneumothorax. There was a full house waiting but Darren obviously couldn't go on. The rest of his bandmates played as a four-piece for the first time in five years, Bernard filling in on guitar as much as he could, as Darren headed off to hospital, where he stayed for several days.

The Fingers still had about a quarter of the tour left to play, so Hoggy turned to his old mate Macca, Cameron McKenzie, to step in for Darren on the remaining dates. Macca had until recently been on the road with the Fingers working as their guitar technician, but he was back at Airlock Studios in Brisbane when he got the call asking him to jump on the next plane down to Melbourne.

'I got there that night,' Macca recalls, 'and I met Ian in the foyer at the hotel they were staying in. We went straight into the bar, which was shut, and we used the stereo in there and went through the set, trying to work out what Darren played. Then I went and visited Darren in hospital the next morning, to learn some of his tricks that we couldn't work out – top-secret tricks that he wasn't that keen on showing me. He was pretty despondent – he thought I was moving in – but he eventually taught me. We had a rehearsal that afternoon and I did a show that night.'

That evening at the 21st Century in Frankston, and for another half-dozen gigs after that, Powderfinger performed with Cameron McKenzie on guitar. 'Macca was awesome and we were very grateful,' Ian says. 'We modified the set-list. Macca learnt maybe 19 songs in one night. It would have been very hard. He got a t-shirt made up that said "12th man". And he even got to play in front of his mum.'

For DZ, the idea of Powderfinger performing without him didn't make him feel any better.

'It was actually quite hard for me,' he says. 'When someone steps in and is up there where you're supposed to be – I felt a bit jealous. I wasn't concerned about my position in the band, just that it should be me.'

DZ need never have worried. Macca definitely wasn't eyeing off his spot. 'I doubt they would have been as great as they were without someone like Darren in there who wrote some of the best songs they've ever had,' Macca says. 'It was awesome fun to play with those guys. After all those years, I got my five minutes. But I seriously doubt I would have enhanced the band. In fact, I would have been a liability. DZ made sure he got better in time to play the Brisbane shows.'

DZ was well and truly back in the groove when the biggest gig in the band's career came around. At the personal behest of Neil Finn, Powderfinger were invited to join You Am I and Custard on the bill of Crowded House's Farewell To The World concert on the steps of the Sydney Opera House on 23 November.

At first, it looked as if they wouldn't be able to make it – the show conflicted with the final dates of their own Allergy Free tour. But Polydor came to the party, chartering a plane to get the Fingers and their crew between shows.

Despite best-laid plans, the Crowded House show was delayed by a day due to a torrential downpour in Sydney, which meant Powderfinger had to fly in on the morning of the concert, play their set, then immediately fly straight back to perform in Byron Bay that same night.

As soon as the Fingers stepped out on stage, they knew that no matter how much drama was involved in making this happen, it was a show they would never forget. There was an ocean of humanity in front of them, believed to number over 100,000 people – some estimated it was double that – packed into the Opera House forecourt, on the stairs and spilling out into the parkland and streets around the iconic building.

Powderfinger played first. The members of Crowded House dropped by their dressing-room to say hi and thanks before they went on. DZ was peaking – Neil Finn was one of his heroes. The guys got to see a little bit of Custard's set but then had to leave to make their flight. They were in a twin-propeller 20-seater Metro, which felt like something out of a WWII movie, and the pilot gave them a thrill by circling over the site of the concert before heading in the direction of Ballina airport.

The Fingers and their crew were having a great time. Sure, they were spewing they didn't get the chance to see Crowded House perform, but here they were on their own chartered flight, a couple of cases of beer on

. . . but here they were on their own chartered flight, a couple of cases of beer on board.

board. Nothing wrong with that at all. Until the plane flew into a lightning storm.

On the approach to Ballina, the pilot informed his passengers that due to the adverse conditions, he would have to attempt what he called a dive-bomb landing. With that, he aimed the plane headfirst at the tarmac. He aborted the first attempt, headed straight up and then straight back down again. At one point, the door to the pilot's cabin flung open, letting everyone on board see what he could see. It wasn't pretty – lightning and sheets of rain.

Instead of fearing for their lives, the band and crew were so pissed that they thought the whole thing was hilarious. They were cracking themselves up by singing 'La Bamba' and other rock songs linked to plane crashes, like Lynyrd Skynyrd's 'Free Bird'. There was no toilet on board, so JC managed to refill an empty two-litre orange juice bottle all on his own. When they eventually got down, the edgy pilot said to Baz: 'I'd never do that again.'

'For me, that afternoon and night had everything,' says Darren. 'I was a massive Crowded House fan, I was probably all googly-eyed supporting one of my favourite bands. Then we went from that high to the fear factor of the flight to Ballina, stormy, super-quick descent to the runway, overshooting it and heading back up, then landing among lightning strikes on the ground, then driving to the Byron Bay show at the Great Northern. It was a pretty crazy day and night, full of fear and elation. It's still one of my most memorable gigs. It was an amazing day.'

There was another memorable gig the following month when Midnight Oil invited the Fingers to join them on the bill of the Woodford Folk Festival. It was a show that had a profound effect on the band. Their set was preceded by a 'welcome to country' ceremony staged by local tribal elders and the Fingers opened their performance with their cover of 'Blackfella/Whitefella'. Then they watched Midnight Oil perform. The whole experience reinforced the concept of blending social consciousness with musicianship of the highest calibre.

The following day, 28 December 1996, the band flew down to Sydney to play the Homebake festival, this time staged in the grounds of the University of Sydney. The Fingers were charged, delivering what JC cites as one of their best-ever performances.

There was a minor controversy in the lead-up to the show. Teaks suggested to Jess that with a hit album and a couple of big singles behind them, perhaps Powderfinger should be playing above Tumbleweed on the bill. Tumbleweed got wind of Teaks's machinations and one of the band members called him up personally, yelling down the phone: 'You've got big balls – don't fuck with Tumbleweed!'

It was inconsequential how big Teaks's balls really were. As 1996 came to an end, there was no arguing that Powderfinger had come of age.

CHAPTER 15

Internationalist

1998

Bernie and his oldest mate, Foggers, were sitting on the balcony of the house they shared in West End early one evening, having a couple of beers, a little high, watching the boats drift past on the river. Their tranquillity was interrupted when, from off in the distance, a party cruise came into view. There was lots of noise and music. As the boat drew closer, they realised there was a cabaret singer performing live onboard and he was singing a cover version of a very familiar song – 'Pick You Up'. 'We were like: "This is the weirdest thing that's *ever* happened,"' Foggers recalls. 'And I said to Bernard, "Do you think maybe this whole music thing is going to work for you?"'

There was no doubt. In late January 1997, Powderfinger headed off on the Big Day Out tour. They played all six dates across Australia and New Zealand in front of some 200,000 people and performed on the main stage for the first time, alongside the likes of Soundgarden, Prodigy, You Am I and the Offspring. After their mid-afternoon slot on the day of the Melbourne event, the Fingers jumped on a private plane to fly up to Cobram on the Murray River to join Silverchair at the Peaches N' Cream festival. They played their set and then flew straight back to Melbourne for the BDO aftershow party that night, where JC performed his magic feat of smashing a marble table in half and taking out the drinks on top without spilling his own beer. JC blamed Bernard for filling him with gin on the plane.

By now, *Double Allergic* had sold over 120,000 copies. This was almost double the numbers achieved by recent releases from the 'Finger's contemporaries like Spiderbait and You Am I. That January, Powderfinger also made their first appearance on Triple J's annual Hottest 100 music poll, with 'Pick You Up' coming in at number six, 'D.A.F' at 18 and 'Living Type' at 32. *Rolling Stone* magazine's annual readers' poll formally acknowledged what Tim Rogers had been spruiking for years, that Bernard Fanning was Australia's best male singer, while Powderfinger was picked out as the brightest hope for '97.

Powderfinger's next album was more than 18 months away at this point but this period saw the band solidify their status as one of the country's hottest 'new' acts and also experience a marked upgrade in their lifestyles. The band members could finally afford to pay themselves a wage of $200 a week. This was so much more than any of them had ever earnt before. They were all still living in shared houses, paying about $60 rent, so the money meant a monumental increase in disposable income.

Even more significantly, by the second half of the year, as *Double Allergic* kept selling and went on to achieve double platinum status, with sales of over 140,000, Powderfinger recouped all the money invested in them by Polydor Records. (*Double Allergic* would go on to reach triple platinum with sales in excess of 250,000 copies.) Being in the black meant the Fingers received their first-ever lump sum royalty cheques – a princely $2500 each. A couple of the guys used the money to buy cars. Revhead JC splurged on a 35-year-old EK Holden for $2000, while Bernard spent the lion's share of his cash on a second-hand piano.

The success also brought about improved travel conditions. Powderfinger could now fly between cities. Initially, they could only afford to fly two members at a time so they used a rotation system. It meant the world of difference and a whole 24 hours out of the van if you got to fly between Adelaide and Brisbane.

In between all the work and travel, the Fingers still managed to find time to focus on the important things in life. The previous year, they teamed up with their mates from Webster and formed the Webfingers cricket squad, to compete in a local Brisbane music industry competition. The Webfingers, which included Paul Fanning and his best mate EZ in the first 11, played a couple of seasons with mixed results. The lowlight, as Bernie would remind everyone forever more, came when JC was bowling and got whacked for 32 off one over, which included three sixes, three fours and two wides. 'I made the second-highest score that day [behind P. Fanning] but no one remembers that,' JC says. Darren also recalls the match. 'I took a sharp bowl to the goolies towards the end of our innnings, but went on to hit the winning runs, in the form of a four if I remember correctly.'

FOLLOWING THE END OF THE BDO FESTIVAL, Powderfinger took a break from touring. Since the start of their gigging commitments for *Double Allergic* the previous August, the band had completed three laps of Australia.

An inevitability of spending so much time in each other's faces out on the road meant that once they got home, aside from the odd cricket game, the band members no longer socialised like they used to. 'At home you stayed home,' says Cogs. 'You tried to stay in contact with the few friends you had left.'

'The dynamic changed,' Bernard agrees. 'I was 20 when I joined and 27 by this time. Where it used to be all-in the whole time, touring like that took its toll on everyone. We were together so much all the time so, in some ways, it became a bit more like a job. We didn't hang out together much when we weren't on the road. That was good and bad in a lot of ways, mostly good that we got to spend time apart, and I was keen to do that, just hang out with my own friends.'

The work, however, didn't stop. The Fingers continued to write and rehearse over at Hoggy's place in East Brisbane and new songs kept spilling out. 'If we weren't on the road, we were writing,' says Bernard. 'Everyone was writing, Darren was writing heaps, tons of writing going on. It was kind of anything goes.'

One of the first of the new songs to come together in the bandroom was an esoteric mid-tempo piece with a peculiar off-kilter rhythm that would end up being titled 'The Day You Come'.

'It was a bit of a breakthrough for us, to sit on a groove like that,' says Ian. 'It took a long time to get right because we were doing something quite different. That whole period was very experimental.'

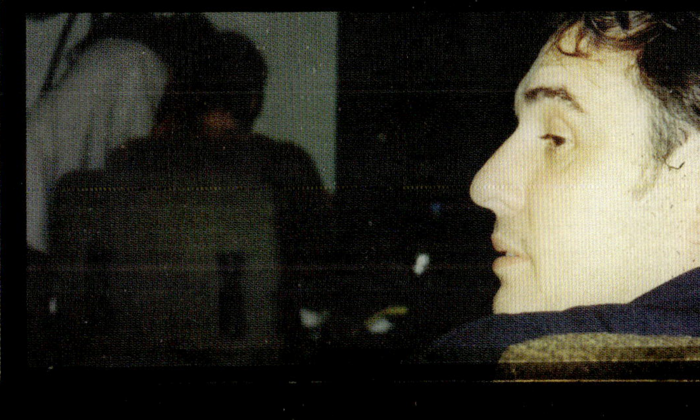

SABIAN

'There was a who's cool and who's not scene and we didn't fit in either.'

'It was a real band song that we all wrote together,' Darren says. 'I think we were still finding our feet or finding our sound, experimenting a bit more than a band normally would after so many years of routine.'

Musically, 'The Day You Come' set the tone for the rest of the writing. 'That was the song that everything else was centred around,' Bernard says. 'And I think it was a massive step up in quality, a big change in sound and approach, with that lush chorus and the falsetto. All smoothness. Yet, to me, that song is quite aggressive. It feels laid-back, but it has an insistence about it, which makes it kind of compelling, and then that big vocal makes it sound like an announcement.'

While the Fingers kept writing, Teaks was strategising the band's next steps and travelled abroad in an attempt to generate interest outside Australia. He'd previously tried getting the band to the UK off the back of *Parables*, but it hadn't come together; now plans were afoot for the Fingers to play their first shows in North America before the year was out.

On the home front, the Fingers had marked out a unique space in Australian pop culture. The band was managing to strike a rare and delicate balance between alternative credibility and mainstream acceptability. You could count on one hand the number of acts who simultaneously have songs being played on both Triple J and 2Day FM.

'We were in this no-man's land where we were starting to get success but we didn't feel we were part of the establishment,' Teaks explains. 'But we were also having too much success and the sound of the band wasn't particularly alternative rock and so it sat between the two camps. We found ourselves in that position by accident but it became the mantra of everything we did. After an initial disquiet, I felt very comfortable working in that space.'

With any success comes a backlash and there were mutterings against the band in some quarters – the Australian Live Show (in reference to lightweight American rockers Live) became a favourite slag-off amongst the cynics. But the Fingers' natural aversion to buying into any notion of what was cool or uncool seemed to immunise them from such petty snipes. That, and distance – the buffer of living in Brisbane, far away from all those music industry types down south who make a career out of professional bitching.

'There was a who's cool and who's not scene and we didn't fit in either,' Cogs says. 'We just thought, "Go with our hearts." We really didn't ever worry whether people thought we were cool or not. When *Double Allergic* happened, we pretty much left any type of scene there was and became what Powderfinger was.

'The funny thing is, we were very wary of it, whether we fit, whether – to put it in business terms – our brand was cool or not. Back then we were touching the mainstream too much and that wasn't cool. You had bands like Regurgitator, Spiderbait, Tumbleweed and, of course, You Am I – the coolest band in the country, what everyone aspired to be. We just didn't sit in there at all.

'We have always been careful about whether people wanted to be associated with us because they thought we were cool. That conversation came up: "What is cool?" "What does it matter?" We were trying to be involved in the right things. Because there was a mainstream side to Australian music and we could have easily gone down that way. It's a horrible way to be, some of it is quite contrived, but we learnt to always ask the questions. We would analyse the fuck out of things. Not just me, it was everyone. I think that's a big reason why we did so well, because we thought so deeply about stuff.'

At the end of May 1997, Teaks's manoeuvrings came together and Powderfinger took off for America, via a couple of shows in New Zealand. 'Good place to go for a holiday,' says JC in reference to the Fingers' career in NZ.

The band landed on the West Coast and quickly settled into an LA state of mind, sipping on Long Island Iced Teas by the hotel pool. It was all pretty exciting, similar to their first wide-eyed visit to Sydney a few years earlier.

Russell Crowe, who was in town shooting *LA Confidential*, showed up at their first show at the Dragonfly nightclub on Santa Monica Boulevard. He came up to the bar after the gig to say hi and invited the Fingers back to his place to play some pinball, but the girl who was looking after the band had hired a limo to show them the sights of the city, so they never got to Rusty's. 'I've always regretted that,' Cogs says. 'I think Russell thought we snubbed him, but it was so nice of him to invite us. He went out of his way to give us some support.' JC and Hoggy regretted it even more – they were outside having a cigarette when the Hollywood star dropped by, so didn't even get to meet him.

'I was pretty sceptical of the whole LA thing, I thought it would be pretty glitzy and wanky,' Bernard told Melbourne's *In Press* afterwards. 'It was a lot better than I expected. The people were really friendly. Also [there was] the Spanish factor, there are so many Mexicans there and that was really exciting for us, because there is not a huge Mexican community in Australia so I had not come by it before. I definitely want to go back. Going somewhere else like that is awesome, because we hadn't been there before, and I hadn't done a flight that long either. I was pretty jet-lagged.'

After LA, the band spent a week and a half driving through Canada, taking in the sights of the Rocky Mountains and Niagara Falls, playing a show a night in towns and cities along the way, encountering a surprising number of vocal Aussie expats at each gig. There were a couple of stumbles during the tour. The band had to cancel two shows when Bernard was unwell. They also had to pay off a little indie band in Vancouver, who had released a CD under the name Powderfinger. But their presence in the country secured a Canadian release for *Double Allergic* and on their last night they played a gig in Toronto with label mates Spiderbait as part of Canadian Music Week before heading to New York City and a special music industry showcase gig at the famed Mercury Lounge. As they say, if you can make it there …

'The show in New York was terrible,' JC says with a moan. 'It's a long way to go to play to five people in the middle of the afternoon.' Aside from that gig, they had a great time in New York, catching up with their old mate Denis Sheahan, and taking full advantage of the city's 'free pour' policy in pubs, which led to someone throwing up in Central Park (JC again). Walking through a street market in the middle of town, they were surprised to hear the saccharine sweet sounds of Brisbane's greatest musical export wafting out of radios. No, not the 'Finger. Or Regurgitator. Or the Saints or Go-Betweens. Rather, Logan City's finest, Savage Garden.

'We almost felt like it was our obligation to get ourselves heard overseas because of the popularity we were gaining in Australia,' Teaks says. 'I was basically just hustling record companies to come and see them. The common theme back then was: "Great band, great songs, but you live in Australia." They were looking for relocation commitments. There was talk of it for a while but, really, none of the band were prepared to make that move.'

The original travel plans had the Fingers heading from New York straight to Europe for a support slot on a tour with their other label mates, Beasts of Bourbon, but that collapsed at the eleventh hour. ('That would have been a scary mismatch,' Bernard says in hindsight.) Instead, they came home and got ready for what would again be their biggest Australian tour to date, the month-long The Word Is Quintet tour, supported by Big Heavy Stuff and Perth's Jebediah.

This time the Fingers could afford to travel in relative luxury. No need to draw straws as they all got to fly between cities, there was a truck for their gear and a Tarago van to get them to the gigs. 'We got modern,' says JC. 'We became one of those proper bands.'

And they were putting on big shows: the Palace Theatre in Melbourne, Thebarton Theatre in Adelaide, three dates at Sydney's Metro Theatre. At one of the Sydney gigs, Hog felt particularly unwell, and had to duck off during 'Glimpse' for a vomit sidestage before coming back to finish the performance. 'You can't call in sick when rock is your job,' notes Hog.

While in Alice Springs, DZ took his *X-Files* obsession to a new level, convincing Cogs and Big Heavy Stuff's bassist Eliot Fish that it was their patriotic duty to find out what the government was really hiding at its secretive Pine Gap facility. 'We jumped into the van at about 2 am and headed out to see how close we could get,' Darren says. 'It was beautiful, a totally clear night. We turned off the car lights at times as we were driving to set the mood, but also to see the stars. We got pretty close, we could see a guy in a tower. In our minds, we were sure he lifted his binoculars up to his eyes like they do in the movies. We were trying to come up with stories to tell him about how we'd been abducted and he had to let us in, we had to talk to someone. But then we decided we better just get out of there.' Remarkably, Darius swears there were no illicit substances involved in this adventure.

During this tour the band commenced its practice of playing extended soundchecks ahead of shows, treating them as portable rehearsal sessions. 'We have got to do some writing,' Bernard told *In Press* before the tour. 'Because we're lucky enough to be headlining we get a soundcheck every day and that's a good time to do it. An hour a day writing, that means we end up with five hours a week ... ideas generated to work on later.'

In August, the month following the tour, the Fingers had three more shows scheduled, one at Melbourne's Story Hall and two more at Sydney's Metro. Only the first show ended up taking place, as Bernard lost his voice halfway through. A new song appeared in the set-list – 'Capoicity', the thematic follow-up to *Double Allergic*'s epic 'Oipic'. This song would find a place on the next record, while the two cancelled Metro shows were rescheduled for later in the year.

At the end of August, the nominations were released for the 11th annual ARIA awards. Powderfinger starred, receiving an incredible seven nominations spanning virtually all the major categories, including Best Group, Album, Single and Song of the Year (for 'D.A.F.'). Finally, a shot at redemption for missing out the previous year – as long as not too many voters had read the interview where Bernie called them all coke-snorting wankers. The Fingers were second in the overall nomination count behind fellow Brisbanites Savage Garden, who garnered a record-breaking 13 nominations.

With the ARIAs still a month away, the Fingers took the opportunity for a quick return trip to Canada, where *Double Allergic* was gaining momentum. They played a handful of shows around the country, including a couple supporting popular local outfit the Pursuit of Happiness, as well as other gigs with an outfit called Moist, which Bernard describes as 'one of the worst bands I have ever seen by miles – they were like a really bad Roxus, if Roxus went bad'.

On 22 September, Powderfinger were back in Sydney and walking the red carpet at the Capitol Theatre for the 1997 ARIA awards. There was no performance this time, they were solely attending as nominees. And what a night it was. Seven nominations ... for zero awards. Savage Garden basically won everything.

Making matters worse, it was the only time that the ARIAs were a dry event, which meant the Fingers had to sit through the whole ceremony without a drink. At the after-party, JC and Hog finally got to the bar, only to realise that they didn't have enough cash between them to buy a drink. Thankfully, Peter Garrett came to the rescue, coming up to offer his commiserations and support and shouting the guys a beer. What more could you ask of a musical idol and/or politician?

The guys weren't heartbroken about going home empty-handed – they thought it was hilarious. Following the event, Squintsy B Jones (aka Bernie), writing in *Egg The Nest*, the band's short-lived fanzine, eagerly reported:

> *BIGGEST LOSERS*
> *With ten nominations and absolutely jack-shit to show for it, rumour has it that Powderfinger have etched their name into the annals of Australian rock & roll as the Biggest Losers In ARIA History. Now, that is something HOT to tell the grandkiddies about. Guitarist Darren Middleton allegedly tried to break up the band after the boys secured the new title, saying: 'I just don't think it gets any better than this,' and added: 'We were hoping for this sort of*

recognition much later in our career but I just can't see what we can do to top this in the future.' Middleton was suitably appeased when the rest of the members promised to become more mediocre on their next album.

FOLLOWING THEIR NOW CUSTOMARY APPEARANCE at the annual Livid festival in the first week of October – alongside the likes of Devo, Dinosaur Jr, Ween and the usual line-up of homegrown suspects – the Fingers locked themselves away in an effort to finish writing the next album.

They re-emerged at the end of the month to play a secret gig at the Crash and Burn in Brisbane under the name of Terry and the Econodogs. It's not the first nor last time they employed this nom de plume. The gig was essentially a road test of the new material, including the first public unveiling of 'The Day You Come'. A couple of the other songs performed that night were destined to end up as b-sides ('Polly', 'Maxwell's Great Mistake'), others transformed into future album tracks ('New Wave' became 'Good Day Ray', 'Vincent' ended up as 'Celebrity Head'), while 'Rule Of Thumb', which Craig Kamber believed was a potential single, was never heard again.

Down at the band's record company headquarters in Sydney, Craig Kamber was negotiating with prospective producers. He was trying to secure the services of Nick Launay, the high-profile English-born producer responsible for a catalogue of classic Australian albums including Midnight Oil's *10, 9, 8 ...*, INXS's *The Swing*, Models' *Out Of Mind, Out Of Sight* and, more recently, Silverchair's *Freak Show*.

Kambo met with Nick Launay's manager in London. Nick was already committed to working with Sydney band Primary (featuring future Sneaky Sound System vocalist Connie Mitchell), followed by the next Silverchair album (*Neon Ballroom*), but they worked out he could slot the new Powderfinger album somewhere in between. The terms and timing were sketched out and Kambo came home with a handshake agreement. However, when Primary's record company reps got wind of what was happening, they put a stop to it.

'Nick had to pull out,' Kambo says. 'He was in and then he was gone. So that threw a cat among the pigeons because we had a schedule, that's what we were working towards, then it was like, "Okay, we have to find somebody at short notice." It was very frustrating. Obviously the band wanted to go, I wanted them to go, Paul Piticco wanted them to get in and make a record so he could start developing the next phase of their career.'

Indeed, Teaks was so frustrated that he decided he'd get the ball rolling himself. Without telling Kambo, he booked time at Melbourne's Sing Sing Studios and asked the band's old mate Magoo if he was up for recording a few songs.

Since producing *Mr Kneebone* two years earlier, Magoo's reputation as a record producer had skyrocketed thanks to his work on Regurgitator's first two albums, *Tu-Plang* and *Unit*.

Powderfinger's reputation had also grown in that time and Magoo was more than pleased to reconnect.

The Fingers had self-produced demos of their latest songs at Airlock and it was decided they'd initially record three tracks with Magoo: 'Good Day Ray', 'Belter' and, of course, 'The Day You Come'.

From what he heard on the demos, Magoo envisioned Powderfinger moving towards something more atmospheric and experimental, along the lines of the recently released and universally praised *OK Computer* by Radiohead.

'I was trying to push them in that direction,' says Magoo. 'I thought the session went really well, but there were times when I felt the democracy was getting in the way of the music.

'We'd spend hours on a guitar sound and thought it sounded great, and then someone, probably most likely Cogsy, would walk into the room and go, "Oh, that's a bit weird." We'd go, "Yeah it is, but weird in a good way." And he'd go, "No, weird in a bad way – I don't like it." It wasn't always Cogsy, but there was a bit of nay-saying going on, which frustrated me. I should have stood up for myself or for whoever was creating that sound and said, "That's your opinion – we're moving on." I gave in a bit and I think it suffered in the mixing.'

Kambo got wind of what was happening and arrived at the studios in Melbourne while the guys were in the process of mixing the three songs. He loved what he heard and had an idea. He'd recently stumbled across a CD called *Interiors* by Brad, the side-project of Pearl Jam guitarist Stone Gossard. As soon as he heard it, Kambo thought to himself: 'Whoever produced this record should produce the next Powderfinger album.' That person was Nick DiDia.

Magoo was not pleased to learn the band was looking for another producer without mentioning anything to him. 'In hindsight, I realised it was Piticco using me as a pawn to get the ball rolling with the record company,' he says. 'Magoo did an awesome job on that,' says Bernard. 'Pretty unlucky to make that recording and then get stepped over, but we still had vestiges of absolute stupidity in those days.'

The New Jersey-bred, Atlanta-based Nick DiDia was best known for his work as an engineer, collaborating with famed American producer Brendan O'Brien on albums by American rock superstars including Pearl Jam, Stone Temple Pilots and the Offspring. With Powderfinger's blessing, Kamber sent a copy of the new songs to Nick DiDia's manager in America.

When Nick received the digital audio tape (DAT), he was in the middle of winding up work on Pearl Jam's *Yield*, so the package sat in his studio unopened for about a month. His manager called to remind him the people in Australia needed to know whether he was interested or not. Nick said he'd have a listen. Another two weeks went by. His manager called again with the message that the Australians had assumed since they hadn't heard back, he wasn't interested. Nick stopped what he was doing and played the DAT. The first song he heard was 'The Day You Come'. And he was blown away.

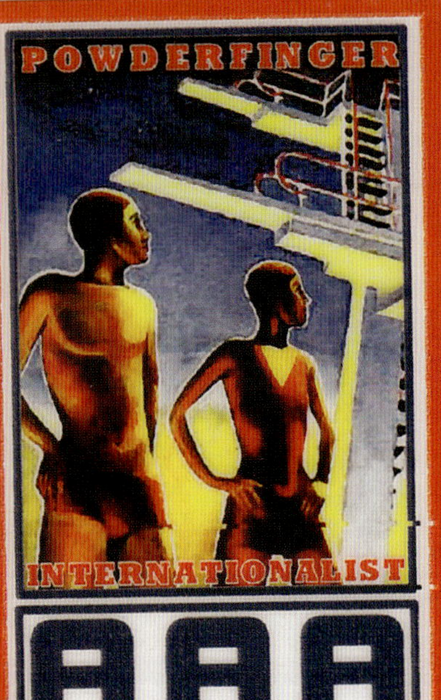

POWDERFINGER

THE INTERNATIONALIST TOUR

GUESTS FROM THE UK

SWERVEDRIVER

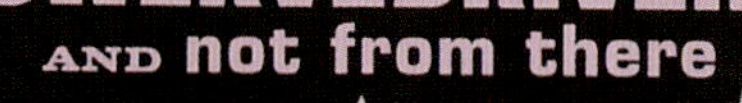

VALHALLA ARTISTS AND IMC PRESENT: THE P2K T

P2K

POWDERFINGER

SOMETHING FOR KATE

ACCESS ALL AREAS

Sun 22nd Nov

Lismore RSL, Lismore

Tickets from - The venue, Music Bizarre, Soundwaves- Byron & ABC Centre - Ballina

TICKETS ON SALE NOW

PRESENTED BY VALHALLA ARTISTS & IMC www.powderfinger.net

NEW ALBUM INTERNATIONALIST OUT NOW

POWDERFINGER - INTERNATIONALIST ALBUM LAUNCH

Name

Date 28/8/98

Venue TIVOLI THEATRE 52 COSTIN ST FORTITUDE VALLEY

Seat 1A

Service Information KARMEN TURNER - 07 3870 3311

Boarding Time 8.30PM

Insert this way at Boarding Gate

POWDERFINGER INTERNATIONALIST

Flight PF 1998

Date 28/8/98

Seat 1A

Seq/Nbr

Boarded YES

BOARDING PASS

'I was like, "Ahh, I can't believe I almost missed this thing,"' says Nick. 'Luckily, when I called and told them "Yeah, I really wanna do this", they hadn't done anything yet, so they're like, "Come on over."'

Before Nick's call, towards the end of 1997, the Fingers had been in a virtual state of suspended animation. Rehearsals and writing sessions continued – the latest new songs included two future singles, 'Already Gone' and 'Passenger' – but in the absence of any touring or recording commitments, most of the guys found themselves external distractions.

Both Bernard and Darren had taken to giving the odd solo performance around Brisbane. Cogsy took leave from the band to go out on a national tour with Regurgitator, acting as stand-in drummer for his mate Martin Lee, who was recuperating after being hit by a car. Meanwhile, Ian had joined forces with one of the legends of the Brisbane music scene, Grant McLennan of the Go-Betweens, for what was meant to be a one-off performance accompanying a visual art installation at the !Metro Arts theatre in Brisbane. Along with Ross McLennan, (the drummer from Turtlebox, no relation to Grant), and Adele Pickvance, (bassist from Dave Graney's band) and keyboardist Matt Murphy (who would soon also play with the Fingers), they became FOC (the Far Out Corporation) and the following year released an eponymous CD, recorded at Airlock.

The Fingers saw out 1997 with another Econodogs performance the week before Christmas, this time as part of a benefit for a Nepalese Eye Camp. Cogsy was still away with the 'Gurge, so his seat was filled by Ross McLennan.

In January 1998, the band went on the road with Homebake, playing Melbourne's Myer Music Bowl, the Gold Coast Parklands and the Domain in Sydney, which ended up being Mudbake II. There was no doubt who the headliners were this time: You Am I, Spiderbait and the 'Finger. Also on the bill were the Victorian female vocal trio Tiddas and Bernard teamed up with the girls to present an acapella version of 'Pick You Up'. Powderfinger finished their sets with a cover of Midnight Oil's 'Hercules'.

Following Homebake, the band's focus finally returned to recording. The third album had the working title of *A Series of Small Victories*, but would ultimately be named *Internationalist*.

Its elongated gestation meant there was an over-abundance of songs to choose from and the success of *Double Allergic* meant virtually no record company budget restrictions this time around.

Nick DiDia flew out and met the band at Sing Sing Studios in Melbourne. The idea was for everyone to see if they wanted to work together. As it turned out, it was love at first sound. 'We hooked it up and he came out for a trial for three days,' says Bernard. 'We worked through a song called "Control Freak", which ended up a b-side. Then he mixed "The Day You Come", which Magoo had recorded, and it was just incredible, how he made it sound and the power he gave to it.'

'We fell in love with Nick,' JC says. 'It was a definite turning point for us. He came back a few weeks later and we went back into Sing Sing. I remember it was probably the best feeling I've had in a session, in terms of a guy like Nick at the helm who got really amazing sounds. He found how to get the best out of us really quickly. It felt really good from the moment we started.'

'Nick was the best thing that happened to us, that's for sure,' says Hog. 'Made us sound as world class as we could. And *Internationalist* was probably our most fun album to make, because we literally did whatever we felt like. It was very schizophrenic – there were punk songs, pop songs, rock songs.'

Nick was just as taken with his new charges. 'I instantly connected with those guys on a musical level,' he says. 'We were all thinking the same thing. And to me they sounded like a real band. It sounds simple, but it's a difficult thing to be a good band. It takes a lot of practice.'

The Fingers loved the way Nick worked – record a song, mix it and move on. Then, once the bones of the album were all in place, go back and enhance. 'We sort of finished the record,' says JC, 'and then he said, "Okay, that's done – now let's have some fun." He said, "In these next two weeks, there are no bad ideas – there are just ideas. Let's add some stuff to it and see what comes up, see what we like." I remember it being pretty open and free.'

They added strings, brass and keyboards. Their new friends Tiddas – three chattering hilarious parrots, as Bernard describes them – were invited to add their angelic tones to 'Passenger' and the album opener, the shuffling and fractured 'Hindley Street'.

'It was a big step up for us,' Bernard says. 'Nick forced us to step up to his level. And it just got better and better as the session went on. The more we got to know him, the more we became friends with him, which happened really quickly. We were really enthusiastic, we wanted to please him, he was our new mate, the boss, and he was very cooperative and very aware that everyone had an equal say.'

By the time the band left the studios, no one was in any doubt that Powderfinger had recorded their best album. It's an opinion that most of the band members still hold today.

Memories are fading
A single voice complaining
While days are stacking up
It's hardly worth debating
The people are frustrated
Drink from poison cup
The system is collapsing
Conscience is relapsing
The damage has been done
On the day you come rising up

Watch the film clip for
'The Day You Come'
www.powderfinger.com/footprints

'THE DAY YOU COME' WAS RELEASED ON 10 AUGUST 1998 and it seemed to leave both fans and critics breathless. Iain Shedden of *The Australian* described it simply as 'one of the best Australian rock songs of the decade'.

Aside from blanket radio coverage for the song, the accompanying lavish video clip by David Barker, shot at the Tivoli Theatre in Brisbane, received endless plays across music television programs.

The song got even further media coverage when it was erroneously interpreted as a slag-off of Pauline Hanson's One Nation Party. 'I don't know where that stuff came from,' Bernard says. 'Probably linked to that idea of intolerance. But it was actually about Aboriginal people. I'm sure I never said this song was about Pauline Hanson. I might have alluded to her talking about the problem we have in Australia.

'But that changed the dynamic a bit in terms of the way people looked at the band, that maybe we were a bit more serious than they thought we were. It was never a trick, we never contrived those things. With *Internationalist*, I started to think you can be more and more honest in telling things that were more real and a bit more raw. Like "Already Gone", just talking about the pressures of life. A lot of my friends had started working and I saw them feeling the pressures of a career path. "Passenger" was a hippy version of that, saying fly away, it's all going to be okay. A bit naive. The key was never saying, "Don't do that, it's bullshit." More suggestions.'

Internationalist was released on 7 September 1998 and debuted at the top of the ARIA national album chart. Despite mocking music reviewers in the song 'Celebrity Head', the album received overwhelming critical praise.

'Every single moment drips with pure musical genius,' extolled Matt Connors in *Time Off*'s five-star review. 'The songwriting, playing and arrangements border on perfection ... Powderfinger have just delivered their own *Revolver*. And like the Beatles, there's plenty more to come.'

'Each song on *Internationalist* has its unique personality, its own musical message,' wrote Tracey Grimson in *Rolling Stone*. '"Passenger" builds from solitary guitar and restrained voice to full-blown rock epic, then throws in horns; "Belter" grates and attacks like the bombs and arrows of Bernard Fanning's lyrics. "Trading Places" is like a deep, relaxing breath; likewise guitarist Darren Middleton's gentle pop number "Over My Head".'

'The record did wonders for us,' says DZ. 'There was a lot more faith in the band from everyone around us. We were excited and we were still young and fresh and pretty keen to crack the world.'

Powderfinger launched *Internationalist* with a special show at the Tivoli Theatre. It marked the beginning of a new era in which the 'Finger was now the biggest band in Australia.

CHAPTER 16
Odyssey Number Five
2000

A month after the release of *Internationalist*, the Fingers were back at the Sydney Opera House, this time performing inside its grand Concert Hall as part of the celebrations for the building's 25th anniversary.

It was another significant gig for the Fingers. Not just because of the historic nature of the occasion, or that it was a Triple J-sponsored event broadcast across the country. And not because it was an acoustic performance – Powderfinger had played the occasional unplugged show around Brisbane as far back as the 'Blue' EP. Nor for the fact that the band brought additional musicians on stage with them in cellist Dave Sills and keyboardist Matt Murphy, the latter becoming a permanent fixture of the band's live shows.

What made this gig so special was, during the performance of 'Private Man' to be precise, Powderfinger discovered the magic of crowd participation. Whilst every 'Finger show had always been an inclusive experience for the audience, no matter what the size, this was the moment Bernard realised he could coax a crowd to do almost anything he wanted.

'It was the first time we got the audience to clap,' Bernard says. 'And it was like, "Fuckin' hell – everyone did it!" That turned a light on in my head. We were learning a lot more about stagecraft, how to put set-lists together, how to present gigs.'

How to present themselves – onstage and off – was somewhat more perplexing. As their popularity and media presence continued to grow, there was a non-verbal agreement between the guys, which manifested into an unspoken mantra, to downplay their image. The days of leather pants, ridiculously long hair and open shirts with vests were obviously long gone, and the band members now believed even expressing emotion in a publicity photograph had the potential to make them all look like wankers.

'We looked like five guys who were about to shoot themselves in the head in almost every photo we had, because that's what we felt like doing,' Bernard says. 'I don't know why we weren't smiling. Photo shoots became this thing everyone hated, we talked about how much we hated them, so we hated them more and more.

'As time went on, we became less vain and more egotistical. That's part of the reason why our photos became so "everyman" and everyone dressed down, no funny haircuts, almost like everyone tried to out-normal each other. The opposite to what a band is supposed to be.'

As Paul Piticco sees it, Powderfinger's non-image – which, of course, ended up becoming their image – was a simple reflection of the band's egalitarian ethos. 'Five people trying to have one vision of what the band was – that concept is central to the psyche of the band,' offers Teaks. 'The visual direction was something they always struggled with. Nobody was in charge going, "Okay, you're all wearing black suits tomorrow." It made for a very common and acceptable image of the band, guys next-door. Nothing abstract or too ostentatious was permitted within the collective vision.' Which explains why we never got to see DZ on stage in his wizard gear.

'I don't think Powderfinger ever really had a vision of itself,' Teaks adds. 'It had ambitions and expectations of itself, but because it was run as such a collective, the vision was never a one-person situation. They knew where they were going, knew that they collectively had to go there, but "which way do we go to get there?" was a common theme that pervaded the band's existence.'

Part of the collective vision meant the band had some basic ground rules in dealing with the press: all members shared media obligations equally and if someone wanted to put the band on a magazine cover, it was all five non-smiling members together or forget it. A welcome by-product of this relative non-celebrity saw the band get through their entire career under the radar of gossipmongers. Sure, the paparazzi probably didn't even know what most of them looked like and, to their credit, none of the band members ever disgraced themselves in public (and let's stress, *in public*). Still, it was something of an achievement considering the level of national recognition they ultimately achieved. On the rare occasion someone did try to lure them into the gossip game, they would simply mock their assailants into retreat.

So, no gossip, no smiley photos, and yet the mass media loved the Fingers. Five thoughtful, intelligent, quick-witted, cheeky, good-looking blokes with a social conscience, producing some of the most popular songs on the radio. What's not to love?

In the absence of a formularised image, Powderfinger always presented a light-hearted, united front to the world. Whenever they were quizzed about what they were really like in private, there were constant quips about storm-outs and spacko attacks, meltdowns and who was going to quit first.

They weren't always kidding. Behind the soundproof walls of the rehearsal room and studios, there was a brewing tension amongst various members dating back almost to the start. You can probably say the same about any band in the history of rock & roll, or any other group of five people working so closely together for so long.

In Powderfinger's case, as time went on, the tension in the bandroom continued to fester. The damned democracy was a big part of the problem. 'So much debate went on over everything,' Bernard says. 'Every decision was so hard won.'

The onset of success did not help relieve any of the underlying stress. It only served to amplify it.

IT WAS HARD TO IMAGINE HOW POWDERFINGER could get any bigger than what they were immediately following the release of *Internationalist*.

The accompanying national tour through November and December 1998 saw the band again playing larger venues, including huge old theatres such as the Enmore in Sydney and the Forum in Melbourne, and kicking off with a sold-out show to 4000 delirious hometown fans at Brisbane's Festival Hall. The new album had already achieved gold status (over 35,000 sales) before they played their first gig. The tour was preceded by an hour-long *Live At The Wireless* broadcast on Triple J, in which the band performed most of the album live to air.

Just prior to taking off on the tour, the Fingers were approached by upcoming Australian film director Gregor Jordan about the possibility of the band contributing a track to his new movie, *Two Hands*, starring veteran Aussie actor Bryan Brown and newcomer Heath Ledger. Gregor was a big fan of the 'Finger. He showed them a snippet of his unfinished film and it proved an instant inspiration.

'I went home that night and wrote "These Days", the body of it,' says Bernard. 'It was directly inspired by the vision, that's where the lyrics came from. Gregor had given us a brief synopsis, showed us a scene and given it some context, how his character was this young naïve guy getting into the crime scene and he'd messed up and was under enormous pressure. That was the seed of the idea.'

The Fingers swiftly worked up an arrangement for the song and went into Sunshine Studios in Brisbane and recorded a version with their live soundman Marky McElligott co-producing along with the band. 'These Days' ended up featuring prominently in the final cut of the movie. The whole experience was the beginning of an enduring relationship with Gregor, who would go on to direct two of Powderfinger's major concert films. Most importantly, 'These Days' became a landmark song in the band's career, providing a bridge between *Internationalist* and the next album.

With their first cinematic dabbling ticked off, the tour was next. Powderfinger's support acts for the *Internationalist* tour were British band Swervedriver and Brisbane alt-rockers Not From There. There was an informal agreement with Swervedriver that they would return the favour by having the Fingers support them on a UK tour. The bands had a great time playing together and became good mates. Steve and Jez, Swervedriver's bassist and drummer, took to accompanying Bernard on 'Living Type', what was meant to be the singer's 'solo' spot on the shows.

During the tour, Darren had a relapse of his lung problem, thankfully the last time it would happen. Macca was once again called upon to fill in for a handful of gigs. The tour ended with two memorable shows in Perth, one outdoors at the Belvoir Ampitheatre in the Swan Valley, in front of some 8000 fans, where an aggravated neighbour, obviously not a fan, started yelling threats at the bands and firing a shotgun into the air during the show. The tour finale was at the Bootleg Brewery on Margaret River. 'You can imagine what happened there,' says Ian with a smirk. Yes, everyone stayed up all night trying to drink the brewery dry. At which point Swervedriver announced they were splitting up. Sorry, Fingers, no quid pro quo.

Following a month off over Christmas, Powderfinger's first engagement of 1999 was the Big Day Out. The festival had taken a break in 1998, but was back with a bill headlined by the freak show trio of Marilyn Manson, Hole and Korn – hardly happy, sunny, summer music. Powderfinger, with 'The Day You Come' polling at number eight on the latest Hottest 100, led the local line-up, performing on the main stage just ahead of nu-metal exponents Korn.

And how did the Fingers get on with their international counterparts?

'By the end, we'd had enough of all the big American fuckhead mentality that went on backstage at the Big Day Out,' says Bernard. 'I remember going on stage in Perth and saying, "We're going to be the last band you see play today that hasn't got a pole up their arse." The crowd just went nuts.'

'You can't do that until you've been on the cover of *Rolling Stone*.'

Later on that same day, Marilyn Manson threw a tanty after being pelted by plastic bottles during his set. He stormed off and his guitarist slashed a large kiddie pool backstage, flooding everyone's dressing-rooms. Earlier in the tour, backstage in Brisbane, Marilyn and Courtney Love put on a faux fight for the benefit of the *Rolling Stone* cameras, chucking around plastic chairs. DZ thought he'd join in and threw a chair of his own. Love screeched at him: 'Who the fuck do you think you are? You can't do that until you've been on the cover of *Rolling Stone*.' Which for DZ and the rest of the Fingers, as it happened, was only a matter of months away.

'I think the Australian bands that year in particular gelled a bit better because the bands at the top were so separate from the rest of us,' JC says. 'Those American metal bands bring a weird energy into the Big Day Out. A real wanker element. It's not friendly.'

It wasn't only international acts that the Fingers deemed to be wankers. A few months later, Bernard found himself embroiled in a public slanging match with New York-based Sydney singer Ben Lee. Lee was going around telling everyone he was God's gift to Australian music. In an interview with Melbourne's *Beat* magazine, Bernard was baited into giving his opinion about Lee and famously labelled him a 'precocious little cunt'. 'It was just something I would say to one of my mates, not make a big deal about it,' says Bernard. 'I was really hungover, but that was no excuse. It taught me to be wary of what you say to newspapers. He and I had a go at each other in the press a few times, and I enjoyed that, it was fun. I ended up ringing him up. To their credit, the Ben Lee camp made up t-shirts with my quote on it. I had so many people saying to me, "Good on ya, mate."'

Following the Big Day Out, the Fingers headed back to the United States. Teaks had based himself in New York for a while to focus on trying to break Powderfinger internationally. They were all very conscious of the fact that they couldn't sustain a long-term career doing endless laps of Australia.

The trip started well, with the band attending the world's biggest annual music convention, South By SouthWest (SXSW) in Austin, Texas, and playing a short set in a tiny but packed room. It was Spring break, the guys were staying five to a room, so why not throw a frat-style party, get drunk and go check out some of the hundreds of other bands in town? From there, it was straight to New York and a show at the infamous CBGBs in Manhattan. They'd played New York for the first time a year earlier with five people in the room. Now, twelve months later, having just performed to crowds as large as 40,000 at the BDO, they had 20 people watching them play. 'We always went from one extreme to another and had to adjust,' JC says.

If there was any mystique playing legendary venues like CBGBs in New York and the Viper Room in LA, Bernard wasn't feeling it. 'CBGBs was a shithole,' he says, 'a terrible, horrible place. Toilets with no doors, a product of too many junkies. What is all the romance about these places? What's so great about a place that is completely decrepit?'

The band then flew across the Atlantic for their first performance in London, a one-off showcase at the Astoria 2 in Soho. The place was packed with about 1000 people (80 per cent Aussies) and it went off. Representatives from the British arm of the 'Finger's record label came to see the gig and they were impressed. The band crossed back over to America for a couple more showcase gigs in LA and New York before heading home to prepare for yet another ambitious Australian tour.

The month-long P2K national tour – with Melbourne band Something For Kate playing support – would see Powderfinger take their own full concert production out on the road for the first time. This meant a truck carrying lights, sound gear and a stage, along with a team of roadies and production crew to set it all up and run the show. Their trusted friend and ally Denis Sheahan, who had been living and working in New York for several years, came home to tour-manage the event.

P2K was a massive financial gamble for the band. If something went horribly wrong, it could potentially ruin them all. But what could possibly go wrong? Well, that's when alarm bells started ringing on several fronts at once.

The first major warning sign that Powderfinger's dream run might be coming to an abrupt end was the buy-out of their parent record company PolyGram by the international multi-media conglomerate, Universal. This led to an instant upheaval in the label's offices across the world. Virtually overnight, over 200 acts were dropped. The Fingers were saved, but it meant that all of Teaks's manoeuvrings to try to get *Internationalist* released in different territories around the world through PolyGram affiliates suddenly came to nought.

At home, there was a clean-out of senior management in the label's Australian head office and a new regime installed. Fortunately, several of the band's key supporters within the label – including their beloved long-serving product manager, Michele Porto, and their publicist, Kate Sutton – got to keep their jobs, but executives like their A&R man Craig Kamber were gone and a new managing director appointed.

Cogs fondly recalls the band's first meeting with the new MD of Universal Music Australia, burly, brusque South African executive Paul Krige. 'Bernie, Teaks and I went down to Sydney,' Cogs says, 'and we went into the Universal offices to meet Paul Krige. We'd recorded "These

MATCHLESS
Something

Days" and put it on the *Two Hands* soundtrack but it hadn't been released yet. Krige goes, [*in a South African accent*] "G'day boys, how you going?" We sat down and the first thing he said to us was: "What's with that fucking song you've just fucking recorded? 'These Days'? It's a piece of shit. What are you going to do with it? Put it on some shit movie, ay?" He was paying out but he was also trying to say, "I'm the boss here." We had a pretty good sense of humour about it. We were pretty Teflon. We were used to getting knocked – that was part of being in Powderfinger.'

Of more immediate concern was the high-risk P2K tour. From the opening night at the Playpen in Cairns on 13 July 1999, it was obvious to Teaks and Jess that if things kept on like they were they'd be in big trouble.

'The most panicked I've ever been about their career was at this point,' says Jess. 'Everything stopped. Tickets stopped selling, everything. I don't think I've ever heard Paul so frantic. You could feel this rising sense that this was pretty fucking serious.'

With the costly tour on the road, there were lots of shows where they were unable to sell more than 50 to 60 per cent of tickets. This meant at many stops around the country, Powderfinger and Something For Kate were playing to half-empty rooms.

'It kind of stalled and I was in a bit of a panic mode,' says Teaks. '"What do we do?" The album started really strong, but then it started dropping off.' Also, the continual surge of new fans that the band had experienced in recent years appeared to plateau and the buzz on the band seemed to be draining. Why? 'We zigged when we should have zagged,' is Teaks's explanation in hindsight.

Since the release of *Internationalist*, 10 months earlier, there were two follow-up singles to 'The Day You Come' – the double a-sided 'Don't Wanna Be Left Out'/'Good Day Ray' and 'Already Gone'. They were all great singles in their own right, and perfect for Triple J, but none had anywhere near the mass appeal of 'The Day You Come'.

And then, in this, Powderfinger's darkest hour, was it providence? Luck? Great marketing? Or simply not one, but two remarkable songs?

On 29 July, the movie *Two Hands* was released and the haunting 'These Days' was suddenly heard everywhere. A little over a week later, a fourth and final single off *Internationalist* went to radio and 'Passenger' became an instant phenomenon.

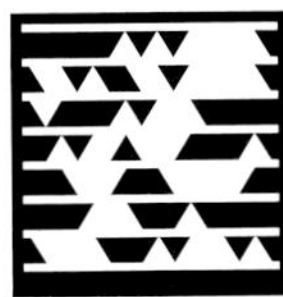

Watch the 'Passenger' film clip.
www.powderfinger.com/footprints

The time had come to start thinking about a new album.

Just like that, everything was back on track. So much so that *Internationalist* sold more copies in the second half of 1999 than it did in the first. It would go on to significantly out-sell *Double Allergic*, with sales of more than 350,000 copies. Everyone could breathe easy again.

The Fingers themselves hadn't been entirely oblivious to the drama, but they weren't going to let it get in the way of enjoying their time on the road with their new best mates, Something For Kate.

'The first time we toured with Something For Kate was awesome,' says Bernard. 'Getting to know the sad giant [Paul Dempsey]. I had an impression of what he was going to be like, and then discovered that he's actually one of the funniest people you will ever meet. You think he is going be politically correct but he is not, he's an animal.'

The sad giant and his band similarly had an unforgettable time. 'The end of that tour was quite ridiculous,' says Paul Dempsey. 'We ended with three shows at the Lookout in Perth and our bandroom was a fully functioning bar, which they left to us. JC and our drummer Clint discovered throughout the course of the tour that they shared a favourite movie – *Cocktail*. They were so excited to finally meet another person whose favourite film it was, so they assumed the roles of Bryan Brown's character and Tom Cruise's character.

'They took over the bar, and they were trying to flip bottles around, reciting entire scenes from the film. It got late and messy and JC was standing up on the bar and he took a really bad spill and landed half in, half out of the sink. He damaged his back pretty badly. I don't think it's ever been the same, actually.'

It wasn't just the fall – it was followed by 'stacks-on' JC with about 20 people piling on top of him. 'We partied ourselves into hospital,' JC confirms.

Bernard was also worse for wear by the end of the month-long jaunt. The band had to cancel the final show because the singer was suffering from what he thought was bronchitis. 'I remember always being tired and finding out afterwards I had glandular fever and I hadn't known about it. I can't believe how hard we worked. The strain on our relationships was pretty severe.'

The band all needed a break. The time had come to start thinking about a new album.

JUST PRIOR TO TAKING OFF ON THE P2K TOUR, the guys had packed up their gear at Ian's place in East Brisbane and had moved into a new rehearsal room, a vacant space above a tattoo parlour up the other end of Stanley Street, even closer to the 'Gabba. Ironically, the new space had nowhere to play cricket.

Financially, things were going well enough that the guys were starting to think about mortgages and, in time, they each bought a home around Brisbane. Ian invested in a semi-rural property on the outskirts of town, which became the permanent home for Airlock Studios.

After a couple of months off to recuperate from all the touring, the band moved into writing mode for the new record. There were a few final public appearances to get out of the way in early October before they could entirely disappear from view – they had their annual appearance at the Livid festival in Brisbane on 2 October (they warmed up with a secret show at the Zoo the night before), followed by the ARIAs.

The 13th annual ARIA Awards were held at the Sydney Entertainment Centre on 12 October 1999 and Powderfinger were nominated for five awards that year. Unsurprisingly, they weren't expecting to win anything. 'We think we're the biggest losers in ARIA history,' Bernard reiterated to the press on the way into the venue. The 'Finger got to perform again, this time a dynamic version of 'Passenger', backed by a brass section and female vocalists. The band members appeared so much more relaxed and confident than during their performance of 'Pick You Up' two years earlier.

Even before the show went live to air, the Fingers broke their ARIA duck when, pre-broadcast, graphic artist Kevin Wilkins won the award for Best Cover Art for his Soviet propaganda-themed design on *Internationalist*. Then, midway through the evening, the band won the first ARIA of its own, taking out the Best Rock Album prize, pipping Silverchair's *Neon Ballroom* and Cold Chisel's comeback record, *The Last Wave Of Summer*. The Fingers lost out in the Best Group category to newcomers the Living End, but then swept the night's two main categories, Record of the Year for 'The Day You Come' and Album of the Year for *Internationalist*. Melbourne's *Age* newspaper described Powderfinger's ARIA Awards redemption as 'heralding a new era of sophisticated Australian rock'.

The following day, the band publicly downplayed the significance of their triumph. The *Courier-Mail* got on to Cogsy and he told them they wanted to avoid any hype. 'We'll just be taking it as it comes,' he said.

Privately, however, this felt like vindication, not so much for the band members, but more for their families, friends and partners, who had sacrificed so much and provided support and faith all the way along.

There was a celebration at Bernard's place. 'We were pumped, all hungover, but we kept going. About 30 people came and the vibe was massive,' he recalls. 'All our families and all our mates were there – it was such a great thing for them to see that reward. My parents couldn't believe it. They were older, not in the rock & roll scene at all, but they were always very encouraging and helpful. The most important thing to Dad was for me not to get a big head.'

With recuperation and celebrations out of the way, it was back to work for the band. So, exactly how do you follow up a best-selling album of the year?

The band decided from the outset that they wanted to produce a more cohesive work as opposed to the stylistically schizophrenic nature of the two previous records. The basic concept was to expand on the lusher elements of *Internationalist*, namely 'Passenger' and 'The Day You Come'. 'We had that cinematic theme in mind, where it would be a somewhat grand album,' says Darren. 'I guess we tried to make a beautiful record.'

There were 'shitloads of half-baked ideas', according to JC, but less than a dozen would be followed through and readied for the recording studio. It wasn't easy. From day one in the new bandroom, the mood was tense. The carefree air that defined the previous two projects had evaporated. Success had brought with it a new tangible sense of strain.

'We claimed at the time that we didn't think about the pressure, but I don't think that's true,' Bernard admits. 'One thing we were good at was toeing the company line, we all had the same story. But it wasn't exactly the truth.'

'We'd be lying if we said we didn't feel any pressure at that point in our career,' JC says. 'The tension was solely because we wanted to be better and we let it get to us for the first time. It wasn't the most fun time. *Double Allergic* and *Internationalist* were fun to write. But then things got more difficult. There were a few clashes. Cogsy and I clashed a bit, definitely.'

Personal tensions were nothing new within Powderfinger. And Cogsy readily admits he was often the source of a lot of them. The band's mischievous joker was also its authoritarian when it came to keeping up standards, or getting his own way, and he had no issue being openly confrontational. He constantly pushed his bandmates to strive for perfection, to the point of tedium or conflict, flying in the face of the considerably more laid-back approach of the other Fingers.

'I was really controlling,' Cogs admits. 'From my perspective, I used to really push them a lot. When we did something, we really had to get it right. We had to get every bit in the song as good as it could possibly be.

'I was a control freak. Bern and I were the two people who would dominate. We wouldn't come in and say, "This is what has to happen right now, this is my idea," but if we liked something, usually it would get done. If something came in and it appealed to our taste, it would go in that direction. But I was very strong-willed. So was Bern, but I was probably even more so than him. I had this weird power in the bandroom where things would go my way, and if they didn't, I would intimidate people into making them happen. Not subtly.'

DZ penned an ode to Cogsy's overbearingness – 'Lemon Sunrise', the closing track on *Internationalist* – although it took Darren a few years to reveal the song's inspiration to its source.

'It isn't a nasty song, it's just an observation,' DZ says. '"You're always right, you're always on time." Cogsy's personality is quite strong and he can be a little impatient and a little bull-headed

at times. "The Bulldog." But he's got a good heart. His intentions have never been malicious or nasty.'

'Cogsy believes clash is a good thing,' says JC. 'Bernard and Cogsy would always win the arguments because they were better skilled at winning arguments, not necessarily because what they're saying is better. Cogsy is a genius at that. Everything has to be discussed in a manner where you lose the point of what you want to do.'

Add to this general tension the weight of following up a hit record and it's hardly surprising there was an explosive atmosphere in the rehearsal room. 'There was a weird siege mentality around the band during that time,where you'd actually be nervous presenting a song,' Bernard says. 'I was, and I know Darren was as well. It was like, "What are they going to do to it?" Seventy-five per cent of the time I thought there were improvements, but certainly not 100 per cent of the time. There was always compromise that went on. When you're 22, it's much easier to compromise, before you have the build-ups you get in the history of a relationship, especially a really long one where you can see the patterns.'

The band briefly emerged from their bullring to see out the year and the century with a series of festival appearances across the country. They played alongside Silverchair at Homebake on the Gold Coast and Sydney, at the Rock-it festival in Perth and also at the Gone South festival in Launceston. The final show in Tasmania was a thrill for Hog and JC, as they got to play on the same bill as one of their idols, the Church.

They were watching the band perform from the side of the stage when JC's mobile phone started ringing in his pocket. It sent waves of interference into the Church's in-ear monitors before he could turn it off. 'They were giving their sound guy all these weird looks,' JC says. 'That night we were having a drink with them on a boat and someone said, "One of the weirdest things happened today – the monitors just went crazy." I was sitting there going beetroot red, but I didn't have the heart to tell them it was me.'

Following a short Christmas break, Powderfinger got back to work. The year 2000 started on a high when, on Australia Day, the results of the Triple J Hottest 100 were released. Powderfinger topped the poll – 'These Days' was voted the most popular song of 1999. Three other Powderfinger songs also made the list with 'Already Gone' at 25, 'Good Day Ray' at 68 and 'Passenger' sneaking in for a second time at 100.

Back inside the Fingers' rehearsal room, the band had already laid down rough versions of 'Waiting For The Sun' (originally called 'My Love') and 'The Metre', but it was only once they began working on 'My Kind Of Scene' and 'My Happiness' that the true vision for the album started taking shape. Both songs were based on riffs that Darren brought in, to which Bernard added melody and lyrics, Cogs and JC developed unique grooves and Hog laid down his signature guitar lines.

'The band makes every song what it is,' says DZ. 'I've said that before but it's so true. "My Happiness" happened really easily. The song itself is so simple. It's perfect in that sense – its arrangement, the way the chords move.'

The appearance of 'My Happiness' helped temporarily soothe nerves in the bandroom – once they had this they knew they had the basic framework for a solid album. But then the record company heard the demo. 'They got wind of it and they were ready to push us into the studio straight away,' JC says. 'And we were like, "Let us write a record first." We went in there with not a full record – only nine or ten songs.'

In early April 2000, Nick DiDia returned to Australia to begin work on Powderfinger's fourth long player. 'It was a no-brainer to work with Nick again,' says Hog. However, the producer wasn't greeted by the same happy-go-lucky outfit he'd met a couple of years earlier.

They were all back in Melbourne's Sing Sing Studios but frazzled nerves quickly resurfaced. Nothing was coming easy. Cogsy's anxieties about the direction of the record had travelled from the bandroom into the studio. He was even clashing with Nick, not that the producer was fazed. It's a big part of a producer's job to be 'simply the other guy in the room', says Nick, and he understood how Cogsy viewed things.

'Cogs and I had our moments,' Nick says with a laugh. 'But Cogs, to me, was always the guy coming purely from a "let's make the song better" perspective. You're doing something you're really passionate about and sometimes there are disagreements. I might say, "You should maybe try to go this way with this song" and name a reference, and sometimes it set off this trigger in his head: "We don't wanna sound like those guys!" I remember making a Beatles reference: "It just needs a Ringo-sort of flowing fill." And Cogsy was like: "Why are we trying to sound like the Beatles?"

'It's all coming from a place of passion, a place of love. He cares so much about all of it, not just his drumming. He cares what the band does, how the band's perceived and how the records are perceived. As we all did.'

However, Cogsy's relentless intensity was beginning to wear thin on several of his bandmates. 'It had been going on for years before that,' says Ian. 'He'd just choose a victim and pick on them. At one stage it was JC and then it was me and then he and Bernard would be antagonistic. It was killing us. It was sapping everyone's energy and creativity.'

The first two weeks in the studio were essentially a write-off. Then, early one afternoon, Nick decided to close the session down and force everyone to go to the pub for a meal and a drink, to have a bit of fun. Cogs resisted – 'I want to stay and do this record!' – but eventually he relented. Nick's tactic did the trick. It was a turning point in the session. 'Finally, we got Cogsy to settle down a bit,' JC says, 'then the recording process picked up again and became a better place to be.'

Of course, the outside world never got as much as a whiff of any internal strife. 'We were good at disguising the tension,' says Bernard. Once everything had calmed down, music media was invited into the studio to report on how the highly anticipated follow-up to *Internationalist* was shaping up. The band told everyone they were making a love record and planned to call it *Let's Fuck*. They eventually settled on a considerably more abstruse title, *Odyssey Number Five*.

Each morning in the final weeks of the session, the band got to the studio a couple of hours ahead of Nick and, working with their engineer 'Double' Dave Davis, jammed with the aim of coming up with some extra songs. 'The reason we called it *Odyssey* was because every jam was called an Odyssey,' says Hog. '"Odyssey #5" the song actually ended up on the record and that's a cool little piece.'

Welcome to the new suburban fables
Dressed up like a tomb inside a cradle
If you're paying peanuts you get monkeys
Better save that silly money for junkets

The band initially used U2's *Achtung Baby* as a sonic reference. The guitars on 'Waiting For The Sun' took inspiration from 'Who's Gonna Ride Your Wild Horses'. 'Then we kind of mined that vein a bit,' Bernard says, 'stayed with the big sounds, wide sounds, not too dirty.'

The first song to get committed to tape was always destined to be the first single, 'My Happiness'. 'Recording that song took quite a while,' says Bernard. 'We did a few different tempos. We got maybe halfway through and it was not right, the tempo was too slow. Nick wasn't happy so we did the whole thing again.'

'My Kind Of Scene' also took some getting right, Bernard initially singing it in falsetto, while 'Like A Dog', the session's rockiest and most political cut, based on a dirty Hoggy riff, went down easy.

It was at Nick's urging that 'These Days' was re-recorded. It took ages and, ultimately, the band always preferred the original version. They were considerably more pleased with how 'Thrilloilogy' turned out, the third instalment in the epic 'oipic' trilogy.

The last song written for the album, the acoustic 'Whatever Makes You Happy', was a tribute from Bernard to his best friend Sean Fogarty's mum, who passed away while the band was in the studio. 'It was an amazing gift,' says Foggers. 'To put on that song and go somewhere that he's created for you.'

'However, Powderfinger are better than any of them.'

Even before the band started recording, they got word that Hollywood star Tom Cruise had become a Powderfinger convert and wanted a song to use on the soundtrack of his new movie, *Mission: Impossible II*, shot mostly in Sydney. The band tried penning a song specifically to suit (with the imaginative working title of 'Mission Impossible') but Cruise decided on 'My Kind Of Scene'. In May 2000, while the Fingers were still in the studio, the soundtrack was released, with a tracklist that included the likes of Metallica, Foo Fighters and Limp Bizkit, and it debuted at number two on the American album charts. It set up an incredible calling card for the Fingers' next North American assault. In the same month back at home, another major accolade: Australian songwriters voted 'Passenger' as the Song of the Year (1999) at the annual APRA songwriting awards.

On 14 August 2000, 'My Happiness' was released and instantly became the biggest hit single of Powderfinger's career, debuting at number four on the charts. *Odyssey Number Five* hit stores on 4 September, and the response from the media and the public was extraordinary. It spent three weeks at number one and ended up as the second-highest-selling album in Australia for the year 2000, just behind the latest Beatles greatest hits set, *One*.

'*Odyssey Number Five* is an embarrassment of orchestrated rock riches,' wrote reviewer Jeff Apter in *Rolling Stone*. '"My Happiness" packs a huge chorus and a message that could very nearly pass as uplifting ... This is orgasm rock: songs that begin with a little acoustic foreplay and then build and swell to huge, soaring climaxes ... So where does this place Powderfinger on the local rock & roll barometer? Have they become grown-up rockers, crafting mood music for those who've outgrown Homebake? The answer probably is yes, and the message lies in Fanning's words: he's now less of an angry young bloke from up north than a fully-grown man concerned with matters of the heart and head.'

'There's an elegance to this album which, if Powderfinger were British, would have them being lauded by those who this year have been seduced by groups such as Doves, Muse and Coldplay,' offered the *Sydney Morning Herald*'s Bernard Zuel. 'Emotional rock, for want of a better term, is back in vogue. However, Powderfinger are better than any of them.'

With *Odyssey Number Five*, Powderfinger struck a commercial and creative peak in their career. With Australia conquered, the world awaited. As long as the Fingers could keep their act together.

CHAPTER 17

Vulture Street

2003

Things seemingly couldn't be going much better for the 'Finger.

Odyssey Number Five would go on to become one of the most popular and successful Australian recordings of all time. It sold over 100,000 copies in its first month of release and ended up selling over half a million copies in Australia alone. The record topped the national charts in September 2000, just as the the world arrived in Sydney for the XXVII Olympic Games and it remained in the top 10 for five months straight.

In October, over 40,000 tickets were snapped up to the Fingers' first live shows in support of the album, kicking off with a warm-up gig in Cogsy's hometown, at the Nambour RSL. The rest of the month-long national tour included four sold-out shows at both the Enmore Theatre in Sydney and the Forum Theatre in Melbourne. 'It felt big,' JC says.

This heightened mainstream acceptance brought an intensified backlash and a new cynicism from some of the band's traditional supporters. In *Time Off* magazine, a review of one of the sold-out shows at Brisbane's Arena snidely concluded 'their new ballads don't have anything like the hooks we've been caught on in the past. Which leaves us with the sound of a band that's coasting.' The magazine also ran an 'I Hate Powderfinger' debate on its letters pages over several weeks.

'We started to get a bit of negative attention,' says Bernard. 'It didn't bother us much, I kept it in my back pocket for when I needed it. We had a lot of support from radio. I can imagine some people must have hated Powderfinger by the time *Odyssey Number Five* came out. If it wasn't your kind of music, it was on every radio station in the country.'

In November, Powderfinger headed back overseas for a quick club tour around the UK, taking in Ireland and Scotland and culminating with a sell-out show to 2000 predominantly expats in the main room of the Astoria in London. It was hardly a luxurious tour befitting Australia's biggest band. The group slept on a dodgy tour bus with a leaking toilet and a driver who refused to keep the generator running when parked at night, despite temperatures outside dropping to minus 10.

Back across the globe and thawing out in Australia's summer, January 2001 saw the Fingers again feature prominently on the Big Day Out bill. A second single was lifted from *Odyssey*, the rocky, bristling 'Like A Dog', a narky social commentary about the oppressiveness of the contemporary national political environment, accompanied by a powerful video starring Aboriginal boxer Anthony Mundine. At the same time, Teaks had secured a high-priority US release for *Odyssey* through the Universal affiliate, Republic Records, the label run by the influential Lipman brothers, Monte and Avery. The band planned to support the release with an extensive North American tour beginning in May.

Despite all this success and the prospect of much more to come, the mood inside the band was still very much on edge. By now all the Fingers were in their early 30s, and almost all of them were struggling with demons of one kind or another.

Bernard was becoming increasingly anxious about performing live on stage and he was also feeling the weight of fame closing in on his private life. 'I was starting to struggle with being recognised and dealing with being in public,' he says. 'People started recognising me around Brisbane and it was picking up pretty much everywhere. It was hard for me and Phillippa socially. It wasn't like I was getting mobbed all the time, but there was this self-consciousness and we started to be a little insular because we were both pretty private. Having people come up and want to talk to you about the band when you only have a precious amount of time together was hard.'

Meanwhile, Hog was out partying whenever possible, making the most of his bachelor status and living it up to the max, perhaps a bit *too* much. He became a bit of a 'loose party cannon', according to Teaks.

DZ was also bordering on enjoying himself more than he should. Although Darren had previously gone as far as giving up drinking for a long stint, he admits he succumbed to 'indulging in rock & roll excesses' during this period. 'I started getting into drugs a lot more,' he says. 'Never anything too heavy, but powders and bits of cardboard with pretty pictures on them. I'd always been a pretty straight little guy, not your wild child, but for a four-year period I was certainly getting involved and experimenting in the distractions that can surround a band doing well.' Darren says he eventually hit a wall, scribbling in his diary that he felt like 'I was on the edge of the toilet bowl, about to fall in if I don't pull myself together.'

This coincided with DZ spending a lot of energy on his latest side-project, Drag, which the other Fingers weren't too pleased about. 'It was a bit of a contentious issue,' Darren says. 'I don't know if they were worried I was going to leave the Fingers for Drag, or that if it did well, I would mentally and emotionally drift away. All I hoped was that it could be a vehicle for me to create and express myself in a less controlled format. I just wanted the chance to do that.'

JC married Tara in December 2000 and, unlike his band mates, he didn't have a care in the world, happiest when he was able to indulge in his favourite pastimes of fishing and golf every chance he got.

Cogs, on the other hand, was not relaxed at all. 'I think the touring of *Odyssey* is what fucked us,' he says. 'The touring of that and the rehearsing, trying to get things right, is where we really started to come to pieces.' Once they hit the road, Cogs tried to remedy the stress by drinking himself into oblivion at any given opportunity. 'That was at the peak of my partying way too hard. I was off my face most of the time, just being a dickhead. Having no regard for life, basically.'

In this fractured and fragile state, Powderfinger joined the 2001 Big Day Out circus.

From the first show in Auckland on 19 January, it become clear to everyone involved with the tour that the international headliners, nu-metal superstars Limp Bizkit, were unquestionably the biggest dufuses the festival had ever hosted. 'Limp Bizkit acted like everywhere they went in the world it was the mean streets of LA,' Bernard says. 'But they were actually in the catering area of Big Day Out. There's ice-cream over there, you're in danger of being smothered by vanilla.'

When the tour arrived in Sydney on Australia Day, 26 January 2001, it was ridiculously hot at the concrete jungle of the Homebush showgrounds that hosted the event. The crowd numbered close to 60,000 and there was lots of drunken teenage angst in the air.

Powderfinger played a powerful set, boosted by receiving news before they went on stage that, for a second year running, they had topped the Triple J Hottest 100 list, this time with 'My Happiness'. ('My Kind Of Scene' came in at number three.) Bernard shared the news with the crowd, adding: 'It's the biggest music poll in the world so we think maybe we're the biggest band in the world.'

But tragedy befell the event later that evening when, during Limp Bizkit's controversial performance, the seething moshpit near the stage collapsed in on itself. Among the crushed music fans pulled out of the crowd by security staff was unconscious 16-year-old Jessica Michalik, who later died in hospital from her injuries.

Accusations of exactly who was to blame were flung around for years to follow. Limp Bizkit immediately left the festival and flew out of the country. The promoters called on Powderfinger to lead a tribute to Jessica at the Adelaide show a couple of days later. The band asked the crowd for a minute's silence during its set. 'Everyone knew what had happened,' Bernard recalls. 'It's powerful when 30,000 people are not making a sound, then we played "These Days" and it was a really strong moment.'

Organisers also asked the Fingers to take over the headlining slot for the remaining dates on the tour, but the band declined the offer. 'We were like, "We can't play after [German metal band] Rammstein – you can't play after the dude walks on stage on fire",' says Hog. 'It's pretty hard to follow that. So we played second last and that worked well.'

At the aftershow drinks in Melbourne, Chris Martin, singer of English band Coldplay, came up to the Fingers to say hi. The two bands had already started to forge a bond and would do battle in some heady backstage cricket throughout the rest of the tour. Chris wanted to air a proposal. His band was heading straight from the last Big Day Out show, in Perth, to the US to start a tour but their support act had cancelled at the last minute. How would Powderfinger feel about joining Coldplay on the tour?

'I was like, "Fuck yeah! Sounds good",' says Hog. 'Eight shows, great fun.' Teaks and his people set about organising visas so that following the Perth Big Day Out on 4 February, the Fingers could fly home, pack, and then join Coldplay in Seattle by 9 February.

'It was a mad scramble to get it happening,' says Bernard. 'We left Brisbane and it was 37 degrees and we got to Seattle and it was minus 4 degrees and snowing. It was a big turnaround, 42 degrees difference, and it's yesterday!'

Coldplay was touring in support of their debut album *Parachutes* and the hit single, 'Yellow', performing to packed rooms across the US. The two bands played Seattle, Portland, the famous Fillmore in San Francisco followed by two nights in Los Angeles. Then Chris Martin got sick and lost his voice ahead of a sold-out showcase performance at the Irving Plaza in New York a couple of days later. When showtime came around, Coldplay asked the Fingers to play a full set to help alleviate the pressure on Chris's voice.

21.08. Berlin
22.08. Köln
24.08. Hamburg
POWDERFINGER
21.08. Berlin
22.08. Köln
24.08. Hamburg
POWDERFINGER
ODYSSEY No 5 TOUR

Powderfinger delivered a blinder of a set to a room full of 1000 people, including many of New York's most influential music business movers and shakers. Their New York City hoodoo had finally been cracked. 'The vibe was unbelievable,' Bernard says. 'We had a great gig. Then Coldplay went on, played two songs and Chris couldn't do any more and they stopped the show. It was a massive deflation.'

The tour limped into Chicago, where Coldplay managed to get through their set, but the Englishmen decided to blow off the last show on the schedule in Canada. The Fingers chose to journey on, playing a free show at the Horseshoe Tavern, a tiny club in Toronto where they'd performed on both their previous visits.

On the tour bus travelling between the two cities, tempers exploded. Sitting in the back, playing a card game called 'Grass' in which everyone takes on the role of a dope peddler ('It's actually really good fun until people get violent,' notes Hog), Cogs made one smartarse comment too many to JC and the bassist finally cracked.

'I can tell you right now, that punch-up had nothing to do with the cards,' says JC. 'It was the result of months and years of torment that finally got me to that point.'

'He might have punched me or slapped me,' says Cogs. 'It was from me niggling him all the time. We were just so sick of each other and I was probably a real prick.'

It wasn't the first time Cogs had pushed one of his bandmates into a physical reaction. There was an altercation between him and Bernie backstage in Tasmania years earlier, during the You Am I tour, where the pair ended up in a push and shove. This time, Bernard was a mere observer and he recognised the signs. 'I thought, "This is gonna get ugly", so I went to my bunk. I think Teaks had to pull them apart. Later, everyone laughed about it a lot over the years.'

The incident acted as a release valve on all the pressure that had built up between JC and Cogs. 'We didn't dwell on it,' says JC. The excitement of what was unfolding overrode any simmering animosities. Things were a lot better from here on, for a while at least.

A MONTH AFTER RETURNING HOME FROM NORTH AMERICA, Powderfinger flew back there again for a quick promotional trip.

Odyssey Number Five was released in the US on 22 March through Republic Records. 'My Happiness' went out to radio a few weeks earlier and everything was seemingly poised to give the band a genuine shot at making a mark on the massive US market.

'We went for it,' Teaks says. 'Republic had picked up the band and they were motivated. They spent money and there was tour support and everything was looking quite promising. "My Happiness" was outright number one most added on US radio. It felt like it was all going to happen.'

Republic paid for a new video clip to be filmed to accompany 'My Happiness'. Apparently the Australian film clip, which followed the journey of a metal slinky, made absolutely no sense to Americans. The band was sent to Universal Studios in Los Angeles to work with Quentin Tarantino's production company, A Band Apart.

The Fingers had a ball shooting the clip. There was a crew of over 50 people working on it and the band members were not allowed to move as much as a guitar case because of union rules. During a break, a few of them jumped on golf buggies and took an unauthorised tour of the studio back lots. Tourists snapped photos of them, thinking they were Hollywood stars. Hog and Teaks drove up to the famous *Psycho* mansion and on the way back, they went to drive over a small bridge when security men came running from everywhere to stop them. They watched on as the bridge collapsed and Jaws jumped out of the water below. 'We would have been eaten by a mechanical shark,' says Hog.

The American clip of 'My Happiness' cost over $200,000 to make, double what the band had spent to record *Odyssey*. It was almost like the 'Reap What You Sow' video all over again, except this time the result was absolute crap. 'It was terrible,' says Teaks. 'Definitely a waste of money. We tried to bury it.'

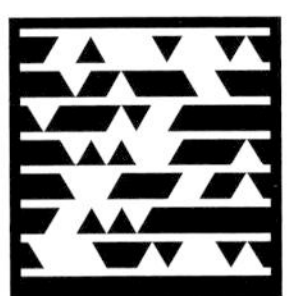

Watch the film clip for 'My Happiness'
www.powderfinger.com/footprints

While still in LA, the band played a one-off free show at the Roxy and then headed over to New York for what was potentially the single most important performance of their career – playing 'My Happiness' live on the *Late Show with David Letterman*.

'It was really nerve-racking,' Ian says. 'People kept saying to us, "More than the whole population of Australia will be watching this." Bernard didn't have a particularly good one.'

'It was a bit of a disaster, we didn't really nail that,' Bernard agrees. 'We were so nervous and it was fucking freezing in the studio.'

The performance wasn't as disastrous as the band made out. JC remembers one of the crew mentioning that if Dave liked the band, he would come over and shake your hands. Which he did.

From there, it was over to Europe for a six-week summer tour, kicking off in the UK with a number of gigs, including a three-night stand at London's Shepherds Bush Empire ('Aussie-mania,' according to Bernard), then off across the rest of Europe; to Holland, Germany, France, Austria and as far up as Switzerland, playing either festivals or small clubs, performing alongside the likes of Muse and Manic Street Preachers.

There was a brief break back in Brisbane before they returned to North America in May. Unlike their previous low-budget exploratory tours, this was the real deal — a five-week, 25-date headline trek across the US and Canada.

Republic Records was still showing the band all the love in the world. 'They are brand new and we have to keep our expectations in check,' label president Avery Lipman explained to *Billboard* magazine. 'We've got to be patient. And I think the band and the record itself is the best marketing tool we have.'

The work was relentless, with barely a day off, but aside from a faulty squeaking air brake on their tour bus, which kept them wide awake during overnight drives between towns, the Fingers travelled in relative comfort. Everywhere they went, they were greeted with chants of 'Aussie-Aussie-Aussie', which wore thin very quickly. In Toronto, more bizarrely, a section of the crowd chanted 'Four-X, Four-X, Four-X'.

There were some big shows on the tour and they reunited with Coldplay at a radio festival at the RFK Stadium in Washington, as well as playing lots of small- to medium-sized gigs with between 300 to 1200 punters. Hog remembers one in Tempe, Arizona, where about 700 people came out to see them perform. The band played 'My Happiness' as the fifth song in their set that night, and after it most of the crowd got up and left. The band didn't make that mistake again. In Dallas, JC went for a walk and came back to the hotel only to find the rest of the band had already left for the venue. He had no idea where they were playing, so he had to phone his parents back in Queensland, who had a copy of the itinerary, to find out where he had to go.

Powderfinger got a glimpse into how big international bands worked during this touring business. If a couple of them had to move between interviews on a press day in New York, they got driven around in a 22-seater stretch limousine. Dinner with the label would include $35 pieces of sushi. If they were playing shows in Canada and had to get to LA and back for a TV appearance, logistics and money were no issue. It was a long way from roadside diners in the Econodog.

And everywhere they went, record company representatives were at hand to reiterate how wonderful they were and how massive they were going to be. The band tried explaining they didn't require the constant affirmations, but it was to no avail. 'I gotta tell you,' one rep said to Bernard, 'the day my father died, I promised myself that I would always be honest with people, and I'm telling you what I think.'

'We were enjoying ourselves,' says Ian. 'It wasn't too traumatic, although it got harder towards the end. The record company was all over us and then, when it appeared it wasn't going to work, they just stopped coming.'

For all the time, money and shows, Powderfinger only sold about 50,000 copies of *Odyssey* in the US. A second single, 'Waiting For The Sun', was taken to radio. 'It wasn't on fire, but we were moving,' Teaks says. 'We felt like we were on an ascendancy.' A new tour was booked for the start of October. And then came September 11. 'That kind of put the kybosh on everything. Everybody forgot about the music industry for four or five months.' The tour was initially postponed, then cancelled. And that, in effect, was the end of Powderfinger's relationship with Republic Records. Teaks packed up his New York office and came home.

In an ironic footnote, the tour receipts for the band's shows with Coldplay were stored at their

American business manager's offices in building seven of the World Trade Center, which was also destroyed on September 11. Teaks had to go to Republic and ask for the money the label had promised in tour support, without any proof of how much the band had spent. 'It was the ultimate "the dog ate my homework" story,' he says. 'I said, "You need to give me $40,000." They said, "Sure, just give us the receipts." And I said, "Well, there's a little problem with that." Luckily, they believed me.'

Canada would remain one of Powderfinger's strongest markets to the end and the band made several return visits to the US in years to come, performing festivals and to loyal pockets of fans across the country. However, after that October tour was cancelled, there was an undeniable sense that the Fingers had missed their one clear shot at cracking America. It was almost miraculous that everything had lined up the way it had in the lead-up to *Odyssey*'s US release and, realistically, it was unlikely to happen again.

AS POWDERFINGER'S INTERNATIONAL ODYSSEY FALTERED, back in Australia, it was starting to feel as if, musically at least, nothing could ever go wrong again. While the band was still away, they received their second straight APRA song of the year award for 'My Happiness'.

The band finally arrived home from their North American jaunt at the start of July. Throughout 2001, the band spent a total of about eight weeks at home in Brisbane. 'It certainly contributed to the downfall of a few of our relationships,' Bernard says.

At the end of July, Powderfinger headlined the inaugural Splendour In The Grass music festival in Byron Bay. This was Teaks and Jess's baby, a boutique winter festival staged in the exact spot where Jess first met Teaks and the band a decade earlier. Splendour was designed as a pop culture counterweight to the (at the time) testosterone-fuelled frenzy of the Big Day Out. The Fingers played a financial and conceptual role in helping set up the event and it was a huge success, going on to become one of the most popular annual events on the Australian music calendar.

Incredibly, this was the first time the Fingers actually headlined a festival and, typically, they felt they could have done a better job of it. 'We didn't have a particularly good gig,' says Hog. 'I'm sure we played okay but after Franti [Michael Franti of Spearhead] vibed up the crowd the way he does, it was pretty hard.' (*Rolling Stone*'s report on Powderfinger's set said 'the response from the 7,500-strong crowd is nothing short of evangelical.')

Immediately following Splendour, the band took off for a couple of shows in New Zealand before heading to one of the world's biggest rock festivals, Fuji Rock in Japan, an event several of the Fingers cite as the highlight of their career. It wasn't that their own performance was particularly memorable (although Bernard did teach himself to say 'you guys rock' in Japanese, which went down a treat). It was that they finally got to see the man who had inspired Powderfinger's existence and even provided their name – Neil Young.

Neil Young and Crazy Horse were one of the festival headliners. Denis, Powderfinger's tour

POWDERFINGER
EUROPE, CANADA
& THE USA
FEBRUARY & MARCH 2004

manager, knew Neil's stage manager and organised permission for the Fingers to watch the Crazy Horse set from the side of the stage. Just before the show, Neil Young's personal manager came up to the Fingers to tell them Neil knew they were there and he had a gift: 'Neil's going to play the song "Powderfinger" – I haven't heard him play it in 17 years.'

'It was really mind-blowing,' Bernard says. '"Hurricane" was the last song.' ('An 18-minute version,' remembers JC, beaming at the memory. He still treasures the set-list he swiped from the stage that day.)

'Seeing that performance up close,' Bernard adds, 'there was lots of interplay between them but little interaction with the audience. They played as a group, which gave us the idea to make our stages smaller and get closer.'

It wasn't the only momentous event that day in Japan. Walking into the venue, Hog ran into an Australian girl, Georgie, who he'd met a few years earlier and who, as it happened, had grown up not too far from Ian's childhood home in Mount Eliza in Victoria. Call it fate or serendipity but Georgie eventually became Mrs Haug.

Meanwhile, Cogs wasn't having such an excellent Japanese adventure. Just before Neil Young's performance, he drunkenly ducked off to have a wee under the main stage. Then, stumbling to get back to his spot before the show started, he literally shirt-fronted the great man himself as he was about to walk out on stage. 'I went bang! "Sorry, man!",' Cogs says. 'And I just thought, "Who is this dirty old stinky roadie?"'

But that was the least of Cogs's worries. The whole time in Japan, he had to avoid Regurgitator, who were also on the Fuji bill and who had a bandroom right next to the Fingers'. About a year earlier, Cogs had made some smartarse remarks about the band in an interview with *Rolling Stone*, after they sacked his mate Martin Lee. Cogs had heard that they weren't too pleased about his comments. He managed not to cross paths with them the whole trip, until everyone got on the plane to leave, and there were the Regurgitator guys in the row in front of him.

Cogs meekly said hi, and the band's manager, Paul Curtis, got up and let Cogsy have it. 'You're fucked! How can you say those things about something you know nothing about? You need to apologise right now.' Cogs genuinely regretted what he'd said and told them so, but he couldn't repair the damage and it was an uncomfortable flight back to Australia. However, all this was frivolous compared to what he was about to face at home.

Cogsy arrived to find his 11-year relationship with Catriona was over. Even at his freewheeling worst, Catriona had always provided Cogs with an anchor. He was devastated and he took a long time to emotionally recover. 'She's so tolerant, a beautiful person,' he says. 'She probably should have kicked my arse a lot earlier on.'

At the same time, Bernard was about to have his world turned inside out. Immediately following Fuji, he'd taken Phillippa away for a week on Heron Island. They had the time of their lives and it provided Bernard with inspiration for a new song, 'Sunsets'. Then the day they got back home,

Bernard's big brother John called with devastating news – he had cancer. Exactly how dire John's situation was wasn't immediately obvious.

'Their songs have become singalong national anthems.'

Powderfinger took off on another European tour, played a handful of German clubs and made festival appearances in England, Scotland and finally in Holland, where the band was building quite a following.

While away, tickets went on sale for the band's New Suburban Fables tour, scheduled for October and November, their first non-festival shows in Australia for the year. The shows sold out as soon as they went on sale. More shows were added and they sold out just as quickly. Three Festival Halls in Brisbane, four Hordern Pavilions in Sydney, four Festival Halls in Melbourne, plus shows in Newcastle, Hobart, Canberra, Adelaide and Perth.

At the start of October, shortly after the band's return from Europe, it was time for the ARIA Awards and Powderfinger won everything; Album of the Year, Best Rock Album, Highest Selling Album, Record of the Year ('My Happiness'), Best Group and Best Artwork. 'Winning is everything,' Bernard joked on the night.

A couple of weeks later, the band took off on their New Suburban Fables tour. Australian rock & roll had not seen a tour on this scale by a local outfit since the heyday of bands such as Cold Chisel, INXS, Midnight Oil and Crowded House. 'Their songs have become singalong national anthems with their live set now a virtual greatest hits collection,' wrote Cameron Adams in Melbourne's *Herald Sun*. 'What they lack in showmanship they make up for in crowd-pleasing songs.' Incredibly, the ARIA Awards and the tour saw *Odyssey Number Five* climb back into the top 10 of the charts, more than a year after its release.

The final show at Brisbane's Festival Hall on 4 November saw the odyssey of *Odyssey* finally over. It had been a historic ride but they were exhausted. The band agreed to take a three-month break and reconvene early in 2002.

There was no holiday for Bernard. For the next few months, along with the rest of his family, he helped nurse John, whose health was rapidly deteriorating. 'We both idolised Johnny,' says Paul Fanning, 'but Bernard's the youngest and it affected him at a deep level. He completely involved himself in Johnny's day-to-day care.'

'That whole experience of looking after someone when they are sick, I'd never done that,' says Bernard. 'My sister is an oncology nurse, so it was particularly difficult for her because she knew what was happening. Until maybe the last week, we were like, "He's going to get through this."'

John Fanning passed away in February 2002 at the age of 42.

Bernard didn't know what to do with himself. Neither he nor any of the other Fingers had ever faced a death in their family. All their parents were still alive (and still married). 'I didn't know

AKG

what I wanted to do anymore, if I wanted to make music,' Bernard says. 'I had a lot of doubts in my life.'

In his grieving, almost subconsciously, songs began to formulate. 'That was the best way to deal with it, to write about it,' he says. 'It was really raw, I was seriously cut up, our whole family was. There was a song called "Dying Day" that I played at a benefit I did with Tim [Rogers, the Woomera Detention Centre benefit at Melbourne's Hi-Fi Bar] which was a few weeks after John died. It was the full tears while you're writing thing. I was just standing in the shower bawling my eyes out, having the song in my head. I wasn't involved in the Catholic Church anymore, still not, but around funerals you get drawn back into that and start looking at things on a universal basis, spiritual stuff.

'With "Since You've Been Gone", I was thinking, "I've got the blues, finally." I've actually got the blues, I've got that pain. I'd lived an easy middle-class existence my whole life up until then, and feeling like, "I know what they mean now."'

There's a truth begging to be told
As the blues grab and take a hold
And I just can't believe when I wake up
That you could be gone

John had told Bernard he mustn't give up on his music. He'd said, 'What you do is really powerful and a lot of people really like it, make sure you keep doing it.'

It would take a while for Bernard to wholeheartedly accept his brother's advice.

IN MARCH 2002, THE BAND RECONVENED in a rented house on North Stradbroke Island. They left their instruments at home. The idea was to spend a week together, relaxing and having some fun; drink, surf, chat about music, the direction of the band and the next album.

'We all talked about making a rock record,' JC says, 'because after playing so many gigs with *Odyssey*, we felt the live set needed a bit more rock injected into it. And we just wanted to do something different and, obviously, we're a rock band.'

'We said we wanted to make a rock record, but what is rock?' says Hog. 'Everyone's got a different idea of what rock is.'

There was lots of passing around of CDs. 'We all had different things in our minds,' Bernard says. 'Hoggy had the Stooges, Darren had Queen, I had Led Zeppelin, so it took a while for us to get the ideas together about what we were going to do and exactly the kind of rock songs we wanted to make.'

After four days on the island, the guys figured they knew where they were going, so they headed off back home to their families. They would meet up again at the bandroom to start rocking out. But it turned out to be nowhere near as easy as they had expected or hoped. They basically spent the rest of the year trying to reinvent rock & roll.

They basically spent the rest of the year trying to reinvent rock & roll.

'We were trying to find this sound and that was a massive struggle,' Cogs says. 'We didn't know what it was. We would talk about it a lot and we would sit down and play things over and over and over. We didn't know what we were looking for. I was really intent on working until we found that thing, whatever it was. A few of the other guys, their argument was, "Well, we shouldn't be trying to push ourselves to get something that we are not natural at. If this doesn't work, we can always rely on what we do naturally." And I just kept pushing and pushing. That caused a bit of tension in the music, I suppose. But the thing is, once we found it, everyone was on board. It was just that eight or nine months where we were trying to find it was really hard.'

There was an escalating riff that JC brought in that everyone intuitively felt held the key. The song '(Baby I've Got You) On My Mind' was slowly built up around it. 'We sat on that groove more than anything we've ever done,' Hog says, 'just trying to work out how to play it so it felt right. We must have driven the people downstairs in the tattoo parlour crazy, endlessly playing that.'

The breakthrough came one day when Darren added some straight power chords into the mix and that proved to be the missing link.

'That was a real turning point for all of those songs,' Hog says. And so after much hard work *Vulture Street* was conceived, Powderfinger's fifth long player.

It had been such a drawn out and often frustrating process that bandroom tensions erupted again. Towards the end of the writing process, everyone had had enough of Cogs.

There was a confrontation, an 'intervention' as Cogs calls it, where they told him that he had to change his behaviour or else. 'I got a talking-to from the band,' says Cogs. 'They told me they weren't going to put up with it anymore. The bad thing was I had just split up with my girlfriend, so it was like my whole life was falling apart. I'd moved out of home and I was living in a unit by myself and I would pretty much spend the day at the bandroom and then go home and watch telly and cry most of the time.

'It had to happen for me. That was really important in my life. And maybe for the band. I don't know if the band was better off for it. We changed a bit. We were better off as friends for all that crap going on. For a while, anyway. We probably would have split up before *Vulture Street* came out if we hadn't talked about things. Darren and Bern were saying they just didn't like coming into rehearsal anymore. And rehearsal was the heart and soul of our band. If that's working then things tended to be okay. And they were saying they thought about giving up. I'm sure I wasn't the only hard part of being in the band, but from my perspective, as far as a band mate goes, I wasn't very helpful.'

In January 2003, Nick DiDia returned and he and the band set up in 301 Studios in Sydney. This time, instead of rushing to get everything done in a week to keep costs down, the band booked out the whole facility for six weeks.

Nick brought an engineer out with him from Atlanta to co-produce the album. Tony Reyes, an accomplished songwriter and musician in his own right, helped the band hone the songs. The Fingers also had a new keyboard player, Lachlan Doley, who would hang around through to the Sunsets tour. Otherwise, this would be a guitar rock album with basically no embellishments.

The stresses from the bandroom didn't follow the Fingers into the studio. There was none of the pressure of following up a hit album because, this time, Powderfinger had nothing to prove. 'It was a good fun recording session,' says Darren. 'We made ourselves comfortable and tried to keep it simple. We turned everything up to at least 11 and just let it go.'

The band set up in the studio's orchestra room and essentially played live. Bernard told Nick he wanted his vocals to sound like those Bowie records from the late 1970s such as *Low* and *Heroes*. As far as Nick was concerned, he'd never heard Bernard sing better. For the singer, this was exactly the sort of record he wanted to be making. 'I was really excited,' Bernard says. 'I had got over the idea of not being a musician anymore and I was really into it.'

When the rowdy and rocking sessions were complete, Bernard, Darren and Hog travelled with Nick back to Atlanta, where Nick's good mate, the celebrated producer Brendan O'Brien, handled the mixing duties.

On *Vulture Street*, the band made good their vision of creating a refined, raucous rock record. They managed to completely recast their sound while producing a work that was unmistakably and uniquely Powderfinger, even harking back to the spirit of their earliest recordings. It was destined to become a fan favourite, as well as Cogsy's personal pick, and the album's four singles – '(Baby I've Got You) On My Mind', 'Since You've Been Gone', 'Love Your Way' and 'Sunsets' – quickly ascended to the status of classic Oz rock anthems.

Watch the clip for '(Baby I've Got You) On My Mind'
www.powderfinger.com/footprints

Vulture Street was one of the most anticipated new Australian recordings of all time, and on release on 6 July 2003, it unsurprisingly debuted at the top of the ARIA charts, spending three weeks at number one and five months in the top 10.

The album reconfirmed Powderfinger's status as the biggest Australian band of its generation. But where could they go from here? No one was sure, but it would take almost five years for the band to make another record together.

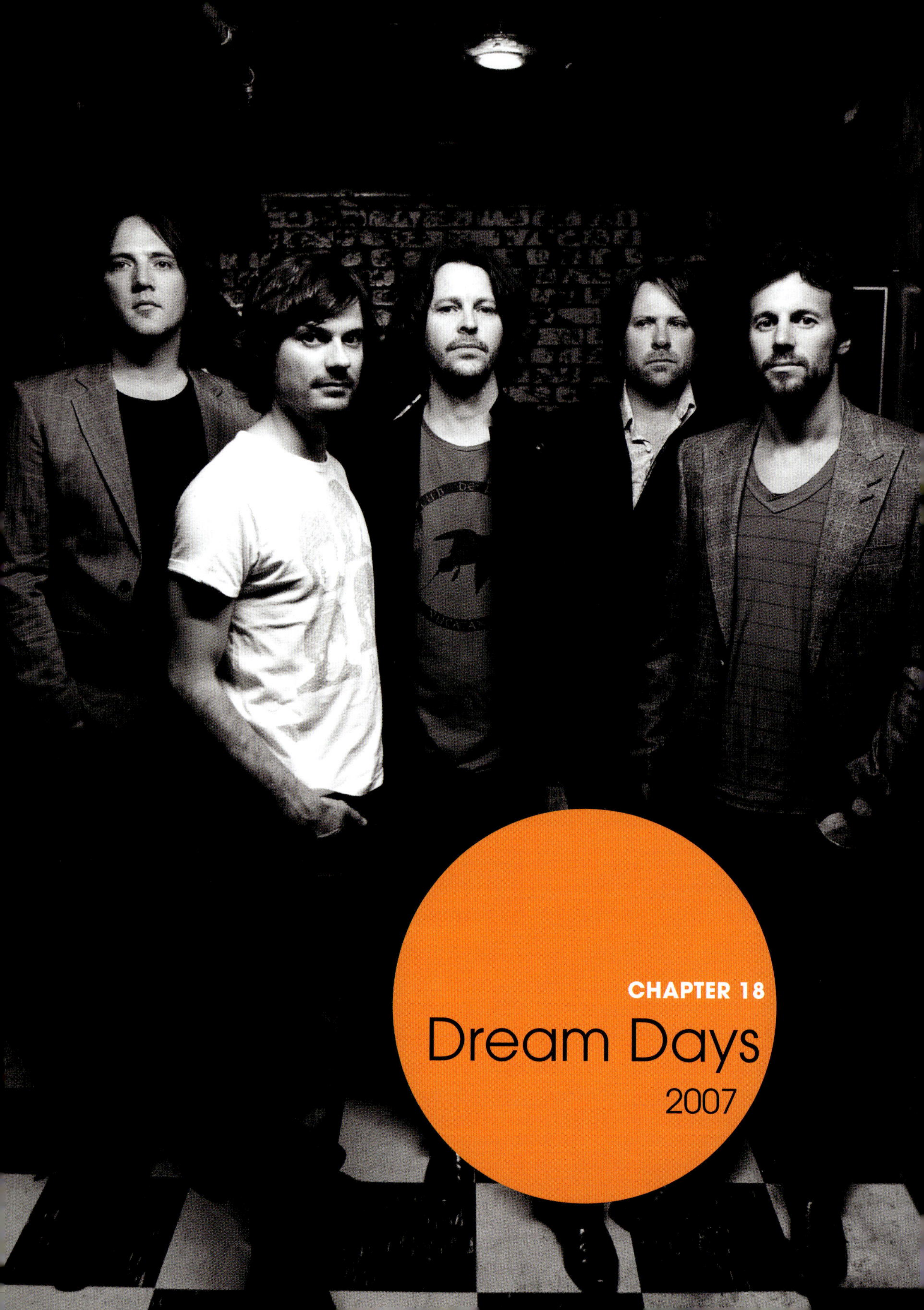

CHAPTER 18

Dream Days

2007

With the release of *Vulture Street*, the Fingers had fulfilled their obligations under the recording contract they'd signed with Polydor/Universal way back in 1994. Despite the agreement almost collapsing after their debut album, it ended up a most beneficial arrangement for all concerned. Almost a decade on, the band was in the enviable position of being at the peak of its earning potential and was free to strike a new deal with whomever it pleased. They chose to stay put.

The team at Universal had obviously played a pivotal role in helping create and sustain Powderfinger's success and, in recent times, the band had forged a close working relationship with George Ash, Universal Music Australia's managing director since 2001. While there were expressions of interest from other labels, there was no way George Ash was going to let his label's biggest act slip away. 'It was critical for the company,' says George. 'The Australian roster was all driven by Powderfinger. To be able to keep working with them was live or die, to a certain extent. They defined our culture in Australia – they were a big part of the image of the company.'

So George made an aggressive offer, which was going to be hard for anyone else to match. In return for a $7 million investment, he wanted a commitment of two more studio albums, plus a couple of compilations.

'That sealed the deal,' Teaks says. 'They were good people. We didn't want to leave but potentially it was the last time the guys would make a record deal so it was about making sure it was rewarding for them. Families had started to appear [Darren and Tamara had the first of their two children, Viola and Arden], so they certainly thought it was time to get paid.'

Being five albums old and the undisputed biggest band in the country wasn't without its drawbacks. Three number one albums in a row, shelves full of ARIAs and the arrival of a new generation of young rocking upstarts, such as Jet and the Vines, were making the 30-something Fingers look like the establishment. It meant that while top 10 singles got easier ('On My Mind' debuted at number nine on the national charts), serious music critics appeared increasingly unwilling to dish out unconditional praise.

Rolling Stone gave *Vulture Street* a four-star review but felt compelled to add: 'What *Vulture Street* lacks is the one soul-power anthem that will ensure it does the same business as its predecessors'. (This about an album featuring 'Since You've Been Gone'?) Reviewer Craig Mathieson writing in *The Age* complained: '*Vulture Street* is commendably well composed and quite enjoyable but lacks for genuine surprises and narrative twists. The album is a touch too self-disciplined.' ('Rockin' Rocks' – too self-disciplined?)

Mainstream reviewers remained less inhibited. 'What puts *Vulture Street* more than a drumbeat ahead of the rest are the elements that leave you in no doubt that they're still Powderfinger,' wrote Sandra Bridekirk in *The Australian*. 'Still a band capable of expressing strong emotions, love and loss, behind the balls, beer and dirty energy.' '*Vulture Street* is a winner,' added Scott Podmore in his five-star review in Melbourne's *Sunday Herald Sun*.

With the band's immediate future contractually locked down, Powderfinger got on with the business of taking *Vulture Street* out to their people. As usual, they put in the preparation and they had a new bandroom to rehearse in. While his band mates had been in Atlanta mixing the album, JC found an old paint factory in the north Brisbane suburb of Albion, which the band bought, soundproofed and christened the Finger Factory.

However, it was their previous rehearsal space above the tattoo parlour in Stanley Street, across the road from the real-life Vulture Street, which was immortalised in the video for 'On My Mind'. Not the actual room itself, but rather a facsimile; the video producers, Fifty Fifty Films, recreated an exact replica of the bandroom in their film studio. 'They even came and took our rubbish bins,' says Hog, 'and they returned them without emptying them out.'

The Fingers had played a bunch of shows the previous year while writing *Vulture Street*, including three weeks worth of club and festival gigs in Europe and North America in the middle of the year, followed by a headlining slot alongside Oasis on the touring Livid festival in Brisbane, Melbourne and Sydney.

By the release of *Vulture Street* at the start of July 2003, it was suddenly almost a year since the Fingers had performed anywhere. They played a short warm-up gig under the name Donkeyboys, supporting Dallas Crane at the Healer in Brisbane, before taking off for a series of one-off launch shows in familiar rooms along the east coast, namely the Tivoli Theatre in Brisbane, the Metro in Sydney and the Hi-Fi Bar in Melbourne. The encore at the Melbourne gig included a rare performance of the closet 'Finger classic 'Let It Grow'.

The band's first big show was a return appearance alongside their old mates Coldplay at Splendour in the Grass on 19 July. It was the same weekend that Chris Martin infamously got arrested for attacking a paparazzo's car after the photographer snapped the singer while he was out surfing. Ian had taken Chris surfing that day. As to what actually happened, Hog seems intent on taking that to his grave.

'We were like, "Hoggy, tell us what happened?"' JC says. 'He wouldn't tell his own band mates. We were like, "What, are you part of Coldplay now?" We wanted the goss. We really hated him for a while over that.'

On stage at Splendour, Powderfinger put on an unforgettable performance ... for all the wrong reasons. With all these new rock songs to play, they had discussed putting on more of a rock 'show' for the fans, rather than simply their trademark stand-and-deliver approach. What better place to try out the new direction than in front of a patriotic rock festival crowd?

'I remember standing there,' Bernard says, 'and "Rockin' Rocks" started, the song kicked in and JC and Hoggy and Darren were all going off, and it sounded like absolute shit. It was bad, a terrible gig. We came straight off stage, got in the van and went back to our hotel. It was a 10-minute drive, but it was horrible, there was deathly silence and lots of tension. The girls were in the van with us, so it was a bad scene.'

However, the band didn't let this one misstep kill off the concept of injecting a bit of rock theatre into their sets. They were very conscious of the fact that they were soon to play the biggest venues of their career and they needed to connect with fans in the bleachers. They had to get it a bit more animated.

Bernard was up for it. 'One major impact my brother's death had on me was I stopped giving a fuck about what people thought,' he says. 'I dropped my inhibitions and that's when our live show really picked up much more energy.'

In September, tickets went on sale for the band's Live On Vulture Street national tour, scheduled for the end of 2003. It would be Powderfinger's first 'arena' tour, playing 10,000-plus-seat venues in the major cities. Again, fans scrambled for tickets. Shows at Brisbane's Riverstage, Melbourne's Rod Laver Arena and the Sydney Entertainment Centre sold out almost instantly, and follow-up shows were added at each venue.

In October, the 17th annual ARIA Awards red carpet was rolled out. It turned out to be Delta Goodrem's night, the newcomer sweeping the pool, except for the prizes that the Fingers managed to wrangle from her grasp, including an unprecedented third consecutive Album of the Year award for *Vulture Street*, plus Best Group, Best Rock Album and Best Cover Art, taking the band's career ARIA haul to 14.

The band immediately headed to Europe for two weeks of shows, including another two nights at London's Shepherds Bush Empire, in support of the UK release of *Vulture Street*, via a new deal with Richard Branson's label, V2 Music.

On their return home, it was straight into Live On Vulture Street, supported by the John Butler Trio. It was an incredible experience for fans and band alike, especially getting the opportunity to play Brisbane's iconic Riverstage for the first time on 29 November. It was such a big deal that on the afternoon of the show, Brisbane Lord Mayor Tim Quinn presented the band with the keys to the city. 'We only give the keys to those who have a very strong association with the city and who have outstanding achievements,' said the mayor. 'I think Powderfinger meets those criteria extremely well.'

'The modern history of Australian rock is made of iconic moments that cement themselves in our collective memory,' wrote Joel Dullroy in Brisbane's *Courier-Mail* the morning after the first Riverstage show. 'Add this one to the list. The band captured the essence of the night when they broke into the triumphant chorus of "Love Your Way" and Brisbane sang it right back to them. The crowd had come for more than just music. They wanted to express their attachment to the band who found a way to bottle the sensation of being young and reckless in Queensland.'

The Sydney shows were filmed and recorded and later released as the band's first concert film and live album, *These Days Live In Concert*. Right across Australia, the Live On Vulture Street tour was an unmitigated triumph.

COMING DOWN FROM THE HIGH OF PLAYING MASSIVE ARENAS to ecstatic fans, the Fingers spent the first half of 2004 overseas, playing mostly tiny clubs, again trying to break through internationally. There was no doubt they were making progress, especially in Europe, where there were ever-expanding fan bases in Germany, Holland and the UK.

In London, they could sell out two nights at the famous Hammersmith Apollo, playing to over 5000 a night. And it was no longer only expats coming to see them. The Fingers unanimously rate one of these shows at the Apollo as their best performance ever as a band. They can't explain exactly why, but 'it so rarely happens when everyone agrees it was a great gig,' JC says.

In May, the Fingers were the personal guests of the soon-to-be Princess Mary of Denmark at a pre-royal wedding concert at a football stadium in Copenhagen in front of 40,000 Danes. Apparently Powderfinger were the Princess's favourite band from her days as a commoner in Australia. The Fingers played four songs. 'Only about 200 people knew who we were,' says Hog, 'but it was cool.' Bernard had given the Princess a couple of *Vulture Street* badges which she wore to the show.

On the second leg of their European dates, they invited Something For Kate along for the ride. During this tour the band invented the game of 'Brawling' to help pass the time, which involved giving another band member a sharp jab to the face when they least expected it. Something For Kate became willing participants. 'We were introduced to it the hard way,' Paul Dempsey says. 'Everyone was just creeping up and punching each other square in the jaw.'

After a final run of dates across Canada, the Fingers came home, by which point their desire to keep touring overseas was gone. In the US, where *Vulture Street* was released through the small independent label Artemis Records, the band was still playing venues like the Roxy in LA and appearing at SXSW, nothing had changed despite all the time and effort they had committed to touring there.

'By that stage,' Bernard says, 'we had been working pretty hard on the road, had done a lot of miles and a lot of gigs and starting over again overseas was really difficult. In the end, that kind of killed overseas touring for us. JC would say, "I don't want to go to Germany and play to 300 people. I don't want to be away for that long, for something that's going to cost us money." He didn't find it very rewarding.'

POWDERFINGER

Dream Days at the Hotel Existence

SUNDAY JULY 6th
O2 Wireless Festival, Hyde Park, London

FRIDAY JULY 11th
The Academy, Dublin, Ireland

SATURDAY JULY 12th
Oxygen Festival, Ireland

SUNDAY JULY 13th
T in The Park Festival, Glasgow, Scotland

powderfinger.com // myspace.com/powderfinger // universalmusic.com.au

'I'm going to make man music, not boy's music.'

'We kept plugging away, but we didn't hold out great hopes of cracking overseas,' says DZ. 'We kind of went, "We'll travel because we've got a bunch of expats in the UK and a few people who will come and see us in LA and New York," but our drive to crack internationally had waned. We looked forward to nurturing what we had in Australia. We worked at putting together better shows to compete with the international bands that would come out and put on big lavish shows.'

'I don't think there is anyone in the band who would tell you they were cut because we didn't crack it overseas,' offers Hog. 'We're just confused as to why so many shit American bands are so popular. We've always been pretty cocky about our music and I know that we have 10 better songs than most of the bands that hit the charts in America.'

There was lots of positive reinforcement for that belief back at home. At the annual APRA songwriting awards in May, Powderfinger were named songwriters of the year, while the Phonographic Performance Company of Australia released statistics showing the band was the most broadcast artist, local or international, on Australian radio.

Following the latest international slog, the Fingers went home to Brisbane and effectively into hibernation for the remainder of 2004. The long breaks were becoming an increasingly common feature of Powderfinger life. 'We tried to be positive and enthusiastic and realised what was needed at this stage was to work and then have a break for the health and safety of the band,' Darren explains. 'We were no longer relentlessly touring and then heading straight back into rehearsing and writing and recording.'

There was only one more public appearance for that year, one show at the Arena in Brisbane in November, a Triple J Live At The Wireless production to coincide with the release of the band's greatest hits set, *Fingerprints: The Best Of Powderfinger 1994–2000*, which flew straight to number two on the charts. The compilation included two new songs, 'Process This', which was actually the first track recorded during the sessions for *Vulture Street* but it had been left off the album, and an entirely new song, 'Bless My Soul'.

In an article he penned for the *Rolling Stone Yearbook* at the time, Bernard explained that 'Bless My Soul' was 'a tribute to the fun we had in Spain on our first visit' during the band's most recent international tour. 'The warmth of the people there was quite overwhelming for us.' Indeed, Bernard spent half the article going on about what an amazing time he had in Madrid. What Bernard didn't know at that point was that the trip would change the course of his life.

On that same tour, sitting in the front seat of the tour bus while driving out of Holland, Bernard began penning a most unPowderfinger song entitled 'The Thrill Is Gone'. 'I was writing a "Dear John" letter to rock & roll, going, "Okay, I have had enough of rock & roll, I'm going to make man music, not boy's music." I remember thinking I was really sick of all the big shows and what a big deal everything was.' But Bernard had to put up with the big shows for a little while longer.

IN JANUARY 2005, POWDERFINGER RESURFACED TO ONCE AGAIN play the Big Day Out, this time headlining alongside the Beastie Boys and System Of A Down (SOAD). They interspersed their BDO performances along the east coast with a series of three side-show gigs at the Brisbane Convention Centre, Sydney's Hordern Pavilion and Melbourne's Festival Hall under the banner of the Rock and Soul Revue.

While on the road, Powderfinger were asked to perform at the extraordinary WaveAid benefit concert at the Sydney Cricket Ground on 29 January, an event hastily put together to raise money for the victims of the devastating Boxing Day tsunami. The impressive all-star bill included Missy Higgins, Nick Cave and the Finn brothers, with Powderfinger slotted in to perform between Silverchair and Midnight Oil, who both re-formed especially for this concert.

On a perfect Sydney summer day, in front of a stadium full of exuberant Oz rock fans, Powderfinger delivered a killer set ... until they got to 'Love Your Way'. 'We played second last, and Midnight Oil headlined,' recalls Cogs. 'We went on and it was pumped up, 50,000 people, SCG. It was one of those gigs where you're thinking, "This is just one of the best shows I'm ever going to be involved in." It was just pumping. We started playing "Love Your Way" and we got three-quarters of the way through the song and I just did this huge stuff-up. I messed it up completely. I actually had to stop in the middle of the song because it just broke down.

'I can probably count on two hands how many stuff-ups I've done in my whole life with Powderfinger. My first reaction was: "Who the fuck was that?" then I realised, "Oh no, that was me!" I just put my head down on the snare and thought, "Oh no!" JC looked at me and said, "What's wrong?"'

JC never let Cogs live it down. 'Our worst one ever,' he says, still wickedly joyous at the memory. 'Bernard said to the crowd, "Hope you like our new ending."'

As they walked off stage, no one was laughing. The band was in a state of shock. 'We played another two songs after the debacle,' Cogs says, 'and when we came off stage, I'm freaked out, and everyone's like, "It's okay! Everything's okay!"'

Just then, there was a commotion at the side of the stage and Denis quickly escorted the band through to the lift to get them back to their dressing-room. A middle-aged guy no one recognised jumped into the lift with them and started growling: 'Nice fucking job, wankers!' Denis, who is quite a tall, well built man, tried to shield the band as this bloke kept yelling: 'You fucking fucked it up, didn't you?' Former short person Bernard arced up: 'Who the fuck are you, mate?' he yelled at the guy. 'I thought Bern was about to smash him,' says Cogs.

'I'm Gary Morris,' says the bloke, 'manager of Midnight Oil, and you guys played 10 fucking minutes over – now we've got to cut our set.'

The following day, Midnight Oil drummer Rob Hirst phoned Bernard to apologise on behalf of his band. A couple of years later, Rob recalled the incident in a story he wrote on Powderfinger for *Rolling Stone* magazine, in which he also noted that the 'Finger reminded him of the Oils, 'not just because we're both five-piece rock bands with a message, melody and macho grunt; we also saw

SUNSET SOUND

the need to reinvent ourselves more than once, and to wrench apart our music, politics and plans.'

Powderfinger's immediate plan was to take a complete year off. They had three more Big Day Out shows to play, the festival wrapping up in Perth on 6 February. It certainly wasn't the most enjoyable BDO they had ever been involved in.

'The atmosphere backstage was poisonous,' says Bernard. 'By then it had become so big and hairy. We were headlining with the Beastie Boys, and they were staying in different hotels to everyone else, but we would run into them and their crew every day in lifts or whatever. And they were the unfriendliest bastards I have ever come across in the music industry. Horrible New York coldness. You would say hello and they would look at you and not respond.

'Then during the final gig, in Perth, we'd finished playing and the Beastie Boys were on stage, and we were like, "Let's get in the car and get out of here and avoid the crowd rush." We were sitting in the van and whoever the Buddhist is from the Beastie Boys [Adam Yauch] comes up to the van's window and goes like this to me [puts his hands together and bows his head]. I just went, "Are you kidding?" I've never been a Beastie Boys fan, so I just stuck up my two middle fingers and gave him a full piece of fuck off.'

And with that, Powderfinger drove off to begin their extended hiatus.

THE IDEA WAS THAT POWDERFINGER WOULD MEET UP again in a year's time and until then the members were free to do whatever they wanted. Cogs took a complete break from music, slowly renovating his house. The other four had plans for side-projects, all of which would be released through Dew Process, the independent record label Teaks had established a couple of years earlier, distributed through Universal.

Darren almost immediately began work on the debut album by Drag, a follow-up to the 2002 EP, *Gas Food Lodging*. The extended line-up of Drag featured Mark McElligott on drums, Matt Murphy on keyboards, and Sean Hartman on bass. Recorded in Byron Bay and in Darren's Lunchbox Studios and produced by David Nicholas, for which he won the 2005 ARIA award for Producer of the Year, *The Way Out* was released in early July and supported with club shows around the country, plus a performance at the 2005 Splendour festival.

Bernard began work on his debut solo album, *Tea & Sympathy*, which would eventually be released on 31 October. In recent years, he'd once again started making the odd musical excursion outside the 'Finger. He'd performed a song with You Am I on the soundtrack of the Australian movie *Dirty Deeds*. He'd also recorded a couple of solo tracks for the most recent Gregor Jordan movie, *Ned Kelly*, again starring Heath Ledger, and Bernard also made a cameo appearance in the film. 'JC started calling me a slashy,' he says. 'Musician-slash-actor.' Most recently, he'd performed as a part of the Wrights alongside Nic Cester for the cover of the Australian classic 'Evie'.

Not long after the Big Day Out, Bernard split from Phillippa, his partner of 12 years. 'I was devastated and also relieved in a lot of ways,' Bernard says. Living alone for the first time in his life, he threw himself into his work, writing and demoing around the clock for two months. In May, he headed to the UK to record the album with famed American producer Tchad Blake at Peter Gabriel's Real World Studios. (Four of the album's tracks were recorded by Mark McElligott in Brisbane.) While in Europe, Bernard reconnected with Andrea Portela Moreno, who he had first met during that visit to Spain. Andrea had worked for the Fingers' European label V2. Friendship developed into something deeper and the pair would eventually marry at the end of 2006.

Upon release, *Tea & Sympathy* proved a phenomenon, debuting at the top of the Australian charts and selling over 350,000 copies. The album won four ARIA awards, including Album of the Year and Male Artist of the Year, while its lead single 'Wish You Well' claimed the top spot on Triple J's Hottest 100. Bernard was also named APRA's Songwriter of the Year.

During the extended hiatus Ian married Georgie in February 2005 and the couple soon had their first child, Ruby. It wasn't until the end of the year that Hog and JC started work on their side-project, a four-piece band called the Predators. On lead vocals was none other than Steven Bishop, Powderfinger's first drummer. It was the original 'Finger reformed, except Bish was upfront so Ross McLennan from FOC was brought in to play drums. The guys recorded a six-track EP, *Pick Up the Pace*, in Ian's Airlock Studios, which was released in July 2006. The Predators played a handful of shows along the east coast, as well as appearing at Splendour in 2006. The guys had a ball. 'Bish had been taking acting lessons,' says Hog, 'so it was pretty funny to see him come flying through the air as a condor.'

As agreed, the Fingers reconvened early in 2006 to begin considering the follow-up to *Vulture Street*.

Not wanting to fall back into bad habits, the decision was made early on not to lock themselves away in the rehearsal studio for months on end as they had done for every previous album; this time they'd exploit the fact that Ian, Darren and Bernard now all had their own home studios. They would get together in twos and threes and work separately on various demos, to avoid the bandroom cabin fever that had led to such stress and volatility during the writing of the previous two albums.

But then, early in the piece, along came a massive wedge. The US record label Lost Highway – home to artists such as Johnny Cash and Lucinda Williams – wanted to release Bernard's *Tea & Sympathy* in America, but they needed a commitment from the singer that he would travel over and perform some shows. Bernard's solo success had already caused an uncomfortable shift in dynamics within the band. They were all glad for him, but it led to fraught conversations about making sure the next Powderfinger release sounded nothing like a Bernard Fanning record. This latest development was a most unwelcome distraction from 'Finger business.

'JC's reaction was, "Oh, fuck!"' Bernard recalls. 'And Cogsy was like, "Mate, if you want a fucking solo career, then go and have it." And that's when the real tension started. It was seen as a bit of a betrayal, like they didn't want me to release it. And I was like, "Come on, it's Lost

Highway, a really good label and I haven't gone around spruiking it like a mad person. They have actually come to us."'

'We were really supportive of his solo career,' say Cogs. 'We were all very congratulatory; I went to see two of his solo shows. But it would have been nice to know earlier that a year off was going to turn into two years off, because we had lives as well and wanted to plan what was going on.'

Adding to the strain was the fact that, to the others, Teaks appeared to be a co-conspirator in all of this, siding with Bernard. 'As far as the rest of us were concerned,' Darren says, 'we were back into Powderfinger time, so we all needed to be onboard and focused.'

Meanwhile, the approach of writing in small groups wasn't working either. There was such a concerted effort to not sound like Bernard that songs were being constantly reworked to death. Ian points to a stillborn song called 'Monkey Mind' which he thought had great potential, but it got demoed half-a-dozen times, to the point where the band killed it off.

In a further effort to shake things up, it was decided that, for the first time in a decade, the band would not collaborate with Nick DiDia. They chose to use the New Jersey-born, Los Angeles-based producer Rob Schnapf, best known for his work with artists like Beck and Elliott Smith, who'd recently produced the first two albums for the Vines. The Fingers also decided they would travel to Rob and spend a couple of months working and living in Los Angeles.

'Everyone thought that LA would be some sort of panacea to the band's troubles,' Teaks says, 'that being in a foreign city would beautify them somewhat, and I don't think it worked. There was a certain sense of let's try something different, let's try a new producer, go to a new place. It was like renewing your wedding vows, but it didn't have the same effect – the sex wasn't as good the second time around.'

In late January 2007, Powderfinger headed to LA. Their families came along too, with the plan to mix in some fun around the work. The band set up in the legendary Sunset Sound Studios, where the Rolling Stones had worked on *Exile on Main Street* and Led Zeppelin had recorded *Led Zep IV*.

Rob Schnapf admits to knowing virtually nothing about the Fingers when he met them, he'd barely listened to any of their previous records. He remembers the first conversation he had with Bernard, where the singer described the band to him as Australia's Hootie and the Blowfish. Rob soon worked out he was joking, but he also quickly realised that this was a band with some serious internal politics simmering away. Initially, the Fingers tried to hide their personal issues from him, not that the producer felt it was any of his business. 'I didn't really give a shit about the internal stuff,' says Rob. 'I just wanted to do what the songs were telling us to do.'

Yet all around him, the Fingers began unravelling. And this time it was different. Bernard and Cogs were increasingly consumed in their own personal war. 'All the fights we had were really juvenile,' Bernard says. '"You did this." "No, I didn't." "Yes, you did." It was like we were in grade three.'

While the pair had separately driven the band's direction in the past, now no one was steering

the ship. Hog and JC stepped up to take a more authoritative role, but that only caused more tension rather than solutions. 'JC used to be pretty easygoing but he ended up being pretty fiery,' says Hog. Both Bernard and Darren felt their relationships with JC were strained for the first time. 'It was a different dynamic,' says Cogs. 'Whatever made things work before, it wasn't happening anymore. We were all lost and confused. We didn't know who was in charge, we didn't know who sat where.'

Exhausted by the constant recasting of ideas, Bernard and Darren essentially relinquished any creative control. 'I felt there was quite a bit of faith lost in the guitarists in the band because of all the time spent demoing,' says Darren. 'Everyone was getting involved in writing the guitar parts. I just kind of threw my hands up in the end and said, "Whatever". I gave up, which is not a good attitude.'

The situation degenerated further when the relationship between Cogs and Rob Schnapf fell apart. While Cogs had his issues with Nick DiDia during previous recording sessions, this was far more serious in his mind. He didn't feel Rob was at all nurturing of anyone's ideas and felt the producer was playing band members off against each other.

'After a few weeks, I just started hating him like crazy,' says Cogs. 'I asked the guys for some back-up and I didn't get any except from Darren. Darren has always been very helpful like that. It was like there were five individuals in the studio rather than a band, and I think Rob exacerbated that situation.'

Rob says he was unaware Cogs felt that way, although he adds he was heavily medicated for much of the session because of a kidney stone and a back injury, so he might have had a numbed perception. 'I heard afterwards how much Cogsy hated it and maybe hated me and I was like, "What? Really?" I had no idea. I was completely unaware of it, but you know what? You're paying me and I'm going to do my job. I'm going to be diplomatic and I'm going to work with everybody, but if you can't tell me that something's bothering you, I can't do anything about that.'

Cogs claims he did talk to Rob. 'I would have been irresponsible if I hadn't tried to talk to him about it. He was just too pig-headed for it to register.'

The other Fingers had no issues with Rob. Bernard and Ian got on with him famously. Ian and Rob even share a birthday.

After two months in Los Angeles, Powderfinger had its sixth album in the can: *Dream Days At The Hotel Existence*. Its weighty title was appropriated from the name of a chapter in the book Bernard was reading at the time, *The Brooklyn Follies* by Paul Auster. ('I fucking hate that title,' notes JC. 'So bloated. I fought against it.')

It was by far the most expensive recording of Powderfinger's career, costing about $250,000. For all the money and anxiety, was it worth it? Was the Powderfinger in Los Angeles experiment ultimately a success? The band is deeply divided on that.

'I am really glad we recorded overseas,' says Ian. 'I had fun, except for the tense moments in the studio. I don't think anyone put in their best performances individually throughout. There are some really good bits that I am really proud of, but we knew when we walked out that it wasn't as good as it could have been. Everyone's creativity was not aligned. But it was still good.'

In fact, Hog and JC rate it as one of their favourite 'Finger records.

Darren doesn't share that opinion. 'I don't think we captured much life out of the band on that record,' he says. 'Just sounds a bit tired.'

'Maybe we should have called it *Dark Days*,' says Bernard.

When *Dream Days* was released on 2 June 2007, it debuted at the top of the charts just like its three predecessors, but it was greeted by the kind of mixed reviews that Powderfinger had not experienced since the release of *Parables*.

Kathy McCabe of Sydney's *Daily Telegraph* gave it four stars, declaring the album 'finds the 'Finger honing their skills as master song craftsmen and players ... The opening track, "Head Up In The Clouds", is spacious, almost psychedelic ... "I Don't Remember" is a signature tune and impossible to shake out of your head. The quintet go '70s with guitars and keys on the climactic rock-out of "Who Really Cares", with superstar keys-for-hire man Benmont Tench defining the song with his organ work. "Nobody Sees" is a haunting piano ballad reminiscent of Coldplay, which showcases just how emotively plaintive Bernard Fanning's vocals can be ... *Dream Days* consolidates their position as one of the country's best-loved bands with an album you will still be playing in a decade.'

Bernard Zuel at the *Sydney Morning Herald* was less impressed, describing *Dream Days* as 'Powderfinger's first dull album'.

The album's first single, the rollicking 'Lost And Running', was overshadowed by controversy surrounding the album track, 'Black Tears'. Legal proceedings concerning the death of Aboriginal man Mulrunji Doomadgee in a police cell on Palm Island on 19 November 2004 meant the band altered the lyrics to head off the lodging of a complaint that they could prove prejudicial to the upcoming court case. The track had to be rerecorded at Bernard's home studio immediately prior to the album's release. 'When I wrote the song there was no trial scheduled. I would prefer the original version was what came out. Hopefully at some stage it will be legally permissible so we can release it,' Bernard said at the time. After an acquittal and three coronial inquests the only thing that is undisputed fact is that Mulrunji Doomadgee died too soon.

POWDERFINGER LAUNCHED *DREAM DAYS* WITH A NOVEL run of media shows staged in hotels in Sydney, Adelaide and Brisbane, along with a couple of theatre gigs in Melbourne and Perth. Then, later in the month, the band held a joint press conference with Silverchair to announce the details of an ambitious co-headlining national tour – Across The Great Divide. Australia's two biggest bands planned to spend two months on the road together, performing in every major Australian centre, plus several rural towns neither band had previously visited.

The tour, which kicked off in Silverchair's hometown of Newcastle on 29 August 2007, was a monumental success, with 220,000 music lovers attending the 28 dates across the country (plus three dates in New Zealand, which weren't such a success). Australian rock fans hadn't experienced anything like it since Midnight Oil and Cold Chisel shared a stage in the early 1980s.

For both the 'Finger and the 'Chair, it was the most fun they'd had on the road in years. 'It was like hanging out with all your schoolmates,' says Cogs. 'That was a really good time. Both of our bands needed to be hanging out with different people. It really helped us to get along. It was awesome.'

The tour was one long party. 'Lots of big benders,' says Silverchair's Chris Joannou. 'Usually, if you get Hoggy and JC together, they are definitely partners in crime, especially when the old Bundy rum comes out. There were also lots of great meals together in restaurants around the country that almost became like family dinners in the end. Doing that tour with those guys was definitely a highlight of my time in Silverchair. It was just a good feeling. Everyone was pretty loose and limber at the end.'

Darren says his favourite memories of the tour were the drives back from the venues to the hotels, both bands sharing the same van. A running joke was forcing Daniel Johns to sing 'Tomorrow', which he'd refused to do for over a decade, and everyone joining in.

The light-hearted mood and prevailing silliness of the trip was immortalised in the *Courier-Mail* when a photo of both bands holding hands and skipping featured on the front page. It had been taken one morning in Cairns as most of the guys had just flown in from Darwin after staying up all night partying.

The tour ended where it started, at the Newcastle Entertainment Centre on 26 October. Two nights later, both bands attended the 21st ARIA Awards in Sydney where they were nominated in virtually exactly the same categories. And the Fingers got their arses whipped by the young 'uns, going home with only the Best Album Cover award.

Still, the Fingers were the happiest they had been in years. However, with only one album remaining on their record contract, everyone's minds would soon turn to the band's long-term future, which, after all the ups and downs, now very much hung in the balance.

TRUNKS

CHAPTER 19

Golden Rule

2009

Bernard was the first to make up his mind that he no longer wanted to be a part of Powderfinger. He came to the decision in his head and heart long before he said it aloud to anyone other than his wife, Andrea.

Following the Across The Great Divide tour, the Fingers travelled to the UK for a run of shows in early December. They performed half-a-dozen concerts, including another two sold-out nights at London's Hammersmith Apollo, and finished up at the Tripod in Dublin.

After those gigs, Bernard and Andrea returned to Madrid for Christmas. The next engagement on the Powderfinger calendar was an appearance at the Clipsal 500 V8 motor race in Adelaide in late February. But then Andrea discovered she needed surgery to treat a congenital heart condition. Her operation was scheduled for February. All the band members had always put Powderfinger first, made countless personal sacrifices over the years. The singer decided he wasn't doing that anymore.

'Andrea had this heart issue and yet I had to fly back from Spain to play a show five days after she had a heart operation,' Bernard says. She was still in hospital and there was no consideration that maybe we should cancel the show because my wife was in hospital on the other side of the world. That was the point where I first started to seriously think, "Okay, am I going to do this anymore? Should I do one more record? Or should I just pull out completely?"

'Eventually I thought, "I have always fulfilled my obligations and I don't want to be in a situation where I'm letting people down." Aside from that, I thought *Dream Days* was average and I didn't want that to be the last thing we did. I really wanted to make a good record, and I think everyone else eventually realised that as well. We could do a lot better.'

In the middle of 2008, the band came together again with a show designed specifically for their most loyal fans. The relatively low-key Upstairs at the Downstairs tour would see the band back in theatres around Australia, performing a dozen concerts in two halves – an acoustic set followed by a rock set. Fan club members got first dibs on tickets via the band's website and they were also asked to help select the songs.

As a result, the set-lists included a couple of obscure b-sides such as 'Sweet Lip' and 'Not The Only One'. The band even teased fans at a few of the gigs by playing the opening of 'Tail'. 'We thought it was a special thing to do,' says JC. 'Traditionally we've always found it hard in our gigs to put in the mellower stuff, so it was a lot of fun,' adds Hog. It was a relief for fans to see their favourite band in such an intimate setting again. 'This is raw Aussie talent at its best,' wrote Lisa Jackson in *Time Off* after the Tivoli Theatre show in Brisbane. 'This energetic gig adds yet another string to the already towering Powderfinger bow.'

In July, they were back in the UK for a quick run of summer festivals. The first show was the O2 Wireless festival in London's Hyde Park, where they performed alongside Ben Harper and Counting Crows in front of 50,000 people. According to JC, Ian had a shocker the night before. He partied all night and turned up to the gig having barely slept. JC says he walked on stage and asked him: 'Is everything alright? I can't hear anything.' JC growled back: 'Everything's fine, don't worry about it.' The pair had a screaming match about it after the set, virtually their only fight ever, but it was all forgotten by the time the band made its final tour appearance at Scotland's massive T in the Park festival a couple of days later.

Once home, the next time the five Fingers came together was in Brisbane on 19 September 2008, for a meeting with Teaks to 'discuss the future'. They were committed and contractually obliged to make another album, but they would be out of contract again after that. So what did they want to do? Things got off to a rocky start when everyone was reminded that after the next 'Finger album, Bernard would make another solo record.

As far as Cogs was concerned, this was the final straw. He felt kept in the dark about these plans. Hog said he couldn't remember being told either. JC backed Bernard up, saying they had all been in the same meeting earlier in the year when it was first discussed.

Regardless, Cogsy believed that, like a sporting team, the success of a rock & roll band requires 110 per cent commitment from its players. That was no longer the case for Powderfinger and it hadn't been for a long time. Also, to Cogs, it seemed like everything in the past couple of years was about keeping Bernard happy for fear he might leave.

'I had spent so much time and effort trying to make things work in the bandroom and I was exhausted. When you're working with someone you know doesn't want to be there it makes it hard. It wasn't only me who added to the tension. I may have been a control freak once but all I was trying to do in the end was keep things positive, keep things moving and nothing I did worked. It didn't help that we had a history of conflict – I seemed to piss people off no matter what way I worded things and I can completely understand why the guys would feel like that. So I got to a point for myself where I gave up. I just thought, "I can't be bothered anymore." I realised it was not meant to be. Psychologically, I think most people had had enough. It wasn't that anything vindictive was happening, it had just run its course.'

Certainly, Bernard didn't want to sign a new recording contract. He wasn't saying he was definitely quitting quite yet, but he didn't want to make a commitment beyond this next record.

A few weeks later he wrote a letter to the other four Fingers to clarify his position, explaining his priority was to live in Spain for a while and he wanted to be open to whatever opportunities that might bring. 'I put in my letter that, after I make another record, I don't know what I want to do myself, I might want to become a butcher. I just honestly don't know. It depends a lot on how things pan out.'

Hog wrote a letter back. He said he understood where Bernard was coming from and began his push for a hiatus. 'I thought he was being flippant,' Ian says. 'He just wanted to do his own thing. Fine. There were moments where the band had almost fallen over before that. I thought we'd be able to keep it together if we had a big break. But no.'

So, with no firm plans to break up, but no commitment beyond the next record, Powderfinger started planning for album number seven.

Despite all the uncertainty, there was still fun to be had as a member of the biggest band in Australia. At the end of September, Powderfinger was invited to the AFL Grand Final to provide the pre-match entertainment at the Melbourne Cricket Ground. From a small stage in the middle of the MCG, watched by 100,000 people in the stadium and another 3.4 million on television, the 'Finger belted out 'On My Mind', spliced with AC/DC's 'Long Way To The Top'. They were accompanied by a live bagpipe troupe, Cogs wore a kilt and DZ finally got to live out his childhood Angus Young fantasies in front of a stadium of people. It was a pretty special day for ex-Melbourne boy Ian Haug too. His AFL team Hawthorn were playing in the grand final. Georgie's dad used to be a Hawthorn player. 'I wore a Hawthorn jersey and we won,' says Hog. 'I was pretty happy about that. My wife's dad was pretty proud about that, too.'

After a few months off, the band reconvened ahead of starting work again and called a truce. The future was still completely up in the air. 'At that stage, nothing was decided,' says Bernard. 'It was like, "Okay, we're going to have to take this under serious consideration, but we are going to make a record, so let's just get in there and make the best possible record we can and try to make it as fun as possible."' They discussed everything that had gone wrong with the last album. Darren made it clear that he didn't want to be involved in a repeat of what happened with *Dream Days*. Everyone agreed they should go back to writing the way they used to, back in the days of *Double Allergic* and *Internationalist*, where people brought in germs of song ideas and the band would build them up. No more fully arranged demos. It was basically the complete opposite to how they had worked on the writing of *Dream Days*.

In January 2009, the band returned to work at the Finger Factory. 'Everyone was trusting each other again and not treading on each other's toes as we had in the past two or three years,' says Darren.

'They were pretty good writing sessions,' Bernard agrees. 'This time I decided I'd write songs at home on my acoustic guitar, not record anything, not even on my phone. I'd commit them to memory, then go and play them to the guys and they could do whatever they wanted, put whatever they wanted over them. I would just have a riff and sing. That's it. The idea was to get everyone to inject as much of themselves into every song. Because I committed to that approach beforehand, I wasn't attached to all these ideas I wanted to be respected.

'Previously, what always pissed me off and one of the reasons why I didn't want to be in the band anymore in terms of writing is that you would spend 20 hours putting a song together and then take it to the band, and before you'd finished doing a pass of that song, people were already changing it in their heads. I'd think, "Show some respect." That approach will piss me off till the day I die.'

'This time it was all live in the bandroom,' says JC. 'We'd record things as we went along. Songs like "Awake", we did once, left it and didn't play it again until we got to the studio. Getting bogged down is one of those things we did really well, and we finally figured out how not to do that. On our seventh record. Never too late.'

For his part, Cogs says he felt somewhat detached from the process. He had started back at university part time, studying international relations, so now the band was no longer his first priority either. 'I just thought I'm going to enjoy it, not make anything too contentious,' he says. 'I'd made up my mind pretty much by then that I wanted to get on with life and do something else.'

After experimenting with another producer on *Dream Days*, the band was in no doubt they wanted to work with Nick DiDia again. They sent him song ideas as they got built up and arranged to have him come to Australia to begin work on the new album in June.

The six months of writing sessions had not been without the odd flare-up – 'Definitely some days of the writing process were horrible,' Ian says – but as Powderfinger prepared to record their seventh studio album, the mood was the most congenial it had been in over a decade.

THE SESSIONS FOR *GOLDEN RULE*, AS IT WOULD COME TO BE NAMED, were designed from the outset to be as stress-free as possible. The band chose to work in the tranquil surrounds of Studios 301 in Byron Bay and all rented beach houses nearby for their families. Even Nick brought his family along from Atlanta.

'*Golden Rule* was a bludge in terms of studio time,' JC says. 'We were working from 11 till 7, so it was pretty good. I'd play golf in the morning, guys were going for a surf. It just felt like it was our time. I had an awesome house on the beach with an outdoor fireplace, it was amazing and I didn't feel guilty. I felt like we'd earned it. I would have done every record there if we could have. With Brisbane only two hours away we could all stay in touch with our normal lives. Andrea and George were pregnant [Andrea with her first child, Gabriela, Georgie with her second, Hugo] at the time and they were able to go home and see their scans. It was awesome. We'd done virtually every other record away – Melbourne, Sydney, Los Angeles – so it was great to be local, and still be removed from your friends so you weren't getting dragged out on weekends, you were still concentrating on what you're doing.'

Inside the studio, in this new era of chilled-out 'Finger diplomacy, the captaincy was willingly handed over to Nick. 'This time he was really in command of the sessions,' says Bernard. 'For the first time, after 20 years, there was a chain of command, where Nick was in charge and everyone else fell in behind. It gave it such a focus and made everyone's roles so much clearer. I think we knew we had a few pretty good songs. "Burn Your Name" had come pretty early, it was actually a leftover riff off another song from *Dream Days*, while "All Of The Dreamers" came when in the studio.'

'The record didn't have the same focus as the other three records we'd made together,' says Nick. 'It wasn't: "This is what this record's going to be!" 'It was more like, "You know what? We all love what we do. We're going to make a new record, let's make it. What's the first song? Let's figure it out." If we did a version of something and it didn't sound right, then we did it again. It was also a situation where it was like, "You want to put horns on some stuff? Let's do it."'

Adding to the fun was 'Gentlemanly Friday', where everyone would turn up to the studio dressed in their dandiest garb; and the odd outrageous act, such as running across the road to the Splendour in the Grass festival to get the crowd to sing the chorus to the song 'Think It Over'. There wasn't much hanging around the studio – the players would show up when needed, but otherwise they'd be out enjoying their surrounds. They were even playing games of cricket again. 'The process had everything going for it to be really relaxed,' says Ian. 'Being in a small town like that, not having too many distractions around, nice studio, working with Nick again, good batch of songs.'

'The experience of making the record was just a lot of fun,' says Nick, 'but in hindsight it was perhaps a little bit melancholy too, because I think they knew that it was probably going to be the last one.'

Indeed, JC remembers packing up the studio at the end of the recording and saying to Darren and Cogs that this might be the last time they walked out of a studio together. 'I was feeling the reality that this could easily be our last session,' JC says.

If so, what a pleasant note to end on. However, sadly, the good times wouldn't last much longer.

After a short break, the band began rehearsals for their upcoming performances. They planned to launch *Golden Rule*, due for release on 13 November 2009, with a publicity stunt – busking in Brisbane, Sydney and Melbourne on the same day. That would be followed by a run of big shows: the Queensland 150th Anniversary show,

Homebake and the Big Day Out. (Twelfth man Macca was on stand-by for the Sydney Homebake show as Ian's wife Georgie was more than a week overdue, ready to give birth to Hugo back in Brisbane.)

At rehearsals, Bernard was stressed. His father was seriously ill and had just entered a nursing home (John Fanning Senior passed away in January 2011). Being back in the Finger Factory was the last place Bernard wanted to be. It was in this sensitive state that he and Cogs had their nastiest confrontations in the whole time they had known each other.

'There were some huge fights that were just horrible. They were just from bad places,' says Cogs. 'I could tell you every little fight that happened, but each one added to the mountain of angst.'

As far as Bernard was concerned, enough was enough. It was over. There was no going back. Powderfinger was broken and could not be fixed. 'That was the moment,' he says. 'I went, "Okay, that's it, I am out.'

UPON ITS NOVEMBER RELEASE, THE RICH AND ADVENTUROUS *GOLDEN RULE* was met with the now customary mixed reviews. Bernard Zuel at the *Sydney Morning Herald*, who had called *Dream Days* 'dull', enthused that the new album 'sounds like it's leaping out of the speakers' and the band 'sound like they are leaping out too. Not just playing harder or faster but piling into their work with an almost childlike enthusiasm. And this time they have material more likely to warrant it: not genius but energised.'

Yes, *Golden Rule* debuted at the top of the ARIA charts – making it five albums in a row, a feat only matched by Silverchair – but it spent only six weeks in the top 10. And while the singles 'All Of The Dreamers', 'Burn Your Name' and 'Sail The Wildest Stretch' still received major airplay on some radio networks, it appeared as if no one other than the band's most fervent fans were still listening. Even Triple J had moved on from Powderfinger.

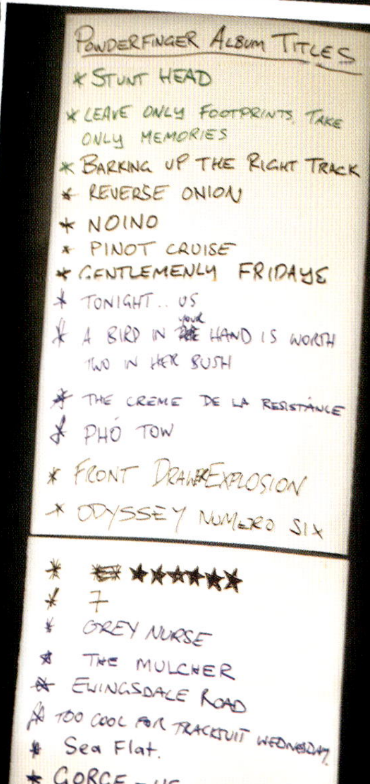

There were mounting signs that if the Fingers hadn't already decided to pull the pin at this point in their illustrious career, perhaps it would have been done for them. The band's one-off hometown comeback show at the Riverstage on 10 December, coinciding with the 150th anniversary of Queensland's foundation, was suffering from sluggish ticket sales, despite a reformed Custard playing support and each ticket coming with a copy of *Golden Rule*.

In January, at the Big Day Out for one last time, the Fingers were starting to feel their age. 'It was like, "Well, we've done this enough times," says JC. 'And it was such a young audience. We were mindful not to play too much old stuff in our set because it would just go over their heads. Most of them were probably 10 years old when "Pick You Up" came out. Actually, they were probably five.'

Even at the height of their popularity a decade earlier, Powderfinger had always promised themselves they would rather stop than become irrelevant. 'Bands do have a use-by date,' Bernard says. 'If you are able to do your absolute best at the end, then that's the exact place to stop, instead of being petered out by unpopularity.'

So perhaps, in the end, it was fate as much as internal turmoil that led Powderfinger to its ultimate triumph – the Sunsets farewell tour.

THERE WAS NO AVOIDING Powderfinger's arrival into Newcastle on 1 September for the start of their final tour ever. They were splashed across the front page of the local newspaper, posing alongside *Fingerbird 1*, the nickname given to the Jetstar airliner inscribed with the band's insignia.

There was a genuinely jubilant atmosphere inside the Newcastle Entertainment Centre for opening night – over 7000 screaming fans totally up for what might be one of the most memorable music nights of their lives: seeing the legendary Powderfinger for the last time.

'Oh, Newcastle, good evening – it's great to be here,' Bernie told the crowd after the one-two opening shot of 'Love Your Way' and 'Waiting For The Sun'. 'We're so happy and relieved to get this tour started. We've always loved playing here. This is a party. It's a celebration. There's nothing sad about it. Let's just all enjoy it.'

That night revealed the shape and mood of the show Powderfinger would take around Australia. They unveiled a huge stage set, a rainbow arch made of lights and high-tech video screens, along with a couple of neat party tricks. Most impressively, they performed a theatrical sleight-of-hand which, halfway through the show while the audience was momentarily distracted by boxer Anthony Mundine on the video screens, saw the band magically reappear on a small B-stage in the middle of the crowd, cranking out 'Like A Dog' as the lights hit them.

At the end of the energetic segment, as Cogs and JC jammed on a crazy piece dubbed 'Drum Thing', Bernard reappeared alone on the main stage to perform his traditional solo spot. With his acoustic guitar and harmonica, the singer alternated night from night between 'Whatever Makes You Happy' and 'Nobody Sees', although he surprised everyone at the third-last show of the tour in Brisbane, even his band mates, by pulling out the obscure hardcore fan favourite, 'Ibis'.

For the most part, it was a 'hits heavy' set, only featuring a couple of songs from Powderfinger's latest album *Golden Rule*. The two-hour show was mainly all about the singalongs, classic 'Finger after classic 'Finger: 'My Kind Of Scene', 'Sunsets', 'My Happiness', 'Since You've Been Gone', 'Passenger', 'On My Mind', 'Pick You Up' and, of course, the emotional finale, 'These Days'. Yes, the soundtrack for a generation of Aussies.

These were the staples of each performance of the tour, but there were also surprises along the way. On different nights, fans might get to hear 'Belter', 'JC', 'D.A.F.', 'Bless My Soul', 'Return Of The Electric Horseman', 'Up & Down & Back Again', 'Rockin' Rocks' or 'Living Type'. Or, if you were really lucky, a rare rendition of the long-abandoned 'Finger gem, 'The Day You Come'.

'Hoggy and I were pushing all the time for more rarities,' Bernard says. 'More album songs rather than just single, single, single. We thought, "Okay, this is your last tour, you can actually have an indulgent section there," but that never got up.'

Towards the end of the Newcastle show, Bernard took a moment to sketch out Powderfinger's history with the city. 'As everyone knows, this is our last tour, so this is our last show in Newcastle,' he announced on stage, initially greeted by boos. 'Alright, if you're going to be like that about it, we'll just get on with it,' he added, half-jokingly. 'We started playing here in 1993, we think, and that was at the Bar On The Hill at the uni. [This was greeted by loud cheers from the crowd.]

'I tell you what, you weren't all there then – there was about seven people there. But we've always loved coming here to Newcastle, we've always had a ball – honestly – and we're really happy to have started our tour here again. So thanks for having us.' Bernie would draw similar historical links with every other town and city the band visited on the tour, he worked out the links among his band mates on the drive into the venue.

A couple of minor technical glitches aside, it was an impressive opening. 'It wasn't the best gig we ever had,' says JC, 'but it was the best starting point for a tour. We were hitting our straps in the first week.'

From there, it was one last two-and-a-half month trek across the nation, sharing this once-in-a-lifetime experience with 300,000 of their fellow Australians. The tour would see the band and crew endure many of the climatic extremes this country has to offer, from scorching temperatures in Darwin to mud and snow in central Victoria. There were countless unforgettable moments, from the piercing screeching crowds in Perth to Bernard spotting an old high school girlfriend in the audience at the Myer Music Bowl in Melbourne or performing a charity gig for Yalari on *Fingerbird 1* in mid-air and raising over $150,000. At least 300,000 memories.

If the Fingers thought Silverchair were party animals, they had obviously never toured with Jet before. Hog and JC nobly did their best to keep up. However, all the hard rocking and some dodgy food caught up with the Jet boys in Rockhampton and they had to cancel their support slot in that city.

In neighbouring Mackay, more than halfway through the tour, Bernard and Cogs spoke for the first time since their blow-up in the rehearsal room. It would be going too far to say they made their peace, but at least they agreed to be civil to each other. Beyond that, all other past anxieties between the Fingers were forgotten in the overwhelming emotional swell of the tour. And it only intensified as the band drew ever closer to the three final sold-out shows at the Riverstage in Brisbane.

The last run of shows through Melbourne, Sydney and Adelaide were truly remarkable. The sight and sound of the full cauldron at Sydney's Acer Arena up on its feet screaming along to 'On My Mind' felt like rock & roll Valhalla. Backstage after the Sydney show, George Ash presented the Fingers with a double-platinum award for *Golden Rule* in a private final gathering of the band's Universal family. He joked that news of the break-up had done wonders for their record sales – God knows what a reunion would do!

As the tour arrived at its final destination in Brisbane, the emotions that the Fingers had managed to keep bottled up began to overflow. All their children, the Mini Fingers, were given their own backstage dressing-room at the Riverstage, along with specially designed laminates. Over the three nights, there was a constant stream of family and friends around, adding to the heightened sense of occasion. The band were on the front pages of the newspapers and there was constant coverage about them and the last three shows on radio and television. It seemed the whole city was peaking towards the inevitable finale.

On the afternoon of their last show, 13 November 2010, the Fingers kept to their tried-and-true routine, heading to the venue early for a 90-minute soundcheck. The band worked through a very bluesy version of 'Since You've Been Gone'. Cogs suggested they play Neil Young's 'Like A Hurricane'. Instead, they dragged up that old mysterious classic, 'Let It Grow', and gave it life one last time. It sounded so good, they shouted out to Marky to press record and played it through again. Finally, Powderfinger had recorded 'Let It Grow'.

'I think this week the whole emotional thing has kicked in,' Bernard explained on the day. 'And also being absolutely bombarded with messages about it being sad. I have a completely different measure for sadness than a band breaking up. Nobody has written to me and said it's a triumph what you're doing. A lot of people have said, "Congratulations, you're going out the way you want". That to me is the key thing. It's so rare for people to be able to choose when they are going to stop, and to celebrate that. To say, "Yeah, we have had a fucking awesome career. We have worked really hard, been really lucky and chosen the right time to go." That's not sad, it's awesome. There is no regret, it's been on my mind for quite a long time. I want to do things differently in my life, I don't want to be ruled by another majority, I want the decisions that I make to be made by Andrea and me, not by a collective.'

During the show that night, the band tried to get all their crew up on stage to take a bow. Immediately after that everyone was invited back to the band's dressing-room for champagne.

'What a ride – what a ride!' screamed Teaks. Hog lifted his glass to everyone: 'To 22 years!'

Bernard and JC jumped up on a chair. The singer encouraged the bass player to say a few words. 'Everyone in this room is so important to us,' he said. 'Sorry to make you work so hard. Thanks for all the early hours, long flights, lack of sleep, some band members' arrogance. It's been very special to have you along for the ride.'

'Seriously,' added Bernie, 'you've been awesome. Good on ya.'

'Frankly, it was such a long time coming,' says Ian now, 'so much buildup, that when we finally got to the last gig, it was sort of, "Thank God it's here." We played pretty well, we enjoyed it, I got a little emotional towards the end, but it was fun. I tried to soak it up, look out and watch people and see their enjoyment. It was pretty surreal.'

'The best time we have ever had in the band by a long way,' says JC.

'This is what we should have done the whole time,' says Cogs, 'be able to look at it and go, "How good is this?" But we could only do that since we decided to split up. But I'm actually really happy that the band's finished. I think if we had kept going for another 10 years, even if we were really happy, I don't think we would have had a chance at a second life when we were 50-year-old musos.'

'It was a grand finale for the band,' says Darren. 'It was a lot of fun. It was a great thing to be a part of. The whole 20 years were a great thing to be a part of. I'll always be grateful.'

And with that, one of the greatest chapters in the history of Australian rock & roll came to a close.

The end of Powderfinger. Well, almost ...

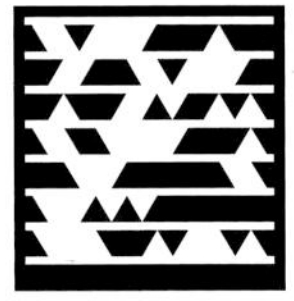

Watch a live version of 'These Days', the song Powderfinger ended their final Sunsets tour concerts with.
www.powderfinger.com/footprints

EPILOGUE

We're Splittin' Terry

A week after the final farewell concert, Powderfinger reformed for one last time, their own break-up party, at the Tivoli Theatre on 20 November 2010. It wasn't an official Powderfinger show. The audience of 900 people was made up strictly of family and friends, each Finger inviting 100 guests, plus colleagues who had helped them along at various points in their career.

Paul Piticco played MC, introducing his band to the stage as 'Brisbane's favourite sons and Australia's favourite rock band – Powderfinger!' There were no video screens, no fancy light show, no histrionics – only a tiny arch with nine lightbulbs lowered behind the band as they started to play, a miniature child's version of their multi-million dollar Sunsets set. 'A *Spinal Tap* moment,' says Ian. 'The crew did that.'

The Fingers put on a rock show for the ages, opening with 'Since You've Been Gone', followed by a curio-filled set-list delving as far back as 'Freedom' from the 'Blue' EP and 'Reap What You Sow' from *Parables*, right through to 'Awake' and 'Burn Your Name' from *Golden Rule*.

It was an hour-long set packed with rare gems. 'This is the best Powderfinger song never recorded,' Bernard said when introducing 'Let It Grow'. 'The Black Crowes ripped us off. So fuck you, Black Crowes!' But the biggest surprise of the night came when Steven Bishop reclaimed the drum stool from Cogs for one song – 'Powderfinger'. 'It was a nice gesture they did for me,' Bish said afterwards. 'It was a bit of closure in a way.'

As the end approached, the band started sharing shots of Sambuca amongst themselves and audience members. Bernie walked up to the back of the stage and poured a drink into Cogsy's mouth as he played.

The singer thanked the gathering for their 'support, wisdom and bullshit over the years,' and then, the last-ever Powderfinger song – 'On My Mind'. Bernard let out a spine-shattering howl, the band delivered one final crescendo, and it was over. A quick bow, a 'see you out there,' and Powderfinger was gone forever.

'It was one of the best gigs I've had for a long time,' says Darren. 'It was just like stepping back in time. It's probably 15 years since my close mates were able to get down to the front row at a show. Even Dad came down the front – Bern gave him a shot.'

This is not how Teaks had envisioned the last chapter of Powderfinger playing out. 'I always wanted it to end at Suncorp Stadium, a big free show,' he says. 'I was going, "We should do the biggest show possible." That was the plan. There was a big debate but I couldn't get the numbers in the band. Another one of my great ideas gone to waste. But this was true to their personalities.'

After the performance, the band members mingled with their friends in the crowd, everyone knew everyone, it was almost like a school reunion according to JC, or a reunion of the old Brisbane scene. But the real final farewell party was scheduled for the following day.

Just the band and their crew, about 15 people in all. It started at lunch and didn't end until the day after. 'It was debaucherous,' says Cogs. 'Just drunk and stupid, lots of hugging. It took me a week and a half to recover.'

In the weeks and months that followed, the Fingers each headed off in their own directions. Family holidays, lounging around. Ian turned his focus to Airlock, working with a couple of new artists. 'I think it's my duty to use my knowledge to mentor people, without being cocky about it,' he says. JC bought himself a boat and began contemplating a career as a race driver. Bernard and his family relocated to Madrid, where he began leisurely writing for a new solo album. Darren and his family took off for an extended vacation across Asia and Europe, while Cogs returned to his studies, as well as working part time at Yalari, which provides educational opportunities for Aboriginal children.

The band's rehearsal room, the Finger Factory in Albion, was destroyed in the Queensland floods of January 2011; the band just managed to get their instruments out before the whole place went under. The floods led to calls for the Fingers to reform, just a month after they broke up, to perform a benefit concert. That was never going to happen. Instead, the band donated one of their final studio recordings, 'I'm On Your Side', to help raise money for those worst affected by the natural disaster. It caused an email stoush between a few of the ex-members, as they argued over whether they should trim the intro before releasing the song. Just like the good old days.

In the middle of 2011, Triple J held a listeners' poll to determine the hottest 100 Australian albums of all time. *Odyssey Number Five* came out on top, *Internationalist* was at number six, *Vulture Street* at 14 and *Double Allergic* at number 41. The Sunsets tour also received the Helpmann Award for Best Australian Contemporary Concert.

For all the awards and accolades, the album sales and record-breaking concert attendances, the true legacy of Powderfinger can be found in their songs.

While the Fingers are now gone, their music lives on forever in hearts, in memories and in stereo.

POWDERFINGER BREAK UP PARTY

ONE PARTY, ONE NIGHT, ONE LAST HANGOVER...

Saturday November 20

The Tivoli Theatre

52 Costin St, Foritude Valley

7pm to late

With special guests DJ FLUENT JB & DJ ASHO

RSVP to .com.au by Friday November 12

STRICTLY INVITATION ONLY - NON TRANSFERABLE

WE WOULD LIKE TO SAY THANK YOU . . .

Powderfinger

To our good friend Dino Scatena, who has worked so hard, talked to everyone and told our story with honesty, humour and his own inimitable style. Thanks mate! To all of our amazing crew, tour and production managers, soundies, stage techs, lighting & video teams and a special mention to the PFC lifer, Brownie – he can actually work miracles. The lovely record company & publishing people we have been lucky enough to work with throughout our career. Everyone past and present from Valhalla and Secret Service, particularly Brian Quinn, Janne Scott, Annette Perkins, Carney Nir and Rachael Dixon. Our studio engineers and producers Nick DiDia, Magoo, Jeff Lovejoy, Andy Baldwin, Tim Whitten, Doug Boehm, Rob Schnapf. All the people who did our vids over the years. To everyone we have met along the way – thanks for sharing a meal and several drinks. Thanks also to Rachel Waggett and Rod Walker, from Stage and Screen. An important person who has been with us always, Jess Ducrou, for having faith in us and teaching us how to have a little bit of class. Lastly, but certainly not least ... Paul Piticco for bringing it all together and making it happen. Much respect.

Ian Haug

My beautiful, supportive, patient and understanding wife, Georgie. My fantastic kids, Ruby and Hugo. Mum and Dad, John and Lynn, for all of their love and support when I was a difficult teenager and onwards. Chris and Greg Haug, for inspiring me musically and showing me it is cool to be smart. All of my friends and musical compadres over the years, particularly Macca. I would like to thank 'the zoo' for being there for us and the whole Brisbane music scene. Ingrid, KP and Gail Neilson for loving me from when I was a private school brat to when I was a stinky hippy. My band mates, Bish, and Cogs, DZ, BF and JC, for sharing a stage with me for all those years. I will always miss it.

John Collins

My beautiful wife Tara, for her patience and understanding and enjoying the journey with me. My awesome girls Grace, Rosie, and Scarlett, it's great to be home.

Mum and Dad for the unwavering support. My brother Jeff, my brother P.C for all his encouragement and teaching me the importance of persistence.

Kevin and Pat and the entire Mahony family and partners for being there when I couldn't be. My great friends for their support and interest in the 'Finger. Bish, Hoggy, Bern, DZ, Cogs and Teaksie for the incredible ride and the opportunity of a lifetime.

Bernard Fanning

To Andrea, Gabriela and the Fanning family. With love.

Marky, Brownie, Pavey, Toph, Denis, Matrix, Rach, Baz, SR and all of the crews that have provided such tireless support over the years. All of my friends, housemates and confidants. Finally, to the rest of the Fingers, thank you, keep a sharp lookout for 'Da Boulders Da Boulders', good luck and buen viaje.

Darren Middleton

Mum and Dad, Chris and Matt ... there from the beginning!!! That castle is coming, Mum, just as I promised all those years ago. My ever-patient and supportive family, Tamara, Viola and Arden, who put up with quite a lot in my self-absorbed life choice. My close old mates, Sandsie and Trav; you guys will never know just how important you have been to me all these years. To my band mates, this has been a journey I will never forget or regret. Cheers to you all.

Jonathan Coghill

To the Coghill family, Sasha, Evie, Tomas and Charli. Also my dear friends and all those who have been so generous and helpful over the life of PF.

To my band mates, Darius, Hoggy, Bernie, JC and Teaks – like brothers we became so close that we took each other for granted. In stepping back I now realise how talented and inspiring each of you are and have been. Thanks for the journey (no, I haven't gone soft ... you're all still bastards).

Dino, thanks for writing a great book, for being a brilliant counsellor and for not vomiting on me when you were carsick during our interview (was it something I said?).

Paul Piticco

Firstly, I would like to thank the Fingers for support and faith in me over the years and allowing me to be a part of their story. Cheers, fellas.

To Lisa, Phoebe, Ivy, Darby and my mum and dad, words cannot justify how much I love you and I can never thank you all enough for the love, support and tolerance you have given me in the pursuit of my dreams.

Dino Scatena

So many people I annoyed to hell during the writing of this book. First and foremost, the love of my life, my best friend, benefactor and wife, who ironically also turned out to be the most patient person I've ever met – the beautiful, incomparable Rachel 'Boobie' Newman. Seriously, how do you put up with me? I owe you a year. Actually, I owe you everything. Love you.

Similarly, my friends and my families, the Scatena and Newman clans. If you still remember who I am, I intend to make up for lost time.

At Hachette: Vanessa Radnidge, our tireless publisher and the second most patient person I know. You've been so committed to this since the first day I met you. Thank you for all the chocolate and pep talks. You're amazing. Also, a big thank you to our book designer Christa Moffitt of Christabella Designs. Beautiful work. And thank you to Karen Ward, Isabel Staas, Fiona Hazard, Anne Macpherson, Jacquie Brown, Helen Holman, Matt Richell, Carolyn Chwalko, Robert Watkins, Asha Krishnayya, Caroline Drake, Kaila Perusco and all at Hachette Australia.

There's a bunch of people who helped make this book possible in various ways. Asho (for getting the ball rolling), Peter Holder (for introducing me to Vanessa), Jenny Anthon (for your keyboard skills), Jackie Hoare (for your scanning skills), the fanatics on the Powderfinger forum (for your research skills – hope you love the book!) and my other Rach, Rachael Dixon (for your endless assistance).

To all the people who gave me their time and memories, thank you. Many of these same people went out of their way to dig up pictures and paraphernalia; your help was priceless. So, additional thanks to Steven Bishop, Jacinta Saunders, Taras Misko, Paul Fanning, Travers Murr, Michele Porto, Carney Nir, Kate Hammond and Jeff Lovejoy.

And finally, Powderfinger and Teaks. Thank you for entrusting me with this. I hope you're all happy and proud with what we've produced. Thank you for all your time, candour and especially for letting me in on the Sunsets tour. It was a truly extraordinary experience I'll never forget.

PHOTO CAPTIONS & CREDITS

Most of the photographs in this book have come from family, friends and the band members' own collections. Many others have also helped record the band over the years and we'd like to thank Dino Scatena, Scott Maughan, Stephen Booth, Steven Bishop, Jacinta Saunders, Kathy Dora, Tony Mott, Ian Jennings, Christopher Morris, Stephen Oxenbury, Cybele Malinowski, Sophie Howarth, John Webber, Sam Charlton, Glen Barnes, Hans-Martin Issler, Katherine Owen, Karin Mayer, Alex Doumany, Jeff Lovejoy, Andrea Smith, Scarlett Page, Travers Murr, Kate Hammond and Anna Warr. Thank you also to Rachael Dixon at Secret Service Artist Management and Michele Porto at Universal Music for their assistance in sourcing photographs. Every effort has been made to identify individual photographers and copyright holders where appropriate, but for some photographs this has not been possible. The publishers would be pleased to hear from any copyright holders who have not been acknowledged.

Page ii **Ian and JC onstage during Alternative Nation festival, 1995** (D.Middleton); p.vi **Promotional photo taken for the launch of the *Transfusion* EP, 1993** (Universal); p.viii **Promotional photo of the band, 2010** (Universal); p.x **Onstage during the Sunsets tour, 2010** (S.Maughan); p.2 **Backstage huddle during the final show of the Sunsets tour** (D.Scatena); p.5 **Darren's son, Arden, giving him a few pre-gig tips, Rod Laver Arena, 2010** (D.Middleton); pp.6–7 **JC hydrating during the Sunsets tour 2010** (S.Maughan); p.9 (top) **Fan's banner, Sunsets tour 2010** (S.Maughan); (*middle*) **DZ soaking up some Darwin sun, Sunsets tour 2010** (D.Middleton); (*bottom right*) **Bernie warming up at Memorial Drive, Adelaide, Sunsets tour 2010** (D.Middleton); (*bottom left*) **Access all areas lanyard, Sunsets tour, 2010** (Secret Service); pp.10–11 **Darren had Denis Sheahan take a few snaps with his camera outside the band's plane, *Fingerbird 1*** (D.Middleton); p.12 **Promotional photo of the band, 2010** (Universal/Cybele Malinowski); p.17 **Quick shot Ian and Darren did for their friends at Maton guitars, soundcheck, Sunsets tour, Sidney Myer Music Bowl, Melbourne** (D.Middleton); p.18 **'Gentlemanly Friday', l to r: Darren, Ian and Bernard trying out some stylish looks whilst making *Golden Rule* in Byron Bay** (D.Middleton); pp.20–21 **JC and Cogsy at soundcheck on the B-stage, Adelaide Memorial Drive show, Sunsets tour, 2010** (D.Middleton); p.23 (*top and bottom*) **At the press conference announcing the decision to end the band and the upcoming Sunsets farewell tour, April 2010** (Anna Warr); p.27 (*top*) **Cogs, DZ and Teaks in South Africa for the World Cup, 2010** (D.Middleton); (*bottom left*) **Cogs 'stuck' in a London phonebox, convinced it was the Tardis** (D.Middleton); (*middle and bottom right*) **Darren and Cogsy thoroughly enjoying the wave pool in Durban, South Africa** (D.Middleton); pp.28–9 **Bernard saying farewell during the Sunsets tour, 2010** (S.Maughan); p.30 **The scene of Powderfinger's first performance at Peter Gartner's house** (Jacinta Saunders); pp.32–3 **The early days** (J.Saunders); p.34 **Ian Haug performing during the Sunsets tour, 2010** (S.Maughan); p.36 (*top, middle, bottom*) **The young Ian Haug** (Haug family collection); p.38 (*top*) **The Haug family: Lynn, Ian, Chris, John and Greg**; (*bottom*) **Ian, Christmas Day, 1984** (Haug family collection); p.41 **The many moods of Ian Haug** (Haug family collection); p.43 (*top*) **Ian performing in the Fossils** (I.Haug); (*bottom*) **The Fossils** (I.Haug); p.44 **Ian in early Powderfinger days** (K.Dora); p.46 **John Collins during the Sunsets tour, 2010** (S.Maughan); p.49 (*top*) **JC at Seaworld**; (*middle*) **the Collins family, l to r: JC, Jeff, Ross, Peter and Cheryl**; (*bottom*) **JC's early fascination with the guitar**; p.51 (*top*) **L to r, brothers Jeff, Peter and John heading off to Beaudesert State Primary School**; (*middle*) **JC boogie-boarding at Greenmount Beach, Coolangatta**; **Peter and JC racing at a fun park at Tweed Heads**; (*bottom*) **JC in his Beaudesert Kingfishers football gear**; p.54 (*top*) **Playing with the Eternal at Michael Hintz's party in 1986**; (*middle and bottom*) **Playing guitar at the Outpost with the Eternal in 1987**; p.55 **At the Outpost** (photos pp.49–55 John Collins); p.56 **JC and Hoggy in full flight at the Metropolis, Brisbane** (K.Dora); p.58 **Steven Bishop, Ian Haug and John Collins** (S.Bishop); p.61 **Hoggy and JC enjoy their favourite drinking game, Ibble Dibble, at JC's house in Chelmer** (J.Saunders); p.64 (*far left,* *top)* **JC**; *(far left, bottom)* **Steven Bishop**; *(left)* **Ian** (S.Bishop); p.67 *(top)* **Fun times were had by all**; *(bottom)* **Steven 'Bish' Bishop** (J.Saunders); p.70 **Bernard performing** (Secret Service); p.73 **'Four Bits' playing for Western Suburbs District Cricket Club, 1978/79**; p.74 *(top)* **Paul and Bern, Bardon Kindy, around 1973**; *(bottom)* **Carmel, Paul and Bernard at St Ignatius Hall with Fr Guy Carlson**; p.76 **St Ignatius U/9 Swimming Champ, 1978**; p.80 *(top)* **Every possible '70s pattern included in the Fanning kitchen**; *(bottom)* **At home, Sherwood Rd, Toowong** (pics pp.73–80 B.Fanning); p.83, **Bernard at the Metropolis, 1992** (K.Dora); p.84, **Publicity shot of the four Fingers: Steve Bishop, Ian Haug, John Collins and Bernard Fanning** (Secret Service); p.87 **Photo shoot with mate Alex Doumany at an old house on Seventeen Mile Rocks Rd, Brisbane, l to r: Ian, John, Bish, Bernard** (A.Doumany); p.88 *(top)* **JC**; *(middle)* **Bernard**; *(bottom)* **Ian** (J.Saunders); p.90 **Sandgate country music festival, Sandgate Australian Rules Football Club, early '90s** (J.Saunders); p.93 *(top)* **Bernard**; *(middle)* **Steven Bishop**; *(bottom)* **Ian** (J.Saunders); pp.94–5 **Publicity shot l to r: Ian, Bish, JC, Bernard** (Secret Service); p.97 **From Seventeen Mile Rocks Rd shoot** (A.Doumany); p.99 **Publicity posters**; p.100 *(top)*, *(bottom)* **Publicity shots of the four-piece 'Finger** (A.Doumany); p.103 **Publicity poster** (Secret Service); p.104 **Darren Middleton** (S.Maughan); p.107 **No photos, please! Two years old**; p.108 *(top)* **Year 7, Darren and friends in band 'drag'**; *(middle)* **Darren, year 7, in school uniform**; *(bottom)* **Darren in his martial arts juniform, having just completed a full jumping spinning kick**; p.112 *(top left and right)* **Darren relaxing after a massive surfing session, and with his famous 'fractured rock' guitar**; *(middle)* **Pirate rehearsing at the Middletons' place**; *(bottom left and right)* **Darren with his brothers Chris and Matt, and with Trav at Boggo Road Gaol, Brisbane, 1993** (photos pp.107–12 D.Middleton); p.116 **Darren circa 1995, with his first nylon-string guitar** (Travers Murr); p.118 **Publicity shot, 1991** (Secret Service); p.121 **The band at Muttaburra for their performance at the local B&S ball** (J.Collins); p.123 **The band's business card, circa 1991** (P.Piticco); pp.124–5 **Publicity shot, 1991** (Secret Service); p.127 *(top)* **The band chilaxing** (S. Bishop); *(bottom left)* **JC and his father Ross celebrating at the Royal Exchange after the band signed with Polydor**; *(right)* **Celebrating at the Royal Exchange** (J.Collins); p.128 **Sara Herald review of Powderfinger show in local music fanzine *B.U.M.S.* (Brisbane Underground Music Scene), March 1991**; pp.132–3 **Powderfinger performing in 1991** (S.Bishop); p.137 **Orient Hotel publicity poster, 1991** (Andrea Smith); p.140 **Jonathan Coghill mid performance** (Secret Service); p.143 *(top)* **Cogs practising 'pregnant man' trick, aged two, Strathpine, Brisbane**; *(middle)* **Weighing up a career as a biker, aged three**; *(bottom)* **Aged eighteen months, off to work for minimum wage to support the family**; p.144 *(top)* **Working out at Bondi, aged five or six**; *(bottom)* **Surfing at Wategos Beach, Byron Bay, on a Christmas camping holiday, aged eight or nine**; p.146 **Bernard Gormley and Jonathan Coghill, self-proclaimed Nambour High School breakdancing champs, 1985**; p.147 *(clockwise from top left)* **Jon and older brother Chris, aged eight and nine; Jon, Christmas 1979; Graham Coghill playing lead guitar; Jon recovering from his bike accident, 1983; The Coghillbillies with Pippin the cat, 1982; Maria, Jon, mum Diana and Chris picnicking at Kondalilla National Park in the Gold Coast hinterland, 1981**; p.148 *(top)* **Jon playing in Powderfinger at the Orient, circa 1991**; *(bottom)* **At the Metropolis, circa 1991–2** (photos pp.143–8 J.Coghill); p.151 **Clark 'Cogs' Kent photo taken by Darren during a photoshoot in 2000** (D.Middleton); p.152 **During publicity shoot, l to r: JC, Cogs, Teaks, Bernard, Ian and Darren** (Secret Service); p.155 **Early publicity photos** (Secret Service); p.158 **Four early publicity shots** (Secret Service); pp.160–61 **Powerfinger Mk IV** (Secret Service); p.164 **Invitation to Powderfinger's debut EP launch, 1992** (Secret Service); p.167 ***Rave* magazine cover featuring Powderfinger, November 1992**; p.168 **Publicity shot 1993** (Secret Service); p.171 **Bernard and JC performing at Newcastle Uni** (K.Owen); p.172 **Publicity shot for *Transfusion* launch, 1993** (Universal); p.175 **Darren performing at Alternative Nation** (Secret Service); pp.176–7 **The band at Metropolis, 1993** (K.Dora); p.180 *(top)* **Band meeting**; *(bottom)* **Early performance** (Secret Service); pp.182–3 **All photos taken after the Boggo Road Gaol concert, 1993** (K.Dora); p.184 **Early days** (I.Haug); p.185 **Cogs, Bernard, Ian, DZ and JC** (I.Haug); p.186 **Invitation to the *Transfusion* EP launch**; p.189 **Powderfinger performing at Metropolis** (K.Dora); p. 190 **Publicity shot, 1994** (Secret Service); p.194 **The band signing with Polydor** (J.Collins); p.200

Bernard and Darren (K.Owen); p.203 **All photos taken at Metropolis studios** (Jeff Lovejoy); p.208 **Invitation to launch of *Parables For Wooden Ears***; p.211 **Publicity shot** (Universal); p.213 **Publicity shot, 1995** (Universal/Sophie Howarth); p.214 **Publicity shot, 1996** (Universal/Sophie Howarth); p.217 ***Mr Kneebone* EP launch invitation** (Secret Service); p.218 **Backstage at Homebake, 1996** (J.Coghill); p.223 **Bernard, DZ, Ian and JC mid-show** (K.Dora); pp.226–27 **Ian and Bernard** (K.Dora); p.231 **Bernard in performance mode** (K.Dora); p.234 *(top)* **Ian**; *(below)* **DZ** (K.Dora); p.241 **The band performing at the Crowded House Farewell to the World Concert at the Opera House, 1996** (Secret Service); p.242, **Taken during a publicity shoot, 1998** (Universal/S.Howarth); p.245 **In the bandroom** *(clockwise from top right)*: **Darren; Bernard, Ian & Darren; Paul Piticco; JC on drums; Ian & Bernard** (J.Coghill); pp.248-49 **Sophie says '*touch your toes*' – photo shoot** (Universal/S.Howarth); p.254 ***Internationalist* memorabilia** (Secret Service); p.258 **Photo shoot for Universal in May 2000** (Universal/Sam Charlton); p.261 **JC during the recording of *Odyssey Number Five*** (D. Middleton); p.265 **Photo shoot for Universal** (Universal/S.Howarth); p.266 *(clockwise from top left)* **During the recording of *Odyssey Number Five* at Sing Sing Studios – JC; Bernard; Nick DiDia; Bernard & Ian waiting outside the studio; DZ recording an acoustic section** (D. Middleton); p.269 **Poster for the P2K tour** (Secret Service); p.271 *(clockwise from top)* **JC rating Darren on the drums; JC; Ian** (D. Middleton); p.272 *(top to bottom)* **Bernard and JC somewhere in the US. All hotel rooms start to look the same; Performing at CBGBs** (I.Haug); **Ian and Darren** (D. Middleton); p.276 **Photo shoot** (Universal/Ian Jennings); p.280 *(Clockwise from top left)* **Ian and JC; hanging outside the tour bus; DJ Bernard in Germany; JC & Cogsy; Darren in Hamburg during the *Odyssey* tour** (Secret Service/D.Middleton); p.285 **US tour poster** (Secret Service); pp.286-87 **Ian Jennings photo** (Universal/Ian Jennings); p.290 **Recording the *Vulture Street* album, Bernard, Ian and Jonathan** (D. Middleton); p.294, **Photo shoot** (Universal); p.296 *(top to bottom)* **JC, Cogs, Darren, Hog** (Secret Service); p.299 ***Dream Days at the Hotel Existence* UK tour poster** (Universal/Secret Service); p.302 *(clockwise from top)* **Outside Sunset Sound Studios during a break from recording** (D.Middleton); **JC and Bernard being interviewed in Hyde Park during the O2 Wireless festival** (Secret Service); **DZ; Bernard in *Dream Days* mode** (D.Middleton); **From the stage looking out at the Hyde Park crowd** (Secret Service); **Cogs backstage at Hyde Park** (D.Middleton); p.306 *(top to bottom)* **Ian, DZ and Bernard while filming the clip for 'Lost And Running'** (Secret Service); p.309 **The 'Finger and the 'Chair photo shoot to promote the joint Across the Great Divide tour** (Universal/Ian Jennings); p.310 **Photo shoot on the mud flats** (Universal/Cybele Malinowski); p.313 *(top)* **Session during the recording of *Golden Rule*, Darren, Bernard, Andrew Morris, Pete Murray and Tim Rogers** (D.Middleton); *(bottom)* **Bernard and DZ sharing a laugh in the bandroom while JC works on a song** (D.Middleton); p.316 *(top to bottom)* **Bernard and DZ; the mixing desk; the advanced microphoning during the recording of *Golden Rule*** (D.Middleton); p.317 *(top to bottom)* **Bernard and Kram from Spiderbait; *Golden Rule* album cover; the suggested titles list for the album that was eventually named *Golden Rule*** (D.Middleton); pp.320-21 **'Gentlemanly Friday', l to r, Nick DiDia, Darren, Cogsy, Ian, Bernard, Paul Pilseniks and JC – a very dashing bunch** (D.Middleton); p.322 **One of the last photo shoots** (Universal/Cybele Malinowski); p.325 **Sunsets farewell** (S.Maughan); p.326, **Performing at the break-up party** (Dino Scatena); p.329 *(clockwise from top left)* **JC says goodbye at the break-up party, Cogsy is in the background** (Kate Hammond); **Rock & roll blood brothers, JC and Hog** (D.Scatena); **Bernard and Darren** (K.Hammond); **The invite every fan wished they had** (Secret Service); **Bish on drums during the break-up party** (D.Scatena); pp.330–31 **The last time** (D.Scatena); pp.340–41, **The final farewell during the Sunsets tour, 2010** (S.Maughan).

INDEX